Who Is White?

Who Is White?

Latinos, Asians, and the New Black/Nonblack Divide

George Yancey

LYNNE
RIENNER
PUBLISHERS

BOULDER
LONDON

Published in the United States of America in 2003 by
Lynne Rienner Publishers, Inc.
1800 30th Street, Boulder, Colorado 80301
www.rienner.com

and in the United Kingdom by
Lynne Rienner Publishers, Inc.
3 Henrietta Street, Covent Garden, London WC2E 8LU

Library of Congress Cataloging-in-Publication Data
Yancey, George A., 1962–
    Who is white? : Latinos, Asians, and the new black/nonblack divide / George Yancey.
        p.   cm.
    Includes bibliographical references and index.
    ISBN 1-58826-123-9 (alk. paper)
    1. United States—Race relations.   2. United States—Population.   3. Minorities—
United States—Social conditions.   4. Whites—Race identity—United States.
5. African Americans—Race identity.   6. Hispanic Americans—Race identity.
7. Asian Americans—Race identity.   8. Hispanic Americans—Cultural assimilation.
9. Asian Americans—Cultural assimilation.   10. Ethnicity—United States.   I. Title.

    E184.A1   Y37   2003
    305.8'00973—dc21

                                                                                    2002190869

British Cataloguing in Publication Data
A Cataloguing in Publication record for this book
is available from the British Library.

Printed and bound in the United States of America

∞   The paper used in this publication meets the requirements
     of the American National Standard for Permanence of
     Paper for Printed Library Materials Z39.48-1984.

     5   4   3   2   1

To Sherelyn, my lover and life companion

Contents

Acknowledgments

The concept of a solo-authored book is a myth. No one writes a book completely on his or her own ability and without the help of others in his or her life. This book is no exception to that reality. Of course, my earliest support came from my family of origin. The key influences were my mother, Rose Taylor, who would not allow me to use any excuses for not performing my best academically, and my grandfather, George M. Yancey, who is the smartest man I ever met and who showed me the importance of seeking knowledge.

This book would not have been possible without a grant from the Lilly Endowment, Inc. Their support of this research has been toprate; without such organizations, our knowledge of society would be much less than it is today. I am also very grateful for the work of the principal investigator of the grant, Michael Emerson, and of my fellow co-investigator, Karen Chai. Beyond their hard work in helping me to gather the data used in this book, they also gave me important feedback to help refine the ideas presented here. I want to thank key individuals at the University of North Texas, Dale Yeatts and David Hartmann, for working with me so that I could make the most of the opportunity to use the Lilly grant. Thanks to Paul Ruggiere for administering the survey through the University of North Texas Survey Research Center and for putting up with the many ways in which I asked, "Is the survey done yet?"

Along the way I received valuable assistance from a variety of sources. Thanks go to Lawrence Neuman, Brad Christenson, Charles Brown, Michael Emerson, and Karen Chai for reading various sections of early drafts of this book. I also thank Woody Doane and an anonymous reviewer who read a later draft of the book and gave me solid critiques and helped me to solidify the arguments.

I want to give special thanks to the wonderful people at Lynne Rienner for their support of this work. I especially want to thank Bridget Julian for her tireless efforts and feedback. Had she not called me out of the blue that summer afternoon to learn about my research and given me positive encouragement along the way, this book probably never would have been written.

Finally, I thank my wife, Sherelyn, who walks by my side in all my endeavors. She encourages me with her love and wisdom as she spends her life working to overcome the racial alienation so pervasive in our society.

1

Alienation and Race in the United States

"By the year 2050 we will not have a majority race in the United States. Whites will be a numerical racial minority, albeit the largest minority, in the country." How many times have we heard a version of those two lines by social observers, political commentators, demographers, or other "experts" on race relations? Evidence of this future numerical minority status for European Americans is based upon the projection of the racial groups shown in Table 1.1. While this projection does not show whites as a numerical minority by 2050, it is clear that soon after this point in time European Americans will no longer be a population majority.[1] The future numerical minority reality of American whites is taken as an unalterable fact in studies of American race/ethnicity. Pronouncements of this coming racial reality are repeated by social scientists and observers so often that many have begun to believe that the shrinking white population is as certain as the rising of the sun each morning. Furthermore, there is no shortage of the important implications. Generally, the speaker of this new American truism goes on to argue that because of this racial diversity, it is important to support multiculturalism, anti-racism, racial reconciliation, and cultural diversity. We have been warned that, because of the shrinking white population, if we do not open up educational opportunities for people of color, in a few decades we will not be able to meet the occupational demands for professional labor. Political commentators warn both political parties, but particularly Republicans, to learn how to reach out to racial minorities if they want to obtain and preserve political power.[2] Political conservatives often react to the notion of a shrinking white

Table 1.1   2000 Census Racial Breakdown and Projected Breakdowns of Racial Groups for 2050, by Percentage

	2000 Census	2050 Projections
European Americans	69.1	52.8
African Americans	12.3	13.2
Hispanic Americans	12.5	24.3
Asian Americans	3.6	8.9
Native Americans	0.9	0.8

Sources: Bureau of the Census 2001: P-20-535; Day 1996.
Note: Figures do not add up to 100 percent due to overlap between groups and individuals who do not fit into any of the categories.

majority with demands to limit legal and illegal immigration into the United States. Given the "fact" that racial minorities are going to be a majority of the population in a few short decades, these suggestions seem particularly relevant if the United States is to thrive in the twenty-first century.

But what if racial minorities do not become the majority population by 2050? I contend that whites are not, in the foreseeable future, going to become a numerical minority. My disagreement with the prediction is not about a certain time frame, nor is it an abstruse argument about how I define this statement; rather, I fundamentally disagree with the prediction as a whole. To illustrate why I believe that this great social certainty is wrong, let me restate the first two sentences with one adjustment. "By the year 1975 we will not have a majority race in the United States. Whites will be a numerical minority, albeit the largest minority, in the country." Now imagine this statement coming from a demographer in 1925. Would this demographer have been correct in his or her assessment? My answer is both yes and no.

In this particular historical context the demographer would have correctly predicted that the groups who were for the most part believed to be "white" in 1925 (only northern and western Europeans) would have been a numerical minority by 1975. The demographer would have correctly observed that there had been a great influx of the Polish, Russians, Ukrainians, and Italians since 1880 and would have correctly foreseen the growth of the Asian and Hispanic population in American society.[3] If one adds these groups to other racial groups who are still not accepted as white today (blacks, Native Americans), then whites would indeed have been a numerical minority by 1975. But this demographer would have been wrong for not anticipating that some of these "nonwhite" groups would become fully "white." By 1975 the eastern and southern Europeans who previously had been treated as racial minorities had become "white."[4] The demographer would be wrong not because of an inability to correctly predict the proper racial and ethnic trends of the day but because the definition of "white" changed over the course of those fifty years. As the children and grandchildren of immigrant European ethnic groups began to intermarry and integrate into the dominant culture, these individuals became accepted as "white." In turn they perceived themselves as members of the majority group and adopted social attitudes that would help them to protect the racial status quo.

The current predictions about whites becoming a numerical minority are wrong not because of incorrect assessments of the growth of racial minorities,[5] but because the definition of who is white is not static. Some individuals who are currently not labeled "white" will be so labeled in 2050. They are individuals whose children and grandchildren will outmarry and integrate into the dominant culture, eventually accepting the social attitudes within the majority culture that supports the racial status quo. Those predicting the new multiracial United States generally overlook this critical piece of the country's changing racial puzzle. They make predictions based upon an assumption that has proven to be very shaky—the assumption is that the way we define who is white, or a majority group member, will not change. It is an assumption that must be challenged if we are going to obtain accurate information about the future of racial reality in the United States.

I believe in many of the ideals and social programs pushed forward by the proponents of what I call the "whites as minority" thesis. I contend that, if done properly, multiculturalism, racial reconciliation, and diversity training have important roles to play in helping the United States overcome its long history of racial abuse. I support efforts to educate children of color and assert that honest dialogue between the racial groups is essential for this country's future success. Given that I share many similar goals with the proponents of this thesis, why should I challenge it if it helps motivate Americans to support racial diversity training, take seriously our responsibility to educate minority kids, and engage in the racial dialogue we so badly need. One reason for this challenge is because there are other extremely useful arguments that can be used to encourage Americans to adopt many of these programs and social changes. Arguments for racial reconciliation or diversity training should be based upon an accurate assessment of racial culture in the United States, not upon the errors in the "whites as minority" thesis.

However, my desire for research accuracy is not a strong enough motivation for me to challenge this thesis as forcefully as I am prepared to do. The fundamental reason why this thesis must be challenged is that it masks an important fact about American race relations—that African Americans experience a degree of alienation unlike that of other racial groups. While many other racial groups may become "white" over the next 50 to 100 years, this transformation is not an option for African Americans because they occupy, and will continue to occupy, the bottom rung in society. The "whites as minority" thesis discounts the ability of nonblack racial minority groups to eventually assimilate into the white majority and thus implicitly assumes that all racial minority groups are in a similar social position in the United States. It postulates that all racial groups will continue to maintain the same level of distinctness they have today and create a country whereby whites are a numerical minority. If this is correct, then all racial minority groups will face the same level of rejection that they have always experienced. History has shown us that this has never been the case. I will illustrate that while the transformation of nonblack minorities into majority group status is occurring, the separation of African Americans from the dominant culture, in spite of efforts by blacks to move into mainstream American culture, is just as strong as it ever has been. These twin processes of nonblack assimilation and black separation will move nonblack and black minorities in opposing directions—reinforcing the racial divide in the United States.

The Process of Assimilation

It is debatable whether assimilation is a desirable goal for racial minority groups. I do not take a position either way. However, understanding the ability of a given minority group to assimilate is necessary for determining the degree of acceptance experienced by that minority group.[6] If a minority group experiences a great deal of acceptance by the mainstream culture, then the members of that group will have the opportunity to assimilate. Majority group members will look upon these individuals favorably as potential neighbors and in-laws. Eventually, members of this minority group are likely to perceive themselves as majority group members and share social attitudes similar to those of dominant group members on racialized issues. Yet if majority group members socially reject a group, then such incorporation into the dominant culture is not an option. Even if assimilation is not desirable to racial minorities, assessing the ability of a group to assimilate is valuable for understanding how much a group will be accepted by the dominant society.[7]

Milton Gordon defines structural assimilation as the entrance of minority groups into primary group relationships with majority group members, and marital assimilation as the intermarriage of minority group members with majority group members without facing any social stigma.[8] He argues that members of a social group must experience structural assimilation before they can experiences marital assimilation, and that marital assimilation must occur before a minority group can be completely assimilated into the dominant society. Comprehensive assimilation into the society, so that former minority group members are full-fledged members of the majority, is called "civic" assimilation. His theoretical process implies that it is possible for a group to experience structural and marital assimilation, but not civic assimilation. The fact that minority groups can live in the same neighborhoods as, and intermarry with, majority group members does not mean that they are fully assimilated into the dominant group.

For the process toward civic assimilation to continue, members of racial minority groups must begin to identify with majority group status. This is what Gordon calls "identificational" assimilation, the next stage beyond marital assimilation.[9] Ashley Doane argues that the worldview of those with a dominant group identity is a presumed perspective on dominant group privilege that leads to a denial of race as a meaningful social force.[10] Building on this argument, it is evident that a useful measure of dominant group identity is when racial minorities adopt social attitudes that support the interest of dominant group members. When former racial minorities adopt social attitudes that support the racial status quo, it is likely that members of that minority group perceive themselves as being able to enjoy the benefits of majority group membership. Social attitudes are an important indicator of whether a minority group has experienced identificational assimilation.

This "straight-line" process of assimilation has recently been criticized. Some of the critics have instead advocated the development of transnational identities, whereby individuals' identities transcend societies and nation-states.[11] Instead of minority racial immigrants eventually developing a majority group identity, they develop an identity that supersedes the racial identities within a given country. However, while there is generally a significant amount of cultural exchange that occurs in the migration of immigrants to the United States, it seems unlikely that most immigrants are able to completely maintain their native identity after living in this country for a significant period of time. Furthermore, second-generation Americans seem less likely to maintain their heritage culture than their first-generation parents, making the existence of a persistent transnational identity unlikely.[12]

A more solid critique of Gordon's straight-line assimilation can be seen in Alejandro Portes and Min Zhou's ideas concerning segmented assimilation.[13] They contend that the way first-generation immigrants are incorporated into the society helps to determine contrasting ways that the second generation accepts the culture and values of the dominant society. Immigrant groups who experience a great deal of discrimination will develop what Portes and Zhou term "reactive ethnicity." From this reactive ethnicity an adversarial stance, which emphasizes discrimination and discounts the dominant values, will emerge from the members in the second-generation racial group. An important implication of this theory is that the adoptation of dominant group values is not correlated with the accumulation of socioeconomic status, and certain racial groups may advance economically in the United States without having to assimilate.

Under the theory of segmented assimilation, immigrant groups that came later into the United States may be more likely to succeed without assimilation than earlier European immigrant groups, because of the different paths these groups have taken into this country. A number of ethnographic studies of recent immigrant groups have supported the idea that assimilation can be unlinked from social mobility.[14] Yet a true final test of assimilation is not possible by examining only first- or second-generation immigrants. The trajectories of these groups may be that they temporarily hold onto their immigrant culture in the first couple of generations before eventually going down the same straight-line path of assimilation that European ethnic groups have experienced. At best, ethnographic tests of first- or second-generation immigrant groups can only predict that early-generation members of a given immigrant group are not likely to soon assimilate into the dominant society. While these ethnographic studies are valuable, testing the relative assimilative tendencies of major racial groups in the United States (European Americans, African Americans, Hispanic Americans, Asian Americans) better assesses the potential of assimilation, since members in these racial categories have been present for more than three generations.

The segmented assimilation thesis and straight-line assimilation may coexist. Later I will show how Gordon's straight-line assimilation theory is useful for explaining the general assimilative potentials for Latino and Asian Americans. This is not to say that recent immigrant groups from these races may exhibit an exception to straight-line assimilation, since they may face a level of local discrimination that creates an adversarial stance among the members of those groups. But on a national basis I will demonstrate that Hispanic and Asian Americans are undergoing a significant level of structural, marital, and identificational assimilation in the United States. However, it seems very plausible that segmented assimilation best describes the rejection experienced by African Americans. There is vast research showing that African Americans face more racial segregation than other racial groups,[15] and do not, or perhaps more precisely cannot, engage in the same level of structural or marital assimilation as nonblack racial minorities.[16] This evidence suggests that the experience of African Americans may be qualitatively different from that of other racial groups, and I speculate that the theory of segmented assimilation explains the African American experience in ways it does not explain the experience of other racial groups. While I will not provide any evidence that African Americans who reject dominant group values are succeeding more than other blacks, I will show that blacks are more likely to reject those values than are Latinos and Asian Americans. This rejection is a reflection of the barriers placed around the majority group society, which do not allow them to become part of the dominant group.

Beyond the critique of segmented assimilation there have been two other schools of thought that tend to criticize the notion of assimilation in general. The first school of thought is primordialism.

Advocates of this perspective contend that racial/ethnic identity is fixed and cannot be altered by interaction with members of other racial/ethnic groups. Harold Isaacs argued that it is important to treat ethnic identity as a form of basic group identity.[17] According to him, such an identity develops from birth and is embedded into a person's basic identity. Isaacs's work, which is built on the ideas of Clifford Geertz and Edward Shils,[18] gave birth to the notion of primordialism—the idea that racial/ethnic identity is unchanging. A seemingly contradictory perspective is the school of circumstantialism. This perspective contends that racial/ethnic groups are interest groups and that members of these groups use their racial identities to pursue their collective interests as a group. To this end, under the proper circumstances, members of distinct groups may adapt some of the elements of their group identities so that they can gain benefits for the group. Under such a perspective, racial identity survives because it is usable for gaining resources and because such identity is flexible enough to adapt to the changing circumstances in society.

Stephen Cornell and Douglass Hartmann offer a promising compromise to these seemingly contradictory perspectives with what they call a "constructionist" approach to racial identity.[19] They argue that racial actors can use their identities in the pursuit of goals, but can do little to shape, reinforce, or transform those identities. Actors simply exploit their identities in the situations that are given to them. Thus while actors have primordial identities that do not undergo much change, they use these identities to accomplish their desired goals. One of the key ways that actors can manipulate their identities for their own purposes is by developing the "thickness" of those identities. Cornell and Hartmann's description of this thickness indicates that it measures the degree of comprehensiveness of the identity. They use the changes in the identity of Italian Americans as an example. In the first part of the twentieth century, Italian Americans had a "thick" Italian identity in that their Italian heritage affected most areas of their social life (where they lived, whom they married, how they voted, etc.). But toward the latter part of the twentieth century this identity became "thin." Most Italian Americans know that they are Italian, but they no longer utilize their identity in such a comprehensive manner. Like many other European ethnic groups, they find it advantageous to adopt a dominant group perspective and to downplay their heritage identity.[20]

The effects of the intellectual attack by primordialists, circumstantialists, and constructionists on the idea of assimilation is that racial identity of minority groups will survive regardless of the degree it interacts with the dominant identity. Primordialism implies that the identity will survive intact, yet such assertions clearly go against common observations that intergroup interactions lead to cultural changes in both majority and minority groups. The circumstantialist and constructionist schools allow for minority racial identity to change, but insist that these changes do not eliminate that identity, since the minority groups opportunistically use their identities to make social gains. Yet the constructionist school in particular implies that one of the most useful ways that members of a minority group use their identity is to reduce the "thickness" of that identity, especially if that minority group can easily merge into the mainstream of society. Consequently this appears to have been the experience for most members of European ethnic groups. But if these groups have such a thin ethnic identity, then are they truly distinct from the majority group? Are not groups such as Polish Americans, German Americans, and Irish Americans all but assimilated into the dominant society? The implications of such an assimilation suggest that the concept of civic assimilation developed by Gordon is not outdated, as some of his critics may argue, but that it is useful for certain groups in the United States. The question remains whether this concept is only useful for European-based groups or whether it may also apply to certain nonblack ethnicities. In the balance of this book, I shall refer to the process by which nonblack groups may enter into the dominant culture as either a process of assimilation or one in which their ethnic/racial identity is "thinned." There are theoretical distinctions between these two concepts, but as far as allowing former minority groups to take on dominant group ideology, the two concepts are closely related and will have the same effect—namely that African Americans will be left at the bottom of the racial hierarchy in the United States. Thus as I discuss the merging of Latino and Asian Americans into the dominant culture, I will freely interchange these two concepts.

To assess whether nonblack racial and ethnic groups can undergo the same type of assimilation as European groups (or at the very least can experience the same type of reduction of thickness in their racial identity), it is important to learn if members of these groups are beginning to approach racial issues from a dominant perspective. If Latino and Asian Americans are beginning to approach racial issues from a majority group perspective, then there is evidence that they have developed a thinner racial identity. This thinness can suggest evidence of some degree of identificational assimilation, since it will show that nonblack minorities are not just living next to and marrying whites, but are also thinking like whites in that they are dismissing the importance of race in the United States. In many ways they are on their way to becoming "white." Whether or not one wishes to label such thinning of racial identity "assimilation," evidence of this thinning should give us reasons to rethink the common statement that European Americans will be a numerical minority by the middle of the twenty-first century.

The Social Construction of Race

Before challenging the "white as minority" myth, I need first to analyze how race is defined in the United States. It is important to examine this issue since I will be attacking commonly held notions of who can be "white." There is a general American assumption that race is a biological concept. Clearly it is not. How Americans define racial membership varies over time. For example, in the early part of the twentieth century, Italian Americans were seen as being physically different from "white" Americans and faced the racial stereotypes of being criminals and being hot-tempered. Today the general American perception of Italian Americans is that they are a different ethnic group than non-Italian Europeans and, while culturally different than some in the majority, are racially the same as whites. Thus Americans tend to associate innate biological differences between different groups as racial differences, while they associate cultural differences as ethnic differences. Actual physical difference is not the key to establishing racial identity, since not all African Americans are darker than all European Americans. African Americans are not labeled "black" because they have a certain degree of skin darkness but because society has decided that individuals with a certain geographical, social heritage should be labeled as such. Instead of being a biological reality, race is socially constructed in American society.

To point out that race does not have a basis in physical reality is not to argue that we are free to ignore race. Race has a social reality that cannot be disregarded. Americans attach social meaning to the perceived biological differences associated with racial differences.

This definition leads to the construction of a racial identity that has profound sociological implications. For example, in selecting a group of jurors for trials, the race of each juror is often used by a lawyer to gauge how the juror might feel about the trial proceedings. This is particularly true if the case is somehow related to race relations (e.g., O. J. Simpson's murder case). The lawyer will ignore socially unimportant biological categories such as hair color and height, because such physical factors generally have little impact on the social perceptions of the potential jurors. But whether a person, and the society around that person, perceives him- or herself as white, black, Latino, or Asian does influence how that person perceives racialized social issues. Merely because race does not have a basis in biology does not mean that a good lawyer can ignore the distinct perceptions that members of different races possess.

Some discussions of the social attitudes of blacks or Hispanics imply that all African Americans or Latino Americans have identical beliefs. This is not the case, as there is a great deal of ideological variability within racial groups. While African Americans clearly are more supportive of Democrats than Republicans, there is still ideological variability among blacks on certain political issues. Surveys of the attitudes of African Americans toward a variety of political issues are likely to discover both great diversity of opinion and high levels of consensus. According to the 1998 National Election Survey, 52.0 percent of African Americans supported the death penalty, 46.7 percent supported school vouchers, and 52.0 percent supported a ban on late-term abortions. On the other hand, 43.4 percent of African Americans opposed the death penalty, 46.7 percent opposed school vouchers, and 40.1 percent opposed a ban on late-term abortions. Yet despite this level of disagreement among blacks on these political issues, the importance of race in American society is still sufficient for the social reality of blacks to influence their attitudes. That same survey also indicated that 78.9 percent of all African Americans gave President Clinton, instead of the Republican Congress, credit for the governmental surplus, and 89.5 percent believed that religion was an important part of their lives. While there is variability within the African American community, there is also some level of ideological agreement that comes from a sense of a shared, racially based social experience.

Perhaps it was Donald Campbell who first postulated that minority groups have different racial attitudes than majority groups because they have contrasting social interests.[21] This assertion implies that to protect their own economic interests, majority group members act in ways that deprive racial minorities of opportunities, and racial minorities attempt to alter the racially based social and economic status quo. African Americans are more likely to perceive unfairness in economic opportunities than are majority group members.[22] This can be seen in the contrasting views blacks have about the role of the government in ensuring economic fairness.[23] These social attitudes reflect the higher social and economic positions of European Americans relative to African Americans. Racial identity is connected to a social reality whereby African Americans suffer economic and social discrimination because of their race; thus it is in the social interests of blacks to advocate for an expanded role in the government in the eradication of racism, while it is in the social interests of majority group members to defend the status quo they benefit from. As long as minority groups do not assimilate into society, we should expect that they will have social attitudes distinct from majority group members, especially on issues where the racial advantage of majority group members is evident.

Because race is a social, not biological, creation, how American society defines majority group status can easily change. If previous racial minorities experienced a definitional change so that they are now seen as part of the majority, then they also will undergo a change in their own outlook on American society. It will become in their social interests to support "white" Americans. Unless accounting for this process, predictions will consistently underestimate the size of future majority groups.

African Americans and the Alienation Thesis

Previous literature suggests that ethnic groups from southern and eastern Europe have already been assimilated into the dominant culture.[24] I will later argue that nonblack racial minority groups are undergoing a similar process. Yet despite their long history in the United States, this process has not occurred for African Americans. There are two possible reasons for the inability of African Americans to assimilate.

The first possible explanation is that African Americans' contributions to the dominant culture are so extensive that they are in fact already a major part of the dominant culture. Charles Moskos and

John Butler argue that there is an Afro-Anglo culture that dominates the United States.[25] They contend that members of the African/ African American culture have influenced European Americans for the last few centuries, with both whites and blacks contributing to their common American culture. As a result of this influence, African Americans have merged their moral vision, spirituality, literature, music, and rhetoric with the European Americans' language, social customs, and legal/political traditions to create the bedrock culture undergirding the United States. Other racial/ethnic minority groups have either assimilated into the mainstream culture (e.g., Irish Americans, Polish Americans) or have not been in the United States long enough to have significantly influenced American culture (e.g., Korean Americans, Cuban Americans).

There is a solid argument to be made that African Americans have made more contributions to the culture of the dominant society through music, literature, and the arts than any other minority racial group. Yet this cultural contribution has only been possible because African Americans have existed as a distinct group in the United States for centuries. Because they have not assimilated, black Americans maintain a distinctness that allows them to contribute to the dominant culture. The Afro-Anglo argument implies that, since African Americans already have a powerful influence in American society, blacks do not fully assimilate because they have chosen not to do so. But I contend that the reason why African Americans maintain this distinctness is that they have been rejected from the dominant culture. When it comes to social status and power within society, African Americans are not part of the core culture but are estranged from whites. This leads to a more accurate way of assessing the inability of African Americans to assimilate into the dominant society: what I term the "alienation" thesis, upon which the premise of this book is built.

The basic claim of the alienation thesis is that African Americans suffered from a qualitatively different level of alienation than did the two other major racial minority groups in American society: Latino and Asian Americans. Because of this alienation, blacks are unable to undergo the process of assimilation generally experienced by other racial groups. Because their ability to become part of the mainstream society has been retarded, the alienation thesis implies that African Americans are destined to remain an outcast race. While other racial groups find their way into dominant group status, blacks will retain their minority group social position. Even if African Americans want to become part of the dominant culture, the barriers they face prevent them from gaining membership in the majority society.[26] The twin major claims of the alienation thesis are that African Americans will continue to suffer a disproportionate level of alienation within American society, and that nonblack racial minorities will begin to accept dominant group status over time. This leads to a prediction that instead of "whites" becoming a numerical minority group in the near future, we are heading toward a black/nonblack society wherein African Americans remain anchored to the bottom of the racial hierarchy in the United States.[27]

Nathan Glazer points out that the persistence of African American culture may be indicative of the inability of African Americans to assimilate.[28] This inability can reflect the alienation of African Americans from the rest of the society. Lawrence Bobo and Vincent Hutchings reinforce this possibility with their finding that African Americans are more likely to have a sense of racial alienation, or group disenfranchisement, and are more likely to perceive other races as group threats, than are European Americans, Hispanic Americans, or Asian Americans.[29] Their analysis implies that nonblack racial minorities do not face the same level of alienation as African Americans and can become incorporated into the dominant group culture. African Americans may share certain cultural values with European Americans since both groups do not have large percentages of first- and second-generation immigrants in their population—which would explain why whites and blacks might have similar tastes in music, religion, language style, and other cultural elements. However, African and European Americans are not likely to agree on social attitudes that pertain to racial power,[30] since African Americans are unable to enjoy the benefits of majority group status. Different social attitudes on racialized topics indicate the degree of alienation that African Americans experience from the dominant racial culture.

It is hardly controversial to suggest that African Americans are alienated from the dominant American racial culture, as a plethora of books examine the extent of this alienation.[31] I am not interested in arguing about the degree of alienation African Americans experience. The controversial part of my argument is the assertion that the largest nonblack racial minority groups in America—Latino Americans and Asian Americans—do not face the same level of alienation as

African Americans. Thus Latinos and Asians have an ability to assimilate that escapes blacks. As they assimilate, or at least develop a thinner racial identity as they accept majority group status, the white/nonwhite dichotomy currently used to understand race relations will eventually need to be replaced with a black/nonblack dichotomy. Instead of evaluating the social acceptance of a group by how "white" they are, it will be more important to assess the social rejection of a group by how "black" they are.

The alienation thesis is not an argument that these nonblack racial groups have escaped prejudice and racism. Clearly Hispanic and Asian Americans do not yet enjoy full status as "white" Americans. Furthermore, in certain ways, Latino Americans and Asian Americans can face more prejudice than African Americans.[32] Prejudice against Hispanic and Asian Americans is still a serious concern in the United States and must be dealt with by those of us who care about racial equality. My argument is that African Americans generally have a level of alienation that is qualitatively greater than that of these minority groups and because of this alienation do not possess the same ability to become incorporated into the dominant culture as nonblack racial minorities. Jonathan Warren and France Winddance Twine have suggested that it is the rejection (alienation) of blacks that serves as the standard by which nonblack racial groups can find acceptance.[33] Because nonblack racial groups can avoid the label of being "black," they can eventually be given a "white" racial identity. African Americans are in a quasi-caste system by which they occupy the lowest level of social prestige in the United States, and it is in the social interests of all nonblack racial groups to keep them at the bottom.

To assess my prediction of the emerging white race, there is a need for data that investigate the degree of structural, marital, and identificational assimilation experienced by Latino, Asian, and African Americans. Such an investigation is the empirical focus of this book.

Assessing Social Attitudes as a Means of Documenting "Alienation"

Detecting the alienation of blacks and the corresponding assimilation of nonblack racial minorities is the key challenge in assessing this alienation thesis. Several observers of racism have argued that the

best way to understand racial inequality is through an analysis of
social structures. For example, Albert Szymanski uses a Marxist perspective to argue that racism is shaped by the ongoing attempts of the
bourgeoisie to keep workers from uniting.[34] Such a perspective contends that individual acts of racism are encouraged by a social structure wherein the capitalist class wants to ensure that white and black
workers fail to realize that their true enemy is the capitalist system.
Another structuralist explanation of racism comes from the school of
internal colonialism. Robert Blauner pushes this perspective with his
argument that the early economic exploitation conducted by
Europeans and European Americans helped to establish a society
where white advantage was institutionalized.[35] Although we no
longer have the type of economic and political colonialization of a
previous time, white privilege remains a constant reality within the
social structures of American society. Finally, Eduardo Bonilla-Silva
argues that a racialized social system approach is the best way to
understand racism.[36] He defines racialized social structures as societies in which economic, political, social, and ideological levels are
partially structured by the placement of actors in racial categories.
Individuals within these racialized social systems receive different
levels of rewards or costs depending on their placement. The contrasting benefits that distinct racial actors receive from this system
provide different motivation for those actors to either change or
maintain the racial status quo.

The brief synopsis in the preceding paragraph is in no way
intended to be an exhaustive or comprehensive description of structuralist explanations of racism. However, it allows for some general
assessment of structuralist theories. Structuralist explanations of the
racial reality in the United States suggest that individuals are caught
up in social structures that perpetuate the racial hierarchy that dominates American society. Contemporary racism is not motivated by
hatred or fear, although clearly such emotions have not disappeared;
rather it is motivated by the subtle desire to maintain privileges for
the majority group. Insensitivity to the plight of racial minorities,
rather than overt attempts to exploit minority group members, is the
key component to the maintenance of racist structures. Because the
privileges of majority group members are largely hidden from the
dominant group, it becomes easier for them to escape accusations of
racism even as they engage in practices and develop attitudes that
enable them to maintain those privileges.[37]

Advocates of these structuralist theories contend that the best way to understand racism is through an assessment of the social structures in American society rather than through an analysis of social attitudes. They argue that social desirability effects prevent dominant group members from exhibiting social attitudes that smack of racial intolerance. It is in the social structures that dominant group members are unwilling to change that racism is manifested. I agree with the proponents of structural racism when they argue that social structures are the key to understanding how contemporary racism is manifested in American society. Yet as even a cursory reading of the different structuralist explanations indicates, there is disagreement as to which social structures are central to the maintenance of racism. Neo-Marxists argue that it is the capitalist structure of American society that perpetuates racism. Internal colonialists contend that structures established by the historical exploitation of the third world are the location of racial inequality. The racialized social system theory postulates that it is important to look at the racial ideology that emerges from social systems.

It is not the purpose of this book to embroil myself in a debate as to which structuralist theory best explains the maintenance of racism. Yet regardless of the structuralist explanation used to assess the racial hierarchy in American society, it can be predicted that efforts by majority group members to maintain their social advantages will lead to distinct social attitudes. Social attitudes are reflections of the social structures that people dwell within—despite the claims of many structuralists that measurements of social attitudes are useless for understanding modern racial stratification (one of the strongest critiques of the use of social attitudes is present in the work of Bonilla-Silva, which I shall deal with in Chapter 4). While I support structuralist explanations of racism, I also contend that the assessment of social attitudes is valuable for asserting whether the alienation of African Americans is a social reality. Even many of the advocates of a structuralist explanation of racism utilize survey research work to illustrate the degree to which majority group members, even as they also strive to project an image of racial tolerance, support the racial status quo.[38] If the alienation thesis is an accurate way to describe the racial reality in the United States, then it should be expected that on key issues dealing with the maintenance of the racial status quo, the social attitudes of whites should differ from those of blacks. Furthermore, if nonblack racial groups such as

Latino and Asian Americans are experiencing more acceptance into the dominant culture, then it can be predicted that their social attitudes on such issues will be more likely to support the maintenance position of European Americans rather than the reformative desires of African Americans. Such differences in social attitudes should be expected regardless of which structuralist theory best explains racial inequality. An examination of social attitudes is an efficient way to assess the possibility that blacks are becoming alienated within the United States.[39]

Examining Nonblack Racial Minorities

To assess whether African Americans suffer from a degree of alienation that escapes nonblack racial minorities, it is vital to examine the social attitudes of, and toward, groups such as Latino and Asian Americans. Traditionally there have been ideological barriers to the study of nonblack minorities. Some observers argue that there is a special history of blacks and whites, which makes this relationship more important than other racial combinations.[40] They believe that there are characteristics of this special relationship—the degree of oppression faced by African Americans, their population size, and their long history in the United States—that can justify a special focus on the racial differences between blacks and majority group members,[41] and that the darker skin color of African Americans may bring about a distinctiveness that attracts more hostility from European Americans than from other racial groups.[42] Given the unique history of slavery, it is reasonable to argue that it is more important to understand white/black differences than those between other racial groups, as white/black relations represent American race relations at their fullest, and often at their worst.

But the emphasis on studying attitudes toward blacks, at the expense of studying attitudes toward other minority racial groups, ignores the social positions of these nonblack minorities in American society. This ignorance makes it impossible to fully understand the social position of blacks. For example, given the relative political power African Americans have achieved in our society,[43] it is possible that blacks have gained, rather than lost, status in the United States. Even though African Americans experience segregation, dominant group members may want to have social relations with blacks as much as they do with other racial minorities, but because of their increased political power, blacks may have created an ideology that theoretically endorses a pluralistic, rather than an assimilationist, framework.[44] Such a reality would crush the alienation thesis, since African Americans would be choosing not to assimilate rather than being unable to assimilate. Only by comparing the attitudes of European Americans toward African Americans with the attitudes of European Americans toward nonblack minority groups can this contention be tested. If majority group members are as accepting of African Americans as they are of other minority groups, then the alienation thesis can be severely challenged. To invalidate the alienation thesis, researchers cannot be limited to an examination of only the perception of African Americans. The failure of the current social scientific surveys to ask questions that include assessments of nonblack minorities leaves social scientists with an incomplete understanding of possible patterns of racial assimilation.

Fortunately, I have been a co-researcher of the 1999–2000 Lilly Survey of American Attitudes and Friendships (LSAF). A more extensive examination of the methodology of this research can be found in the book's appendix, but it is worth noting that this survey oversampled Hispanic and Asian Americans to allow for the comparison of the social attitudes of these two groups to whites and blacks. The LSAF also allows me to examine the attitudes of respondents toward these nonblack racial groups. In short, this survey enables me to more deeply explore the alienation of African Americans.

Overview

Chapter 2 examines the historical assimilation of racial/ethnic groups. Through this analysis I will show how previous immigrant groups have become "white" or at the very least have thinned their racial attitudes. I will also look at the assimilative process already taking place for Latino and Asian Americans and then examine the historical alienation of African Americans—contending that blacks were not given the chance to assimilate like other American racial/ethnic groups. This has led to a situation whereby African Americans face a much higher level of alienation in our society than do other racial minority groups. Finally, I will look at contemporary attitudes toward racial groups by using the LSAF data to illustrate that Americans perceive blacks to be the group who experience the most discrimination in the United States.

Chapter 3 concentrates on a discussion of residential and marital segregation, and also explores the social attitudes that support this segregation. If the alienation thesis is viable, then nonblack minorities as well as European Americans should be more hesitant to support intermarriage with blacks and having blacks as neighbors. Research from the LSAF indicates that there is a clear black/nonblack racial dichotomy that shows up in measures of social attitudes toward exogamy and residential integration. Research from a study by Camille Zubrinsky-Charles will strengthen this work, as it illustrates that nonblack minorities tend to reject blacks as potential neighbors. Thus African Americans face a level of rejection not experienced by other racial minorities.

Chapter 4 concentrates on research that documents the basic difference in social attitudes between African Americans and European Americans. African Americans tend to adopt more progressive attitudes than European Americans on issues that affect disenfranchised racial groups, are more supportive of talking about racial issues, and are more supportive of integrated churches. The LSAF data are used to show that on key issues, the social attitudes of Latino Americans and Asian Americans tend to be as close to a European American perspective as to an African American outlook, or even closer. I will use the evidence from this chapter to argue that these nonblack racial groups are not only assimilating into the dominant group residentially and maritally, but also are beginning to identify with whites by adopting attitudes similar to those of majority group members.

Chapter 5 focuses on how a process that allows Latino and Asian Americans into the dominant society may occur. I speculate that we are heading into a society where nonblack racial groups will eventually become incorporated into the dominant culture and, for all practical purposes, become "white." This process will be especially strong among the children and grandchildren of today's first- and second-generation nonblack minorities. I will also lay out the assumptions that I have used in asserting that this process will take place. If my assumptions are sound, then the process described in this chapter is very likely to take place.

In conclusion, Chapter 6 examines the implications of the arguments presented in this book. The main racial issue in the United States has been, and will continue to be, the divide between blacks and whites. As they attempted to assess for American racial reality, researchers must account for this divide. But an important question remains: Who is white? In the past, our understanding of race has been shaped by a white/nonwhite dichotomy, but I assert that a black/nonblack dichotomy is the best way to approach studies of race and ethnicity. It is important to evaluate how the acceptance of a black/nonblack dichotomy may change such studies. Finally, I speculate about some of the political, social, and cultural implications that will likely emerge in the coming black/nonblack society and investigate public policy implications.

A research caveat is in order. Within the context of the following chapters, I will strive to utilize tables that are not statistically complicated and will generally compare the means of the different groups to examine the extent of the differences between them. In this manner I hope to communicate the results of this research to a wide audience in a way that does not necessitate having a sophisticated understanding of statistics. Nevertheless, for those readers with more technical expertise, I include in the book's appendix some of the findings that have undergone more rigorous statistical testing.

For the most part I will employ a broad usage of racial terminology. I freely interchange the term "African American" with "black," and "Latino" with "Hispanic." Nevertheless, I will not always freely interchange "European American" with "white," since the former term indicates a person with a European ancestry, while the latter term, I argue, will soon have a more expanded meaning. While I freely use the term "European American" when discussing current and past assessments of majority group members, it is my contention that this term will soon be outdated as a way of describing the racial majority, since nonblack minorities will assimilate into the dominant society.

Notes

1. There is evidence that many Americans already believe that whites are a minority of the U.S. population (Nadeau, Niemi, and Levine 1993).

2. In the 2000 elections the Republicans made a big push to attract nonwhites. They nominated George W. Bush, a governor who had been relatively successful in attracting nonwhite voters in Texas, and staged a convention where racial minorities were paraded on the center stage in an effort to change the Republicans' image as being a "whites-only" club. Even after the election, President Bush engaged in a quasi-quota system of appointing racial minorities as cabinet members, unlike his father and Republican presidents before him, who adhered to a more pure "color-blind" model for

appointments. That the Republicans were largely unsuccessful in their bid to attract racial minorities does not detract from the fact that they take seriously concerns about a shrinking white voting population.

3. It can be argued that "Latino American" denotes an ethnicity, not a race. Yet a common American social perception of Hispanics is that they are a distinct racial group. While race is a biological fallacy, it is an important social construction, and I believe that this perception has important implications for Americans labeled as "Latino." Thus I will discuss the contemporary Latino American population as a distinct race rather than as an ethnic group.

4. Some researchers, such as Mary Waters (1990, 1999) and Richard Alba (1990), argue that these groups have never completely assimilated. These researchers contend that ethnic identity is still somewhat salient for European ethnic groups. This argument should not distract from the fact that a great deal of assimilation has occurred for these groups. The evidence of this assimilation is so strong that by the middle of the twentieth century, social scientists were already dismissing ethnicity as a way of retaining cultural maintenance for Europeans and instead focused upon religious differences (Kennedy 1944; Herberg 1955; Gordon 1964). Furthermore, even if these European groups have been able to maintain some of their ethnic distinctness, it is clear that they do not have minority status in American society. At least when it comes to having a position of power, European ethnic groups have completely assimilated into the mainstream.

5. Latino Americans surpassed all expectations about the size of their growth from 1990 to 2000 (Grieco and Cassidy 2001), and today this group is larger than African Americans.

6. Lewis and Yancey 1995; Porterfield 1978.

7. According to Paul Metzger (1971), early social scientists believed that racism was incompatible with the features of modern society and thus assimilation was inevitable for all minority groups.

8. Gordon 1964.

9. Gordon also postulates that there are two stages between identificational assimilation and civic assimilation. Those stages are attitudinal receptional assimilation, where there is a lack of stereotyping and prejudice between majority and minority group members; and behavioral receptional assimilation, where there is a lack of discrimination between majority and minority group members. These latter two stages are very closely related to civic assimilation, since when majority group members no longer stereotype or discriminate against a certain minority group, acceptance into majority group status is not likely to be far behind. Since both concepts are closely related to civic assimilation, I will not attempt to deal with attitudinal or behavioral receptional assimilation.

10. Doane 1997.

11. See, for example, Lie 1995.

12. Waters's examination of first-generation West Indians (1999) found little evidence of this transnational identity. Yet, as she argues, if there is a racial group that has a strong motivation to maintain their ethnic identity

and avoid an American identity it is the West Indians, who perceive African Americans as having a lower status than black immigrants. If West Indians are unlikely to develop an identity that transcends race, then it seems less likely that other racial groups are able to sustain a transnational identity.

13. Portes and Zhou 1993.

14. Gibson 1989; Suarez-Orozco 1987; Matute-Bianchi 1991.

15. James 1994; Massey and Denton 1996, 1987, 1988; Lewis and Yancey 1995; Merton 1941; Herring and Amissah 1997.

16. Massey and Denton 1996; James 1994; Lewis and Yancey 1995; Spickard 1989.

17. Isaacs 1975.

18. Geertz 1963; Shils 1957.

19. Cornell and Hartmann 1998.

20. The tendency for European ethnic groups to downplay the importance of their ethnicity is well documented in Waters 1990.

21. Campbell 1965.

22. Gallup Organization 1997; ABC/Washington Post Poll 1989; Kinder and Sanders 1996.

23. Kluegel 1990; Schuman et al. 1997; Schuman and Steeh 1996.

24. Alba 1995; Fairchild 1925; Kennedy 1944.

25. Moskos and Butler 1996.

26. Metzger (1971) argues that the early propensity of sociologists was to search for the possible functions of the African American community so that they could explain the inability of blacks to experience assimilation. But such a perspective fails to consider the power dynamics that operate to maintain the disenfranchisement of African Americans. Likewise, I contend that it is much easier to explain the alienation of African Americans by looking at how external social forces have operated to keep them out of the dominant society rather than attempting to utilize internal cultural reasons for their estrangement. The evidence in this book will tend to support the former, rather then the latter, explanation.

27. This alienation thesis concerns the general placing of racial groups. We should expect that certain Hispanic and Asian ethnicities will be more likely to assimilate than others. My argument is that the members in these two racial groups will generally be more likely than African Americans to experience acceptance as part of the majority group and to adopt the attitudes of the majority group on racialized issues.

28. Glazer 1993.

29. Bobo and Hutchings 1996.

30. Fang, Sidanius, and Pratto 1998; Emerson and Smith 2000; Kinder and Sanders 1996; Dawson 2000.

31. Carr 1997; Hacker 1992; Feagin and Sikes 1994; Kozol 1992; Robinson 2001; Bell 1992; West 1994; Manning 2000; Oliver and Shapiro 1995.

32. For example, Phil Nash and Frank Wu (1997) illustrate that the controversy over fundraising for the Democratic Party led to a scrutiny of Asian Americans that members of other racial groups escaped.

33. Warren and Twine 1997.
34. Szymanski 1983.
35. Blauner 1972.
36. Bonilla-Silva 2001.
37. McIntosh 2002; Bonilla-Silva 2001; Dalton 2002.
38. Bonilla-Silva 2001; Virtanen and Huddy 1998; Emerson, Smith, and Sikkink 1999; Kluegel 1990; Bobo 2000; Pettigrew 2000; Sears, Henry, and Kosterman 2000.
39. Of course, none of this is to argue that we should not assess how social structures in American society may be changing, or have changed, in such a way as to perpetuate the racial alienation of African Americans and to accommodate the entrance of Hispanic and Asian Americans into the dominant society. Clearly, such an analysis would be an incredibly valuable extension to this present study. I am merely illustrating that the assessment of social attitudes to discover whether the alienation thesis has merit is especially valuable given that there is still significant debate as to which social structures are the best sources of modern racism.
40. Moskos and Butler 1996; Lieberson 1980; Hacker 1992.
41. Of all the major racial groups in the United States, only African Americans have historically experienced the ravages of slavery on a consistent basis. It can be plausibly argued that, with the exception of Native Americans, no racial group in the United States has historically suffered the amount of racial oppression that African Americans have faced. However, unlike Native Americans, African Americans still have sufficient numbers to create the visibility necessary to produce aversive reactions from majority group members. This is important since there is evidence that the number of minorities present in a given area is correlated to the level of racial hostility a group receives (Olzak, Shanahan, and West 1994; Giles and Hertz 1994; Taylor 1998). Given this social history and constant threat some perceive from the African American community, it can be hypothesized that blacks will face more racial animosity than other racial groups.
42. Douglas Massey and Nancy Denton (1996) argue that skin color is a major force behind the type of residential segregation African Americans face. They demonstrate this by comparing light-skinned and dark-skinned Puerto Ricans, the latter of whom endure more segregation. Extrapolating this to black/white relations allows for the possible hypothesis that darker skin acts as a signal of African heritage. Latinos with dark skin can suffer some of the stigma that African Americans generally endure.
43. According to the National Roster of Black Elected Officials (1997), the number of such officials nearly quadrupled from 1972 to 1996 (from 2,264 to 8,395). Mexican Americans have also increased in representation, to 5,466 Latino officials in 1994 (National Roster of Hispanic Elected Officials), 4,276 of whom were in the five southwestern states, where most Mexican Americans live. It seems plausible to argue that most majority group members are less likely to be represented by a Hispanic American political official than by an African American political official.
44. It can be argued that the acceptance of pluralism is unlikely for a

group that is geographically dispersed, shares the language and religion of the majority group, and has experienced irregular but progressive advancement of socioeconomic status. Those qualities characterize African Americans. Yet despite this expectation, it is possible that African Americans have historically experienced a great deal of social rejection that enables them to become comfortable with separation from the majority group. In such a scenario, blacks may continue to keep majority group members out of their social spheres even as they progressively receive less social rejection from the dominant group.

2

How to Become White

It is natural to believe that the way things are today is the way they have always been. For example, today individuals tend to choose their prospective spouses without significant interference by family members. However, arranged marriages were historically the cultural norm for many societies,[1] and until recently we have had a system in the United States known as "calling," whereby the parents of young women could weed out all undesirable suitors.[2] Even though parental involvement in spousal choice today is relatively minimal, this has not always been the case. Social customs and norms are subject to change, and those changes often bring new customs and norms later generations will consider "natural." Likewise, we generally take it for granted that the racial structure of today is a natural outgrowth of the racial differences of the past. But European ethnic groups that today are considered white were once thought of as being different from majority group members, and it seemed "natural" for Americans to perceive them as ethnic or racial minorities. Over time, members of those groups lost their minority status and were accepted into majority group society.

The future racial structure in the United States is very likely to be different. To predict this future, it is advisable to understand the past. Because we often assume that the racial structure has not historically changed, it is easy to believe that our future will be similar to the present. When we forget that certain European groups were once treated as minority group members, there is a tendency to accept a static concept of whiteness. It is only when we recognize that the definition of majority group status is dynamic and evolving that we can conceptualize a future where notions of whiteness will change. Because of the dynamic and expansive nature of majority group status, it is reasonable to predict that individuals who are not defined as white today will be defined as white in the future.

Merely predicting that there are groups who will gain majority status is not sufficient for understanding the future American racial structure. Clearly some groups have a much better chance to become "white" than other groups. To discover which groups are likely to become white, it is important to look for clues in the past transformation of formerly nonwhite groups. What is the general pattern of those who were once minority groups but now are considered white? Which groups today best fit into that pattern and which groups seem unable to move toward majority group status?

Such questions are vital to understanding the future of American race relations, and this chapter will attempt to answer them. I will first define the basic concepts of assimilation and cultural pluralism. I then look at the historical evidence surrounding the assimilation, or the thinning of the racial/ethnic identities, of European ethnic groups. This will put me in a position to explore the assimilation experienced by Latino and Asian Americans. In doing so, I demonstrate that these nonblack minority groups are following a similar path that European ethnic immigrants followed in years past. Then I will look at the historical evidence concerning African Americans and their inability to find social acceptance. This examination will document the historical alienation African Americans have experienced, using an elaboration of the "one-drop rule" to show the exceptionality of the black experience. Finally, I will look at data from the 1999–2000 Lilly Survey of American Attitudes and Friendships (LSAF) documenting the fact that Americans realize the degree to which African Americans experience greater discrimination (alienation) in the United States and thus provide the theoretical bases for my claim that blacks suffer greater alienation than do other racial groups. It is this alienation that will keep their racial identities "thick" in comparison to Hispanic and Asian Americans, who are in the process of moving into majority group status.

Assimilation or Cultural Pluralism?

When different racial groups experience relative equality, two types of race relations become possible.[3] Either the two racial groups will culturally merge, or they will remain distinct. These two paths, which represent contrasting ways that race relations may be conceptualized, are called assimilation and cultural pluralism. Assimilation can be defined as "the process by which a subordinate individual or group takes on the characteristics of the dominant group and is eventually accepted as part of that group."[4] Assimilation can be readily seen in the tendency of second- and third-generation immigrants to adopt cultural aspects of the United States,[5] and to speak English as opposed to their native tongue.[6] Cultural pluralism can be defined as "a situation in which each ethnic group preserves its own traditions, language, customs and lifestyle."[7] Pluralism can be readily seen in the ethnic enclaves that have persisted in the United States,[8] as well as in the tendency of some racial minorities to maintain primary relationships only with members of their racial in-group.

Currently there is a debate as to whether assimilation or cultural pluralism should, or will, dominate future race relations.[9] Nathan Glazer has contended that assimilation is an inevitable process that occurs due to the natural social process of intergroup relations.[10] If that is the true, then it seems reasonable that the best way to plan for future race relations is to prepare Americans for this assimilative process. However, I have documented some of the arguments against the inevitability of assimilation, and the proponents of cultural pluralism argue that it is desirable to preserve the distinct cultures of various racial and ethnic groups.[11] Therefore, we have seen a rise in multicultural programs that have been designed, in part, to further the ideas of cultural pluralism,[12] and as I noted in Chapter 1, several researchers question whether Milton Gordon's type of straight-line assimilation actually occurs.[13] Such critics can perceive pluralism as a better way to understand intergroup interaction, since this theory allows for the different experiences of contrasting racial groups— rather than an inevitable process toward assimilation as suggested by Gordon.

I take no sides in this debate. Yet it is reasonable to argue that the theoretical benefits of assimilation (e.g., majority group status for minority group members, greater acceptance of minority out-groups) are likely tied to whether assimilation takes place in an "Anglo-conformist" model, whereby minority group members lose their distinctive nature and merely imitate the majority group culture, or whether assimilation takes place in a "melting-pot" model, whereby both majority and minority groups are altered to form a novel culture. An Anglo-conformist model is one that is less respectful to the culture of minority group members, while a melting-pot model offers minority group members the opportunity to gain an equal status in the construction of a new American culture.

Gordon's theoretical perspective would predict that, over time, former new immigrant groups will adopt many of the cultural patterns of the host group, penetrate the social structures of the dominant group, intermarry and live among members of the dominant group, begin to think like members of the dominant group, and then finally become dominant group members. Cultural pluralists argue that such a process is the cultural genocide of minority groups. While Gordon's predictions may be correct for some minority groups, I contend that this assimilative pattern is not an option available to all racial groups. A racial/ethnic group has the option of fighting to maintain its distinctive culture only if that group has the ability to become incorporated into the dominant society. If a racial/ethnic group is not allowed to assimilate into the dominant society, then that group has no choice but to accept cultural pluralism and remain distinct from the majority. It is easier to opt out of participation in majority group membership than to choose to be included in the dominant society, because minority group members control the first option while the second option depends upon acceptance by majority group members. For groups without the opportunity to assimilate, the question of whether such assimilation is desirable is irrelevant. The debate over the desirability of assimilation or cultural pluralism is meaningful only to groups with the opportunity to assimilate into the dominant culture.

The Historical Assimilation of European Ethnic Groups

If I walked up to a German American today and asked that person about his or her race, that person would likely identify him- or herself as white or European American. If I had done this in the early 1800s, that person would likely have identified him- or herself as German. These different answers offer us an illustration of how thin racial identity has become for European ethnic groups. It is not that contemporary European ethnic groups do not understand that they have a different ethnicity than other Europeans. Rather it is the case that their ethnicity is not very salient to their current racial identity. These groups have assimilated into the dominant culture to such a degree that previous ethnic identities are little more than an afterthought. It is well established historically that many Europeans who were once considered minorities have eventually obtained dominant group status.[14] While some theorists may question whether these European ethnic groups have assimilated completely into a "white" identity,[15] there is no question that southern and eastern European ethnic groups enjoy the privileges of majority group status, sharing the top position in America's racial hierarchy with other Europeans, and there is strong evidence that for many European Americans an ethnic identity separate from majority group status no longer exists.[16] To understand which contemporary minority groups may have the opportunity to assimilate and gain access to such racial power, it is important to document this process among European ethnic groups.

To understand the contemporary racial pecking order, it is vital to comprehend how the concept of today's "white" race has developed. The early majority group, the English Americans, were not defined as such. After the Revolutionary War, English Americans relegated all non-English Europeans in the United States to second-class status. While these European ethnic groups did not suffer the same degree of rejection that non-Europeans faced, they were still not granted the full privileges of majority status. The English were not only the dominant group in social power, but they were the numerical majority. In 1790 about 63 percent of the U.S. population claimed nationality of descent from the British Isles.[17] While other Europeans generally faced prejudice and discrimination, these experiences were uncommon for English immigrants.[18]

As immigration brought more non-English Europeans to the New World, the English begin to exhibit a typical reaction of the majority group toward an encroaching minority group—they resisted immigration. The Federalists, the political conservatives of their day, feared that the poor immigrants would swell the ranks of their political opponents.[19] This reaction set the stage for the nativist movements of that time. But these movements were not successful in maintaining the numerical dominance of the English Americans. In response to this immigration and their numeric loss, the English began to accept northern and western Europeans into the dominant culture. This process began with ethnic groups who were more culturally similar to the English—the Welsh and the Scandinavians. The majority group then incorporated other northern/western European groups—such as the French and Germans, who possessed more cultural distinctness—into dominant group status. Perhaps due to their long conflict with the English, the Irish resisted assimilation longer than most other northern/western European groups, but eventually even they become part of the majority group.[20] In time the English were no longer a numerical majority in the United States, but they still were part of the core of a larger majority group called "white."

But the United States was not just attractive to northern/western Europeans. Immigrants from the southern and eastern parts of Europe experienced a degree of political and social unrest that influenced many of them to come to the United States. The immigration was slow during the early part of the nineteenth century, but accelerated in the later part of that century and peaked in the early portion of the twentieth. The coalition of northern/western European groups who were known as "whites" began to experience the threat of being outnumbered. Just as the English had done before them, the majority group of this period developed nativist reactions to the high number of southern and eastern Europeans who were entering the country. Fears of the increase in immigration led to the National Origins Quota Act of 1921, which greatly limited immigration from southern/eastern Europe. Yet these measures were not enough to head off the eventual shrinking of the northern/western European population relative to other racial groups, and a process of accepting southern/eastern Europeans began to develop.

Because they enjoy majority group status today, it is easy to ignore the degree of discrimination and racism that southern/eastern Europeans historically faced. Leonard Dinnerstein and David Reimers document much of the early discrimination and cruelty faced by European ethnic groups in the latter part of the nineteenth century.[21] They illustrate that the early Italians were despised and sometimes forced to go to all-black schools, Greeks faced physical attacks, and the Polish were thought of as being animals instead of humans. To the majority group members of that day, Europeans from southern/eastern Europe were at the very least an inferior form of "whites," if not an inferior race altogether. Because Americans place individuals from these ethnic groups fully into the dominant group today, it is easy to forget that at one time these individuals were considered alien to the dominant group, just as Latino and Asian Americans are today. In the middle of the nineteenth century these European ethnic groups were seen as "unassimilable" and distinct,[22] and Deanna Pagnini and S. Philip Morgan argue that the prohibitions against outmarriage experienced by these groups created a "caste-like" reality for southern/eastern Europeans.[23]

In time an "Americanization" movement competed with this racism.[24] This movement emphasized the need of immigrants to quickly fit into American society. Immigrants were expected to speak only English, lose the vestiges of their old culture, and avoid ethnic organizations. This emphasis lessened some of the discrimination these ethnic groups faced, and helped preserve the stability of the dominant Anglo American culture. Southern/eastern Europeans began a process of assimilation that would serve to defend the interests of the dominant group by lessening the number of minority group members, and toward the end of the twentieth century southern/eastern Europeans were no longer considered to be distinct from the majority group. For many of them their country of origin became merely an ethnic designation that did not have a great deal of importance to their social identity.

Exploring the creation of a majority group culture and identity is vital for assessing how that culture may envelop future racial/ethnic groups. An excellent examination into the formation of ethnic identity in European Americans is a study undertaken by Mary Waters.[25] She conducted interviews of Italian, Polish, and Irish Roman Catholics in an attempt to examine the effects of the ethnic resurgence in the 1970s. Waters found that the ethnic identity of her subjects did not affect much of their everyday life. Rather, ethnicity tended to be voluntary and was influential in only superficial ways— such as celebrating certain holidays or cooking an ethnic meal. Waters illustrates that ethnic identity does not have the same global effect upon the social place of European ethnics as racial identity does for racial minorities. In this sense, European ethnic identity has become very thin. Furthermore, instead of building a strong personal and social identity upon their ethnic origins, southern/eastern Europeans use their ethnic origins to legitimate a philosophy that defends majority group status. They do so by asserting that their ethnic group has been able to overcome racial discrimination and succeed in the United States, which means that the same should be possible for racial minorities. Waters suggests that the voluntary nature of their ethnic identity makes it difficult for whites to perceive that racial identity is not voluntary, and many of her respondents were unaware of the degree of importance skin color continues to play in the lives of racial minorities.

I will more thoroughly investigate the implications of majority group identity in Chapter 4, but at this point it is important to introduce the concept of "white privilege."[26] This concept is related to the generally unrecognized advantages majority group members have in the United States. Much research in "whiteness" studies documents how this concept is related to an ideology among dominant group members that enables them to preserve the racial status quo. White privilege is a staple within majority group ideology and plays a central role in the racial identity of majority group members. The construction of a white identity is at least partially based upon how that identity helps dominant group members to defend their racial privilege.[27] As a result of the construction of a white identity, southern/eastern European ethnic groups who formerly faced powerful oppression have also incorporated an ideology that is supportive of white privilege. For example, Michael Omi and Howard Winant illustrate how European ethnic groups who were formerly excluded from dominant group status developed attitudes, such as the rejection of non-European groups, that helped promote them into a majority group status.[28] Whereas historically the cultural norms that buttress these ethnic cultures generally differed from majority group ideology, contemporary ethnic cultural values support the ideology of the dominant culture.

Waters's work suggests that the contemporary ethnic identity of European Americans is peripheral to their core philosophy. Other work has suggested that there is a core philosophy among European Americans, part of which is the defense of white privilege.[29] Majority group members still recognize that they have an ethnicity, but the voluntary and peripheral nature of this ethnicity makes it a tool supporting contemporary majority group ideology. This is in stark contrast to the thickness of white ethnic identity earlier in U.S. history. Due to the discrimination and nativism faced by these European ethnics, their minority identity was a core part of their culture. The transition of ethnic identity from its central role among American ethnics to its current voluntary status can illustrate how minority groups of this day can eventually lose the centrality of their minority identity and accept majority group status.

Noel Ignatiev uses the Irish as an example of how a European ethnic group can come into the United States as a minority group and then over time adopt majority group status.[30] He argues that this assimilation was achieved in part because of the willingness of the

Irish to reject their former support of abolitionism and to adopt an antiblack stance. Based on his work, it can be argued that part of the process by which the Irish were able leave their minority group status was through the acceptance of an important part of the dominant group ideology of that day—acknowledging the inferiority of blacks. The notion that the Irish, as well as other European ethnic groups,[31] have undergone a process by which they have gained the status of becoming "white" has until recently been a presumed assumption within historical research. The only real question for such historians is why these groups were able to gain majority group status.

However, the idea that European ethnic groups were ever white has recently come under attack. Some historians have called into question the idea that these groups were ever seen as not being white. Eric Arnesen is a powerful supporter of this position.[32] He contends that southern/eastern European ethnic groups were always considered to be white, although it is clearly the case that they were viewed as inferior to northern/western Europeans. Historians such as Noel Ignatiev, Matthew Jacobson, and David Roediger have argued that the process by which European immigrant groups have gained majority group status is one of racial transformation and they have generally been credited for their exploration of the historical constructiveness of race.[33] Yet Eric Arnesen and Adolph Reed dismiss the evidence that these groups were ever considered to be nonwhite.[34] Barbara Fields takes this argument even further as she argues that because only African Americans were subject to the inflexibility of the one-drop rule, racial categories have historically served to distinguish who is black from who is not.[35] Whether she is correct in her assessment of a historical black/nonblack dichotomy, her observation is appreciated, as I will later illustrate how this dichotomy is part of the future of American race relations.

Whether the nineteenth-century southern/eastern Europeans were considered to be an inferior type of "white" or a different race than the majority group of their day, certain facts are undisputed about their interaction with the latter. First, these European groups were seen as inferior to the dominant group when they first arrived in the United States. Even if they were not considered to be racially different from northern/western Europeans, they still faced discrimination, violence, segregation, and social rejection. Second, in time the members of these groups accepted ideas of white supremacy. This acceptance of white supremacy, even among those who may not have been considered white, was a factor in helping these groups to gain more acceptance in the dominant society. Third, today members of these groups are clearly seen as white. For contemporary students of race/ethnic studies, the question is whether these groups were transformed from a clear nonwhite status to become white or whether they gained their social position by improving their status within the white racial classification.

These observations suggest that there was motivation for any European ethnic group to accept this ideology, so that they could maintain a superior position to African Americans.[36] Regardless of whether they have partial "white" status or not, as European groups moved closer to full acceptance into the dominant group status, the ideology of white supremacy became acceptable. This trend is not different from the acceptance of color-blind forms of racism today by nonblack racial/ethnic groups. In fact, Mary Waters's work illustrates how the these groups can use their former minority status to condemn the inability of blacks to improve their socioeconomic standing.[37] The acceptance of dominant group ideologies is related to the fact that these European groups believed themselves to be at least partially white and began to enter into the stage of identificational assimilation described by Milton Gordon.[38] Even at a point in our history when the ethnic identities of these groups had not "thinned" enough for them to have completely lost their distinctions from "whites," they were incorporated far enough into the dominant culture that they began to accept some of the majority group ideologies. For example, in the latter part of the nineteenth century, ideological distinctions between the Irish and majority group members still existed. The Irish were a big part of a labor movement that was consistently more progressive than the political ideology of whites in general. But as the Irish ethnic identities thinned out, much of this distinction has finally disappeared, illustrating that while there will be ideological movement toward the positions of majority group members by racial group members who are in the identificational stages of assimilation, some distinctions between minority group members and majority group members will likely remain until members of the former have been fully incorporated into the dominant culture. The acceptance of the ideology of the dominant group does not happen overnight.

A general pattern emerges from a historical understanding of European ethnic groups. These groups come to the United States as immigrants and are segregated from the dominant group. The ethnic group then initially faces discrimination and racism. But these groups become so numerous that they become a threat to the dominant group, which then must take measures to neutralize that threat. Thus over time these groups begin to structurally and culturally assimilate into the dominant culture. Their ethnic identities become thinner. They begin to accept the ideology of the majority group culture. This acceptance is linked to the perception of the minority group that they are gaining full majority group status. Eventually these groups attain majority group status, which serves both the current majority group and the ethnic minority group. It serves the minority group since its members gain social status and escape future racism. It serves the majority group since its members can maintain their numerical advantage over other racial minorities by incorporating former minority European ethnics.

As we look into the near future it appears that the European Americans who have been labeled as white will be outnumbered by those who are not part of the majority group. Historically, when the dominant group has been numerically challenged, it reacts first with nativist/antiminority racism before an assimilation process eventually begins that incorporates some of the minority groups into the dominant group. Milton Gordon's pattern of assimilation predicts that residential and marital assimilation will take place before identificational assimilation. If we want to predict who are likely to become the majority group members of the future, we have to look for groups that are experiencing residential and marital assimilation as well as beginning to accept the ideology of majority group culture. An examination of the two major nonblack minority groups in the United States, Hispanic and Asian Americans, will provide evidence that this pattern has started—ensuring the continued numerical dominance of the majority group.

Latino and Asian American Assimilation

The similar phenotypes of European ethnic groups to the majority group members of their day undoubtedly made it easier for those groups to experience acceptance than for contemporary Hispanic and Asian Americans. But it is a mistake to believe that complete assimilation of groups who are not European is impossible because of phenotype differences. While Latino and Asian Americans have clearly not experienced a thinning of their racial attitudes to the same degree as European ethnic groups, there is evidence that these groups are experiencing certain levels of acceptance and incorporation into the dominant culture. The important question is whether there are limitations of this incorporation. As long as they are undergoing the process documented in the previous section—that is, structural assimilation followed by acceptance of the ideological framework of majority group members—then civic assimilation is not only possible but also likely.

Many of the groups that we call "Hispanic" were created by the racial intermixing of Spanish and Native Americans, with smatterings of Africans thrown into the mix. Thus, within several Hispanic American ethnic groups are individuals who are partially European American. Yet this partial European heritage has not protected Latino Americans from racism. Mexicans, established throughout the southwestern and western United States before European Americans, were dispossessed of their land. Mexican Americans continue to face nativist reactions to their presence because they illustrated a numerical threat to the dominant group culture. Other Hispanic groups do not necessarily have the same claim to the land that is now called the "United States" as do Mexican Americans. Cubans, Nicaraguans, Puerto Ricans, and Guatemalans do not have as strong a historical origin in the United States as Mexicans. Many of these groups also differ from Mexican Americans in their "racial" makeup. For example, the group we call "Puerto Ricans" became established on the island of Puerto Rico, not in the area that is today known as the United States. In Puerto Rico, the early Native American populations were decimated and Africans were imported as slaves to take their place; thus the genetic mixing of Puerto Ricans contains a much heavier influx of Africans and a much lesser degree of Native American influence. It is also important to observe how long Hispanics groups have been in the United States. Other Central American groups such as the Salvadorians, Nicaraguans, and Guatemalans have come to the United States relatively late in its history. Many of these individuals immigrated after 1978 due to internal wars and political strife in their own countries. Clearly, such groups will be less likely to acculturate into the dominant society than Latino groups that have been here for at least a couple of generations, such as Mexican Americans and Puerto Ricans.

Despite these differences, non-Mexican Latino Americans and

Mexican Americans share certain traits that link their fates and lead to the tendency to classify these different ethnic groups into a single racial group. First, they share the Spanish language, which has been a continuing source of tension between Latino Americans and majority group members. Second, they have a country of origin that is very close to the United States. Without an ocean to separate the immigrants from Latin and Caribbean America from their homeland, it becomes much easier for those immigrants to keep in contact with their primary culture. This proximity also makes it more difficult for the majority group culture to totally assimilate members of these groups into the dominant society. The third trait that binds these groups together is the fact that there are varying degrees of European representation in their genetic ancestry. Perhaps because of the presence of Europeans within their ancestry, Hispanics are considered in the U.S. census as a separate ethnic rather than racial group, despite the amount of racism that Latino Americans have endured.[39] An argument can be made that the undisputed presence of European Americans in the genetic heritage of most Latino Americans will increase their tendency to assimilate.[40] Even for Latino Americans who do not have a strong presence of European genetic stock (i.e., those of darker skin color), the fact that other types of racial mixing have clearly occurred within their country of origin can serve to point out to them that they are not part of a "pure" race. Such knowledge may eventually help members of Hispanic groups to accept a change from minority status to majority group status.

These traits help to define the unique social position Latino Americans possess in the United States. Their potential European heritage can make it easier for them to experience social acceptance. Thus, while the advocates of an "internal colonialism" model have postulated that European American imperialism worked to perpetuate the residential segregation of Hispanic Americans,[41] there appears to be a limit to this segregation. Douglas Massey and Nancy Denton have documented the degree of residential segregation that African Americans experience within the United States.[42] They developed five dimensions of segregation. When a group experiences at least four of these dimensions, Massey and Denton argue that its members are experiencing "hypersegregation." They estimate that about a third of all African Americans live in areas where they are experiencing hypersegregation, but go on to note that there is not a single metropolitan area where Hispanic Americans are experiencing hyperseg-regation. The segregation of Hispanic Americans that does exist is likely tied to their economic conditions and will decrease if they can exhibit economic social mobility.[43]

Research into the marital assimilation of Hispanic Americans tells a similar story. There is a long-term trend toward more outmar-riage for Hispanic Americans,[44] and the longer a Hispanic stays in the United States the higher the probability of outmarriage.[45] Mario Barrera argues that there is a considerable amount of outmarriage taking place among Hispanic Americans and that those at higher lev-els of social class are especially likely to outmarry.[46] This correlation is much like the one noted for residential assimilation and suggests that as Hispanic Americans move into middle-class status, marital assimilation will increase at a faster rate. These residential and mari-tal changes within the Latino American community have altered it so much that as early as 1970 Fernando Penalosa suggested that Hispanics were starting to resemble the European immigrant group of a generation ago.[47] The implication of this observation is that the eventual acceptance of Latinos as "whites" is more likely than their continual existence as a minority group.

Yet the proximity of Latino Americans may operate to prevent easy assimilation. Because they do not have an ocean separating them from the American continent, it is all but impossible to stem the immigration of Hispanics. This proximity can also make it easier for those who immigrate into the United States to maintain their cultural heritage. The constant influx of newly arrived Latino immigrants guarantees the presence of "authentic" Hispanic communities in the United States. The presence of such strong Latino cultures provides a possible alternative for Hispanic Americans to the acceptance of dominant group values. As long as first- and second-generation immigrants make up a significant portion of the Latino population and the individuals in this population live in racially segregated com-munities, there will be a powerful counterforce to the possible assim-ilation of Hispanic Americans.

In sum, Hispanic Americans bring unique challenges to the idea of assimilation. Because of their potential European heritage they may experience a level of social acceptance that escapes other racial minorities. Yet the proximity of their host cultures can operate to neutralize some of this assimilation. To assess the prospects of future racial identificational assimilation for Hispanics, these unique aspects must be taken into account.

These aspects differ somewhat from the experiences of Asian Americans. While clearly there are a variety of nations represented among Asian Americans, the introduction of these ethnic groups into the United States tends to follow a similar path of voluntary migration. The historical introduction of Asian Americans is a better fit for the traditional immigration model than the patterns experienced by Hispanic Americans, since like the European ethnic immigrant, the Asian immigrant voluntarily chose to come to the United States to flee oppressive conditions. Unlike the tyrannical conditions of slavery or imperialism that other racial minority groups were forced to endure as they were introduced into the United States, immigration for most Asians was an opportunity for advancement.[48] This is not to state that Asian Americans were not subject to discrimination and oppression themselves once they came to the United States. But it is important to note that Asians generally came to the United States because they were leaving situations in their host countries that were perceived as worse than the possible discrimination they would face in the United States, and like the European ethnic groups before them, Asian Americans came into the United States under less harsh conditions than African Americans. This type of an introduction has led them to experience less alienation from the majority group.

The Asian immigrant experience is similar to that of southern/ eastern Europeans in other critical ways. For example, Asian immigrants came from a relatively wide variety of countries, and just as Americans historically group Europeans from certain countries together as a single racial group, the same trend has occurred for Asian Americans. This has meant that Asian Americans with vastly different cultural backgrounds experienced similar levels of rejection and acceptance from other Americans. Another important similarity between Asian and southern/eastern European immigrants is that members from many counties within both groups came to the United States at roughly the same time. The bulk of southern/eastern European immigration took place in the last part of the nineteenth century and the early part of the twentieth, with the 1921 National Origins Quota Act ending this large influx. The big push of Asian Americans occurred toward the end of the twentieth century as war, economic opportunities, and civil unrest served to dislodge many Asians from their host nations. In both cases the individuals from several host countries entered the United States within a given amount of time, and thus experienced similar social conditions that shaped their racial reality. An argument that the immigration experiences of Asians are similar to the immigration experiences of European ethnic groups has some basis in social reality.

However, it is a mistake to underestimate the degree of racism Asian Americans still face in the United States. Their experience differs from that of the European ethnics in that the phenotypic distinctions between Asian Americans and majority group members today are much more distinct than between southern/eastern European immigrants and the majority group of their day. Furthermore, the contemporary nature of this immigration means that the dominant society has not had the opportunity to adjust to the presence of Asians in the United States and Asians have not yet had the opportunity to become acculturated. There are some Asian ethnic groups, such as the Hmong, who are almost entirely first generation. Thus Asian Americans in general will continue to occupy a minority group status and suffer racism through stereotyping, violence, and discrimination.[49]

In time, the novelty of the introduction of Asians into American culture will disappear. The real challenge for assimilation is for Asian Americans to overcome phenotypic differences between themselves and European Americans. While southern/eastern Europeans could, and sometimes were, historically perceived as being biologically distinct from northern/western Europeans, they were still a closer phenotypical match to the majority group than individuals with Asian ancestry are to majority group members today. Given their similar history of immigration into the United States, if Asian Americans overcome the perceptions that they are biologically different from majority group members, then it can be argued that Asian Americans will eventually assimilate into the dominant group society in the same way that southern/eastern European ethnic groups have become "white."

The preceding section should not be taken to imply that Latino and Asian Americans do not continue to face discrimination today. Even as the Irish and other European ethnic groups underwent the process of assimilation, they still faced racism and nativism by the dominant group. Likewise, Hispanic and Asian Americans are likely to face racism and anti-immigration rhetoric for some time to come. It is common for the majority group to first resist immigration and use racism in an attempt to contain the numerical growth of minority groups. But when this does not work, the majority group adjusts to the growing presence of these minority groups by incorporating some of them into the dominant society. Such was the path of the southern/eastern Europeans, and I contend that this is the path that Hispanic and Asian Americans are currently walking.

Hispanic Americans and Asian Americans face different issues if they are to lose the thickness of their identities. The proximity of the host cultures of Hispanic Americans makes it more difficult for them to separate from their native cultures. Asian Americans lack the potential European genetic heritage that increases their ability to experience acceptance from the dominant culture. Both issues are linked to whether these racial minority groups will learn to perceive themselves as members of the majority group. If Latino Americans perceive themselves as members of the majority group, then those who live within the United States for a few generations will separate themselves from their native cultures, despite the presence of immigrant Hispanics. If Asian Americans overcome the perception that they are biologically different from majority group members, then the relatively high level of economic and educational success that they enjoy makes it likely that they will soon accept majority group status.[50]

It is important to point out that these assertions are made about Hispanic and Asian Americans in general. Clearly it is the case that some of the Latino and Asian ethnic groups will have a greater ability to assimilate than others. Those groups who have been in the United States for a longer period of time and have enjoyed more economic and educational success will have an easier time incorporating themselves into the dominant culture. Thus one should expect Mexican Americans to have a better chance to thin their racial identity than other Hispanic ethnic groups,[51] and among the Asians one can expect the Chinese and Japanese to become incorporated into the dominant culture more easily than recent Asian groups such as the Hmong. But while the alienation thesis may well be incorrect when examining specific Latino and Asian ethnicities, I still argue that it is accurate when we look at these nonblack groups in general, who are not subject to the type of alienation that African Americans face. The history of ethnic assimilation suggests that most Latino and Asian

Americans will soon experience identificational assimilation if they are able to avoid being continually alienated from the dominant society.

When that transformation is complete, our perception of the "whiteness" of Hispanic and Asian Americans will seem as natural as the current perceptions of "whiteness" we have of Italian or Irish Americans. Hispanic and Asian Americans will be relegated to an ethnic category that is voluntary for members of those groups. In the concluding chapter I will explore the implications of the assimilation of Latino and Asian Americans for racial/ethnic studies. However, it is also vital to recognize that the possible assimilation of African Americans has stagnated and that they do not have the opportunity to convert their racial status into a voluntary ethnicity. This makes it crucial to examine the alienation blacks continue to face.

The Historical Alienation of African Americans

While other groups have been able to lose the thickness of their racial/ethnic identities, or are currently assimilating into the dominant culture, this has not been the case for African Americans. There are important historical reasons why blacks have failed to assimilate into the majority group culture and why they show no evidence of being able to assimilate in the foreseeable future. The overarching feature of African American history is slavery, and the American slave system set the tone for the future racism and alienation toward African Americans. To justify slavery, European Americans developed a philosophical system of white superiority that reduced African Americans to a subhuman status. This status made it necessary to keep blacks separate from whites, even after slaves were freed. The phenomenon of slavery created the social conditions that supported the continual alienation of blacks. The extreme residential segregation in the North as well as the caste system of Jim Crow in the South are natural extensions to the historical chattel slavery of African Americans.

Slavery interrupted the natural progression of African Americans toward assimilation or attitudinal thinning. Other racial groups were allowed to adjust to the dominant culture relatively soon after their entrance, which led to their experiencing increasingly higher levels of acceptance by majority group members. In these groups, early alienation slowly gave way to less overt hostility by the dominant society. As the dominant culture accepted members of the minority groups, those minorities were encouraged to adopt the cultural norms of the majority group. This process of minority group assimilation into majority group culture and majority group acceptance by minority group members continues until the former racial minorities identify themselves, and are accepted, as majority group members. Yet this process was not possible for African Americans. Slavery made it necessary for majority group members to maintain a caste system for African Americans that deprived them of any possible social acceptance, and despite the adoption by African slaves of many European American cultural aspects, such as Christianity, they were unable to engage in the process of assimilation that other racial and ethnic groups experienced.

The interruption created by slavery was not overcome by emancipation. By the end of the Civil War, African Americans had been defined as less than human for such a long time that it was no longer possible to allow them to assimilate. European Americans had invested too much social prestige in their superiority over African Americans to permit them to attain social equality. This resistance was clearly demonstrated in the unwillingness of whites to defend the civil rights of newly freed blacks soon after the war. Thus the Hayes Compromise eliminated Reconstruction and delivered blacks to the horrors of Jim Crow, whose social policy was based on the historical idea developed during slavery that African Americans were generally inferior to European Americans. This notion led to a philosophy of social pollution that kept majority group members from interacting with blacks on an egalitarian basis. This exclusion differed by degrees, but not in nature, in white/black relations in the North. Even after the modern civil rights movement, the hesitation of whites to interact with blacks has been transformed from a formal restriction against interracial relations to an informal reluctance of whites to live next to African Americans and to intermarry with them.[52] Given the persistence of the notion of black inferiority and social pollution, it is not surprising that, unlike the experiences of European ethnic groups and Hispanics, African Americans who have been in this country for several generations are still unable to engage in wide-scale residential integration or socially acceptable interracial marriage.

Even though the ideology of overt white superiority has fallen out of favor, the racial distinctions envisioned in this ideology have perpetuated the notion that African Americans are biologically distinct from European Americans. While laws that support racism and segregation have been stricken from the books, this ideology can still manifest itself through more subtle forms of prejudice that lead to the rejection of African Americans as potential neighbors, coworkers, or marital partners.[53] African Americans remain persistently alienated from majority group members, having no option of assimilating into the dominant society, and because of that alienation they are not able to move into dominant group status. Thus they retain a racial identity that is connected to a notion of racial purity.

Mary Waters's work with West Indian immigrants illustrates the degree of alienation African Americans suffer, and the difficulty that blacks have assimilating into the dominant society.[54] She illustrates how these black immigrants come to the United States with optimism, nonattention to racism, a desire to save money, and other social values that contribute to their initial economic success. Much of this is due to their experience with a West Indian culture where racism against blacks is a problem, but not the systemic dysfunction that it is in the United States. West Indians simply have not experienced the level of racial alienation that American blacks have faced. This allows them to develop social attitudes that are in contrast to the more adversarial stance that native African Americans tend to have. Yet as these immigrants encounter the alienation their skin color brings, they find that their hard-won relative success is followed by a pattern of downward mobility for their children—who then tend to take on the adversarial pattern of other black Americans. Waters documents how the racial realities of discrimination and educational segregation the West Indians face begin to alter their previously optimistic attitudes toward American success, especially among their children, who have a more limited experience of a previous West Indian experience. Her research indicates that the ability of immigrants to eventually adopt the dominant social values is shaped, at least partially, by the structural and institutional forces they experience. Because of their African phenotype, West Indian immigrants are unable to sustain the social beliefs necessary to incorporate themselves into the dominant culture.

It can be argued that this type of alienation has not been suffered by African Americans alone. There is a powerful argument to be made that Native Americans have suffered more at the hands of the majority group members than have African Americans.[55] Just as

European Americans had motivation for dehumanizing African Americans to use them as slaves, they had ample motivation for dehumanizing Native Americans so that their land could be taken. The data presented in this book only allow me to compare the alienation of blacks to the possible assimilation of Hispanic and Asian Americans. It is plausible that Native Americans suffer the same amount of alienation that African Americans have endured, making it impossible for them to eventually obtain majority group status. Yet I do not believe that this is the case. Some Indians appear to easily assimilate into the dominant culture, while others live in a situation of cultural pluralism. The key as to which racial pattern prevails is whether Native Americans live on a reservation. Research has indicated that Native Americans outmarry at a much greater rate than African Americans,[56] and this rate is especially high for Native Americans who do not live on a reservation. Perhaps this outmarriage is a result of the fact that nonreservation Native Americans cannot easily find other Native Americans to marry, but it is also a result of the relative acceptance of whites of marriage with Native Americans. This high rate of intermarriage illustrates that whites do not reject Native Americans as potential marital partners as readily as they reject blacks. Since Native Americans who do not live on a reservation have undergone a high degree of marital assimilation, I suspect they will soon undergo the process of identificational assimilation as well. Living on a reservation may allow some Native Americans to retain their heritage culture, and to live in relative isolation from majority group members, but those who leave the reservation seem likely to experience some degree of assimilation—much like the experiences of Hispanic and Asian Americans. While there may always be groups of Native Americans living on reservations who refuse to assimilate, those who leave the reservation appear to have a choice about whether to develop a thin racial identity. That choice is denied to African Americans.

Blacks live in a racial reality whereby their social status is fixed. It is fixed because they have historically experienced a degree of alienation that ties their racial identity more completely to the historical ravages of racism than for other minority groups. Because of this alienation, even today African Americans are unable to escape the racialized social position given to them or their lower racial identity. The racial identity of African Americans has a more important role in establishing the social and economic outcomes within their lives compared to the racial identities of other groups. The saliency of this identity can be illustrated by an exploration of the one-drop rule, a concept that has generally been applied only to African Americans.

The One-Drop Rule and the Saliency of an African American Identity

The power of the one-drop rule can be illustrated within my own personal life. I am an African American married to a white woman. Presently we have no children. When we discuss the possibility of having a child, my wife often asks a very relevant question. She wants to know why a child born to us would be perceived as black, but not white. After all, she is a white woman and the child would come from her womb. She will contribute as much of the DNA as I will. In fact, because I, like most African Americans, have some European American genetic ancestry, and she, to the best of our knowledge, does not have any African American genetic ancestry, a child of ours would have more "white" genes than "black" genes. But she is aware of the social rules of our society, which state that a child from a black/white union can be considered black, but never white.

My wife's question touches upon a cornerstone of American racial reality: the static nature of African American identity. In recent years there has been a movement toward granting multiracial individuals the right of self-definition.[57] This movement has made it easier for individuals with multiple racial ancestries to identify themselves as multiracial. However, even with the progress that this social movement has made, it is still clear that mixed-race individuals who have a white/black ancestry are not free to define themselves as white, although they are free to identify themselves as black.[58] This social phenomenon is not an accident. It is the cumulative result of the historical racism that has plagued African Americans. The system of slavery required a steady source of slaves. As this system moved from one of indentured servanthood, or temporary slavery, to one of lifetime oppression, a need developed to differentiate between white workers and black slaves. To meet this need it was important to define who was black, so that Africans and African Americans could be condemned to slavery. The need was met with the development of the one-drop rule, which stipulated that individuals with any amount of African ancestry had to be labeled "black."[59] The rule had the dual effect of discouraging respectable white/black romantic unions, since the children of such unions would be condemned to slave status, as well as providing a growing source of future slaves through the rape and sexual coercion of black women slaves.

The one-drop rule is a rule only for African Americans. F. James Davis illustrates that it has never been consistently applied to any other racial group in America.[60] For example, when Native Americans married European Americans, their offspring were not thought to be pure Native Americans, but instead were generally conceptualized as being of a mixed race.[61] Historically, this "in-between" status has meant that while the offspring did not enjoy the full benefits of majority group status, neither were they seen as being purely Native American. The fact that black/white unions produce offspring who have been, and to a lesser degree still are today, fully characterized as being black indicates the higher degree of persistence of black identity when compared to Native American identity. This persistence is a manifestation of the alienation suffered by African Americans, since it denotes a social prestige caste system whereby African Americans are unable to escape their lower racial status.

Because of the one-drop rule, there was a strong barrier blacks had to overcome if they were to lose their racial status. Unlike the European immigrants, who could eventually become "white" if given enough time, African Americans are stuck in their lower caste. The only exception to this is when the child of a white/black union possesses a sufficient degree of European phenotype that he or she is able to "pass" as white. While such an option may have been attractive to light-skinned individuals, given the degree of oppression that African Americans had to face, it is an option that meant leaving one's family and friends as well as keeping a secret from future friends, associates, and sometimes even lovers. It would be a mistake to underestimate the degree of sacrifice that goes with such a decision. The difficulty of moving out of the black race trapped African Americans at the bottom of the racial hierarchy and is still a dominant feature of black racial reality in the United States.

The presence of the one-drop rule illustrates the unique status of racial identity among African Americans. At times, individuals with a minuscule amount of African genetic heritage were defined as black,[62] and being black trumped all other possible racial identities. To be black has been, and I argue continues to be, a prison that can be used to maintain a minority group's estrangement from the rest of society.[63] The exceptional nature of black identity is important to the preservation of white privilege, since this identity provides dominant group members with an out-group by which a definition of whiteness can be formed. In other words, to be white is to not be black. The resilience of the black identity indicates how important this definition of whiteness is to Americans. For this out-group to be maintained, blacks simply cannot be allowed to escape their racial status—as European ethnic groups can and, as I will argue, as Hispanics and Asians will eventually be allowed to do. The persistence of the one-drop rule, and its enfranchisement to such an extent that even African American activist organizations defend it,[64] exhibit its foundational nature in American racial reality.

Who Faces the Greatest Oppression?

Understanding our racial history is vital for comprehending current racial reality. But despite the importance of historical knowledge, there is still a need to verify notions of historical alienation by an examination of current racial reality. The bulk of this contemporary examination will take place in the next two chapters, but since it is the purpose of this chapter to establish the historical and theoretical underpinnings of the alienation that African Americans experience, I want to illustrate that this alienation is a social fact that Americans already understand. To do this I propose the question: Which racial group is worse off today?

Of course there are many ways to attempt to answer this question. A researcher can make a careful examination of the relative economic, educational, and political power each group has. This will allow the researcher to appreciate how structural racism has affected different racial groups in a contrasting manner. Comparisons of these types of structural measures for different racial groups have been done in previous work. I shall allude to the results of this work at the end of this section. But I would like to do something a little more creative. I want to see how Americans in general rate the level of discrimination each racial group continues to face.

To accomplish this task I will rely upon the LSAF. In the LSAF survey, respondents were asked if they thought that any one racial group faces more discrimination than all other groups. For those who stated that there is a group that experiences more discrimination, there was a follow-up question that asked which group faces the greatest amount of discrimination. For this second question, the respondents were given five choices: whites, blacks, Hispanics, Asians, or American Indians.

Some respondents believe that no single racial group suffers more than any other racial group. This may be linked to the fact that Americans tend to attach themselves to an ideology of individualism,[65] which postulates that individuals who work hard are able to succeed and those who are lazy or inefficient will generally fail. Under such an ideology, race does not matter to an individual's success or failure. This ideology can also be linked to the general belief of some white Americans that racial equality is the cultural norm in the United States.[66] Since this is a common belief among majority group members, it should be expected that European Americans are more supportive of the idea that no race suffers more than other races. While this question is not a direct measure of the tendency of European Americans to accept a color-blind ideology, clearly having a color-blind ideology and a faith in American racial equality would lower the ability of an individual to perceive any single group as being worse off than other groups.

While such a finding may illustrate notions of color blindness among majority group members, it does not reveal the presence of racial alienation that blacks may suffer. The second question will be instructive in accomplishing this task. If African Americans are truly alienated from the dominant culture, then this alienation should be generally evident to all Americans. The presence of this alienation should lead many Americans to believe that today, even after the civil rights movement, African Americans are worse off than other racial groups.

Historical racism is correlated to the degree of alienation a racial group faces today. But it is subjective to argue that a certain racial group has suffered more, and continues to suffer more, than other groups. Was the enslavement of Africans and African Americans worse than the attempts at exterminating Native Americans? The enslavement of blacks may have been less heinous than the wars against the Native Americans since blacks were allowed to survive in relatively large numbers, but the resulting treaties from those wars have produced tribal rights for contemporary Native Americans that are not enjoyed by African Americans. A reasonable argument can be made for either blacks or Native Americans as the group that suffers the most from historical and contemporary discrimination. Racial discrimination is not limited to blacks and Native Americans. Although ethnic groups from southern and eastern Europe have historically faced a great deal of discrimination, it is also clear that these groups have been accepted into the majority culture to such an extent that it is difficult to argue that they currently suffer more discrimination than other racial groups. The discrimination faced by Hispanic and Asian Americans is more intense than that faced by European ethnic groups today. But if the alienation thesis is correct, then the discrimination faced by blacks, and possibly Native Americans, is arguably more intense than discrimination faced by Hispanics and Asian Americans. This is not to ignore the fact that there are instances in American history when the level of disenfranchisement of Latinos and Asians rivaled, or even surpassed, that of blacks or Native Americans. For example, the use of the relocation centers in the 1940s placed a burden upon Japanese Americans that neither African nor Native Americans had to face at that time. Furthermore, Latinos and Asians are subject to an anti-immigrant backlash and a language bias that generally escapes blacks and Native Americans. Yet I argue that these groups are in the process of assimilating into the dominant society—much like the European ethnic groups of an earlier time. This assimilation means that these groups are gaining more privileges of majority group status, relative to the alienation experienced by African Americans. If this is true, then despite the degree of discrimination Latino and Asian Americans continue to face, there should be a perception that they currently face less discrimination than African Americans.

Given the level of discrimination that blacks have historically experienced, I hypothesize that respondents across different racial groups will perceive African Americans as facing the highest level of discrimination today. This should be particularly true when African Americans are compared to European, Latino, or Asian Americans. This prediction is less certain as it concerns Native Americans, because they suffer from historical racial atrocities as bad as or worse than those suffered by African Americans and because the system of reservations in the United States may perpetuate a segregation that prevents some Native Americans from gaining social acceptance. However, as I noted earlier, there is evidence that Native Americans who do not live on reservations may be more likely to assimilate than African Americans, and so some Native Americans may be able to obtain a degree of majority group status.

A second hypothesis is that racial groups will be extremely likely to perceive their own racial in-group as facing more discrimination. A theory of social group interest postulates two reasons for this possibility.[67] First, obtaining a victim status for themselves can enable members of a group to make claims upon societal resources. For example, if whites can be seen as victims of affirmative action, then European Americans will have an easier time eradicating that program, which will direct resources away from racial minorities and toward the European Americans. But if whites are not seen as victims, then they lose an important weapon to use against this governmental program. This social reality can account for the development of the "reverse discrimination" argument that many majority group members now use against affirmative action.[68] Second, it seems likely that individuals will be more sensitive to discrimination against members of their own racial group than to discrimination against individuals of other races. It is easier for individuals to justify why other groups face discrimination, since it is discrimination against one's one group that is deemed threatening to one's well-being.

Before looking at which group is perceived as having to endure the most discrimination, it is insightful to look at the percentage of individuals who believe that one race faces more discrimination than other races. The data in Table 2.1 compare the percentage of European Americans, African Americans, Hispanic Americans, and Asian Americans who believe that one racial group suffers more discrimination than other groups. As I hypothesized above, whites are less likely to believe that any racial group has suffered more discrimination than other racial groups (only 64.5 percent believed that one group suffers more, while over 70 percent of each of the other racial groups have that belief). This is consistent with a tendency for whites to accept a color-blind philosophy, since this perspective makes it easier for them to dismiss the possibility that one racial group faces a higher level of discrimination. On the other hand, it should be expected that people of color would be quick to recognize the fact that racial minorities suffer more from discrimination than majority group members. While this is true, racial minorities are not equally as likely to recognize this social fact. African Americans (78.1 percent) are the group most likely to recognize that discrimination can

Table 2.1   **European Americans, African Americans, Hispanic Americans, and Asian Americans Who Believe That One Group Suffers More Discrimination Than Other Groups, by Percentage**

One Group Suffers More	European Americans	African Americans	Hispanic Americans	Asian Americans
Yes	64.5	78.1[c]	72.5[bd]	70.3[ad]
	(1,006)	(226)	(211)	(130)
No	35.5	21.9	27.5	29.7
	(553)	(63)	(80)	(55)

Source: LSAF.
Notes: Numbers of respondents are in parentheses.
a. Significantly different from European Americans at 0.1 level.
b. Significantly different from European Americans at 0.01 level.
c. Significantly different from European Americans at 0.001 level.
d. Significantly different from African Americans at 0.1 level.

affect a single group more than other groups, followed by Hispanic Americans (72.5 percent) and Asian Americans (70.3 percent). The difference in percentages between the two nonblack minority racial groups and African Americans is about the same as it is between these two racial groups and European Americans. The findings in this table suggests that while nonblack racial minorities are more likely than European Americans to recognize that certain racial groups suffer more from discrimination, they may be less likely to recognize this tendency than blacks. The propensity of nonblack racial minorities to disagree with blacks on key racial issues will be further documented in Chapter 4, yet even here it can be argued that nonblack minorities are more likely to adopt a color-blind attitude than African Americans. Later I will argue that this propensity illustrates a growing acceptance, largely missing among African Americans, of majority group identity by Latino and Asian Americans.

Among those who do perceive that one racial group suffers more than other groups, there are important trends as to which group suffers the most. Table 2.2 shows the results of the question of which racial group faces the most discrimination. There is clear evidence supporting my first prediction in that only Hispanic Americans fail to rank African Americans as the group who have suffered the most discrimination. In fact, while the difference is not significant, Asian Americans are more likely than African Americans themselves to

Table 2.2   Groups Who European Americans, African Americans, Hispanic Americans, and Asian Americans Believe Have Suffered the Most Discrimination, by Percentage

Groups Listed	European Americans	African Americans	Hispanic Americans	Asian Americans	Total
Whites	5.1	1.8	4.3	4.6	4.5
	(51)	(4)	(9)	(6)	(70)
Blacks	53.3	62.8[a]	39.5[cd]	67.4[be]	54.0
	(533)	(142)	(83)	(87)	(845)
Hispanics	9.4	8.9	40.0[cd]	3.1[e]	12.9
	(94)	(20)	(84)	(4)	(202)
Asians	2.7	3.5	3.3	10.9	3.6
	(27)	(8)	(7)	(14)	(56)
Indians	29.5	23.0	12.9[a]	14.0	25.0
	(295)	(52)	(27)	(18)	(392)

Source: LSAF.
Notes: Numbers of respondents are in parentheses.
a. Significantly different from European Americans with 95 percent confidence.
b. Significantly different from European Americans with 99 percent confidence.
c. Significantly different from European Americans with 99.9 percent confidence.
d. Significantly different from African Americans with 99.9 percent confidence.
e. Significantly different from Hispanic Americans with 99.9 percent confidence.

state that blacks suffer more discrimination than other racial groups (67.4 percent to 62.7 percent). The total percentages indicate that blacks are more than twice as likely to be perceived as facing the most discrimination than the second-place group—Indians (54 percent to 25.1 percent).

If we eliminate blacks from consideration, then in all groups except Hispanic Americans, more individuals perceived Native Americans as the group most likely to suffer discrimination. These findings suggest that the historical slavery and extermination respectively faced by blacks and Native Americans affect the perceptions of Americans toward the level of discrimination these groups face. Yet it is difficult to argue that the racism of slavery is so much worse than the racism of extermination that twice the number of people should perceive the group who suffered slavery to be worse off than the group who suffered extermination attempts. To account for the greater tendency of African Americans to be perceived as facing more discrimination than Native Americans, I must take into consideration the possibility that Native Americans experience more contemporary acceptance than African Americans.[69]

At the other end of the spectrum, European Americans and Asian Americans are the groups whom the fewest people perceived as being most discriminated against. This finding is likely the result of the higher social status of European Americans and the Asian Americans' image of a "model minority."[70] All respondents place these two groups toward the lower end of the spectrum of perceived discrimination, with Hispanics in the middle, and blacks/Native Americans at the higher end. My results are reflective of previous comparisons of structural economic and educational variables of these racial groups, since European Americans and Asian Americans have higher economic/educational status than other racial groups, African Americans and Native Americans have lower economic/educational status than other racial groups, and Hispanic Americans tend to score in the middle.[71] It seems that Americans' perceptions of discrimination are a fairly accurate reflection of the economic reality of these five groups, and so using the method of obtaining a subjective assessment of discrimination from Americans reveals a similar hierarchical order that a structural analysis of racism would produce.

Hispanic Americans are most likely to rank themselves as the group who have faced the most discrimination. While this is anomalous to the first hypothesis, it does help fulfill the second prediction—that members of racial groups are more likely to perceive themselves as victims. This second trend can be seen clearly seen in that European Americans, Hispanic Americans, and Asian Americans each are more likely than other racial groups to rank their own group as the one most discriminated against, even if this difference is not always significant. For example, 11.1 percent of Asian Americans perceive themselves as the group most discriminated against, in contrast to only 2.7 percent of European Americans, 3.4 percent of African Americans, and 3.2 percent of Hispanic Americans who perceive Asian Americans in that way. Interestingly, European Americans are almost twice as likely to perceive themselves as facing the most discrimination than they are to perceive Asian Americans in such a manner (5.1 percent versus 2.7 percent), despite the continuing institutional discrimination Asian Americans face.

The evidence in Table 2.2 indicates that African Americans face more contemporary alienation than other racial groups. Even though the contemporary economic conditions of African Americans are not significantly worse than those of Native Americans, blacks are more than twice as likely to be perceived as facing more discrimination than other groups. The level of discrimination that African Americans are perceived as experiencing is not merely a reflection of the depressed economic conditions they live within, but rather is also the result of the special lower status of African Americans, which reflects the greater alienation they continue to suffer. It is this alienation that keeps African Americans from experiencing the acceptance necessary for them to undergo the process of assimilation.

Yet just because Americans perceive that African Americans face more discrimination than other racial groups does not mean that blacks are alienated from other racial groups. There are other possible explanations for this perception. The perception can be based upon discrimination that is a temporary phenomenon and will change if African Americans begin to develop a thinner racial identity. However, African Americans have been present in the United States since the country's inception, and there is little possibility that they will soon assimilate or develop a thin racial identity. Another possibility is that Americans are incorrect in their assessment of the social discrimination against blacks. Yet as I noted, Americans are fairly accurate in their assessment of the economic plight of the distinct racial groups. I contend that they are also accurate in their assessment of the special plight blacks face. Finally, one can argue that the respondents are only assessing economic discrimination, but not social alienation. However, in the following chapter I will demonstrate that the social alienation of African Americans is just as real in the United States as the economic disparity that they experience. Furthermore, if Table 2.2 only measured the relative economic disparities of the different racial groups, then Native Americans, who are at least as economically deprived as African Americans, should have scores similar to those of blacks. I contend that these findings reflect Americans' recognition that African Americans are experiencing an alienation that makes them unable to gain the level of acceptance other racial groups enjoy.

It is important to put the results of these findings into context with the theoretical constructs that have been developed. The alienation that African Americans experience is a result of their historical inability to incorporate themselves into the dominant society and has resulted in the perception by most Americans that blacks experience more discrimination than other groups. This belief, I contend, is reflective of the alienation that Americans either overtly or implicitly recognize as a feature of black racial reality. This alienation makes it unlikely that African Americans will experience assimilation in the near future or be able to develop a thin racial identity. This argument is further buttressed by the fact that blacks are less likely to outmarry or live in integrated neighborhoods than individuals of other races.[72] Yet if Americans acknowledge the alienation of African Americans, do they also support that alienation with attitudes that keep blacks separated from other races? The evidence of the LSAF suggests that they do. In the next chapter I will begin to explore the ways that the social attitudes of nonblacks support the marital and residential segregation of African Americans.

Notes

1. Cherlin 1996: 225.
2. Bailey 1988.
3. It can be argued that racial groups do not experience relative equality in the United States, and I do not dispute the fact that discrimination is a common feature of American society. Yet overt legal discrimination is not nearly as commonplace as it once was, and overt types of discrimination are today discouraged. This is in contrast to the days of Jim Crow, Zoot Suit riots, or Japanese internment camps, when assimilation or egalitarian cultural pluralism was not possible. There is enough legal or political equality today that we can at least talk about the possibility of assimilation or cultural pluralism.
4. Schaefer 1998: 24.
5. Spickard 1989; Alba 1995.
6. Alba 1995; de la Garza 1992.
7. Patchen 1999: 275.
8. Portes and Bach 1985; Logan, Alba, and McNulty 1994.
9. Lyman 1992; Metzger 1971.
10. Glazer 1993. However, it should also be pointed out that Glazer believes that American discriminatory and prejudicial attitudes have stunted the assimilation process for blacks. He implies that a limit to the power of assimilative forces does exist for African Americans.
11. Gutmann 1994; Choi, Callaghan, and Murphy 1995; McKeever and Klineberg 1999.
12. Parrillo 1997: 539; Downey 1999; Kymlicka 1996.
13. Lie 1995; Portes and Zhou 1993.
14. Waters 1990; Ignatiev 1995; Alba 1990; Kennedy 1944; Herberg 1955.
15. Waters 1990; Gans 1992.
16. Gallagher, 2002a.
17. See Parrillo 1997: tab. 5.1.

18. For example, Rowland Berthoff (1953) reports that the English were rarely ridiculed on the vaudeville stage—unlike the experiences of other European ethnic groups.

19. This is very similar to some of the arguments from the contemporary conservative party in the United States—the Republicans, some of whom argue that illegitimate efforts to increase the number of immigrants are the result of Democrats attempting to bring in individuals who are more likely to vote for Democrats (Alvarez 1997; Field 1997). A fear of the voting power of immigrants seems to be a constant worry of the political party that does not electorally benefit from the immigrant vote.

20. Unlike many of the immigrant groups in the nineteenth century, the Irish experienced little occupational or social mobility. But after the turn of the century they made slow but steady progress toward assimilation. According to Nathan Glazer and Patrick Moynihan (1963), between the 1940s and the 1960s the Irish begin to leave the working class in mass numbers, and with the election of John F. Kennedy, an Irish Catholic, it is fair to argue that the Irish experienced near total assimilation by the end of the 1960s. At the very least, it can be argued that by the 1960s the Irish shared in the power structure of the United States as much as other European ethnic groups.

21. Dinnerstein and Reimers 1982. See also Lewis 1971 for information about the discrimination experienced by the Irish.

22. Waters 2000.

23. Pagnini and Morgan 1990.

24. Pavalko 1981.

25. Waters 1990.

26. McIntosh 2002.

27. Hartigen 1999; Giroux 1997.

28. Omi and Winant 1994.

29. Wildman and Davis 2002; Lipsitz 1998; McIntosh 2002; Twine 1997.

30. Ignatiev 1995.

31. David Roediger (1991) makes a similar argument for European groups in general.

32. Arnesen 2001.

33. Ignatiev 1995; Jacobson 1998; Roediger 1991.

34. Arnesen 2001; Reed 2001.

35. Fields 2001.

36. This argument for how racist actions can be justified is seen in Scott and Lyman 1968; and Mason 1970.

37. Waters 1990.

38. Gordon 1964.

39. Latinos were not always so classified. In the 1930s they were considered a separate race on the U.S. census.

40. Clearly there is within the genetic heritage of most African Americans the presence European ancestry as well. However, African and European Americans generally do not historically or contemporarily

acknowledge this presence, allowing the illusion of biological racial differences between whites and blacks to be maintained.

41. Parrillo 1997: 435.

42. Massey and Denton 1996.

43. It is not a certainty that Hispanics will enjoy upward socioeconomic mobility in the near future. Matthew McKeever and Stephen Klineberg (1999) found that third-generation Hispanics in the Houston, Texas, area were not any more likely than second-generation Hispanics to have higher wages or education. However, these Hispanics also do not exhibit the adversarial culture that the theorists of segmented assimilation predict, nor are they worse off than the second-generation Hispanics. If these findings are generalizable to Hispanics at large, then it is possible that their social mobility can plateau, which may slow down some of the possible residential assimilation that they experience.

44. Bradshaw and Bean 1970; Alvirez and Bean 1976.

45. Grebler, Moore, and Guzman 1970; Moore and Pachon 1985.

46. Barrera 1988.

47. Penalosa 1970.

48. Ogbu 1978.

49. On stereotyping, see Ohnuma 1991; Hurh 1994; and Kitano and Daniels 1988: 176. On violence, see Yip 1997; and Parrillo 1997: 307–308. On discrimination, see Lee 1993; and Kang 1995.

50. There is little dispute that Asian Americans generally enjoy a higher level of socioeconomic status than other racial minority groups (Kitano and Daniels 1988; Kasarda 1992). Some have argued that this has contributed to a model minority myth that can create stress for Asian Americans (Ohnuma 1991; Takagi 1992). But this criticism does not eliminate the fact that Asian Americans have an educational and economic status that is more similar to that of European Americans than to that of African Americans—providing a theoretically easier path to assimilation for Asian Americans than for Hispanic or African Americans.

51. Among Hispanic Americans it is also important to examine the degree of African heritage present in each group. As I suggested in Chapter 1's endnote 42, Puerto Ricans are more likely to have African heritage than are Mexicans. The socially "polluting" nature of African heritage may help determine which Latino ethnic groups will be able to thin their racial identities in the near future.

52. Emerson, Yancey, and Chai 2001; Herring and Amissah 1997.

53. Symbolic racism can be defined as racism whereby majority group members have aversive emotional perceptions of racial minorities, expressed through symbolic issues rather than through overt prejudice. Because of social desirability effects, and because symbolic racism operates in subtle ways through the avoidance and stereotyping of African Americans (Kluegel 1990; Kovel 1984) rather than through overt expressions of discrimination, this type of racism is more commonplace than overt expressions of racial hatred.

54. Waters 1999.

55. While there are many scholars who can be cited to illustrate the fate of Native Americans, one of the best-known classical works has been written by Dee Brown (1970), who documents the degree of suffering inflicted on Native Americans by European Americans in the latter part of the nineteenth century.

56. Karl Eschbach (1995) finds that the outmarriage rates among Native Americans range from 16 percent in the Southwest to 82 percent in the Midwest. This is in contrast to the 3 percent outmarriage rate for African American men and the 1 percent outmarriage rate for African American women (McDaniel 1996).

57. Rockquemore and Brunsma 2002; Dalmage 2000; Root 1996.

58. Mary Waters (1998) finds powerful evidence that white/black children are much less likely to be identified as white by their parents than are children of other types of white/minority interracial mixings. For example, only 22 percent of all white-father/black-mother couples identified their children as white, but 51 percent of the white/Native American, 67 percent of the white/Japanese, and 61 percent of the white/Chinese pairings identified their children as white.

59. Davis 1991.

60. Ibid.

61. Ibid.

62. Walter White, the president of the National Association for the Advancement of Colored People (NAACP) from 1931 to 1955, is an excellent example of the power of the one-drop rule. Many anthropologists argue that he could be no more than 1/64th African (Davis 1991). He reportedly had light skin, fair hair, and blue eyes, but had been raised in the Deep South and experienced racism as a "black" man. It is of further interest that he created controversy with his second marriage, to a white woman, which was then characterized in the black community as an interracial marriage. This is in spite of the fact that genetically he was a closer skin-color match with his white wife than with the black critics who saw the marriage as a betrayal.

63. Another interesting piece of evidence of this claim is the fact that among whites, women are more likely than men to marry blacks, while the reverse is true for outmarriage to most every other racial group (e.g., white men are more likely than white women to marry Asians). Why this may be the case can be linked to Maria Root's assertion (2001) that male privilege allows men to retain their patriarchal status and power despite the race of their wife. Root goes on to argue that white women are likely to lose some of their racial status in interracial marriages, regardless of the race of their spouse. I would build on her argument by contending that this is only accurate when the male marries a member of a nonblack minority group. Because of the overwhelming rejection that blacks experience, I contend that even male privilege cannot fully survive intermarriage with an African American. Because they have more societal power, white men have more to lose in a marriage with a black than do white women. But white women, who lose some of their racial status in marriages with nonblack partners, have more to lose in marriages with nonblacks than do white men. This con-

trasting potential cost for white men and white women can account for different sex combinations for whites in marriages with blacks as compared to marriages with other minorities.

64. The resistance of black political organizations to the multiracial category is one of the ways that African Americans indicated an adherence to the one-drop rule. This resistance is linked to the desire of such organizations to force multiracial individuals to identify themselves as blacks and can be seen in statements by leaders in the NAACP in the late 1990s, which postulated a fear of the multiracial category since it could dilute the political strength of African Americans (Lindsey 2000).

65. Bellah et al. 1985.

66. Schuman et al. 1997.

67. Group interest theory basically postulates that members of racial groups take actions and develop attitudes that further the interest of their own racial group (Bobo 1983; Pettigrew 1985) as well as protect the individuals in that group.

68. Schneider 1996; O'Sullivan 2000; Loury 1998.

69. Another possible explanation for this tendency is the fact that Native Americans enjoy certain treaty rights that other racial groups do not. Americans who are aware of these treaty rights might rank the discrimination faced by blacks higher than that faced by Native Americans. While this may explain at least part of the difference in the perception of the discrimination faced by these two groups, it seems unlikely that the existence of treaty rights is the only reason, since in-depth knowledge about treaty rights does not seem to be widespread. Having taught in Wisconsin, where there is a relatively high percentage of Native Americans, and Texas, where there is a low percentage of Native Americans, I can attest to the fact that Wisconsinites are much more aware of Native American treaty issues than Texans.

70. Winnick 1990; Petersen 1971.

71. For quantitative support of this assertion, see Yetman 1999: statistical appendix, tab. 19.

72. Heaton and Jacobson 2000; Korgen 1998; Massey and Denton 1996.

3

"They Are Okay—Just Keep Them Away from Me": Residential and Marital Segregation Patterns

In the last chapter I argued that the largest American nonblack racial minority groups—Latino and Asian Americans—experience a degree of assimilation that escapes African Americans. It is my contention that the movement of these racial groups is similar to the movement of previous European ethnic groups into a full majority group racial status. If pluralism was a desired value for these European ethnic groups, then this movement can be seen as the destruction of their native cultures. If assimilation was a desired value, then this movement can be seen as a mechanism that enabled these former minority groups to gain societal equality. I argued that this process has traditionally been an option for European ethnic groups and soon will be an option for Latino and Asian Americans, but it is an option denied to African Americans because of the alienation they continue to experience. This chapter will illustrate this alienation by examining the social attitudes that support the residential and marital acceptance received by nonblack racial minorities while also documenting the resistance faced by African Americans.

Understanding these social attitudes is crucial if researchers are to comprehend why residential and marital segregation have persisted in the United States. There have been suggestions that African Americans have not assimilated into the dominant culture because they have chosen to self-segregate.[1] This self-segregation can most readily be seen on college campuses, where African Americans tend to isolate into their own dorms, cafeterias, and social clubs.[2] According to this perspective, the African American preference to interact within their own racial group explains their tendency to endogamously marry and live in segregated neighborhoods.

Yet the proponents of this argument do not take into consideration the fact that one of the powerful priorities of the modern civil rights movement has been to create a racially integrated society.[3] While the failure of Americans to support this integration fueled a movement toward pluralism and black nationalism within today's civil rights organizations,[4] this pluralism has not completely negated the desires of many African Americans for social inclusion. I hypothesize that African Americans desire integration as much as, or more than, other racial groups, but are unable to experience this integration because of the rejection they have experienced. Furthermore, the rejection of African Americans is not merely by European Americans, but is also present within the social attitudes of nonblack minority groups.

If African Americans are segregated because of rejection by whites and other racial groups, then they are clearly on the bottom rung of the racial ladder in the United States. The alienation thesis suggests that all nonblack groups, not just racial minorities, make up the next and highest rung of the ladder, so that the American racial social hierarchy is bilevel, with blacks on the bottom and everyone else on top. Such social organization challenges the "whites as minority" thesis in its illustration that Hispanic and Asian Americans are merging into the dominant culture and that this merging is supported attitudinally as well as residentially and maritally. The propensity of individuals to approach or withdraw from members of other races is a dimension that has been termed "social distance," a concept I will define in the next section. I will then discuss prevailing theories of the informal racial hierarchy in the United States, and examine social attitudes toward interracial marriage and residential integration as measures of social distance. Finally, I will determine if there is a consensus on how the informal racial hierarchy in the United States is shaped, as well as discuss the larger implications of this hierarchy.

The Concept of Social Distance

How comfortable are we when we interact with people of other races? Do nonwhites approve of European Americans who join their social clubs? Are non-Hispanics comfortable working closely with Hispanic Americans? Are non-Asians willing to have Asian Americans move in next door? How willing are nonblacks to let their daughters date or marry an African American? These questions highlight the social uneasiness many Americans have about interacting with members of other races. The concept of social distance measures these levels of uneasiness. Higher levels of social distance mean that people will attempt to distance themselves from members of another race and will likely seek out ways to exclude them from their lives. They may leave jobs rather than work alongside members of the rejected group, or inhibit intermarriage between members of their family and members of the rejected group. On the other hand, when groups possess less social distance to other groups, members of both groups are more likely to accept each other. This lower level of social distance makes it easier for a minority group to eventually become accepted into the dominant culture.

Emory Bogardus developed the earliest version of the social distance scale, which contains measurements of seven possible types of relationships to determine how close to him- or herself the respondent will allow out-group members.[5] Assume that we are exploring how much social distance there is between European Americans and Hispanic Americans. The seven levels of acceptance used to measure social distance would be (1) whether European Americans would allow their kin to marry Hispanic Americans; (2) whether European Americans would have Hispanic Americans in their clubs as personal chums; (3) whether European Americans would accept Hispanic Americans living next to them as neighbors; (4) whether European Americans would accept working with Hispanic Americans at their jobs; (5) whether European Americans would allow Hispanic Americans to become citizens of their country; (6) whether European Americans would allow Hispanic Americans to visit their country; and (7) whether European Americans would exclude Hispanic Americans from their country. The respondent is assigned a score of 1 if he or she would not oppose any of these seven levels of social interaction, which is interpreted to mean that the respondent perceives no social distance between him- or herself and the potential out-group. On the other hand, the respondent is assigned a score of 7 if he or she opposes all seven levels of social interaction. Higher numbers indicate more social distance. Studies of social distance take the average of such scores from many members in each racial group to examine how comfortable people are with different out-groups.

Carolyn Owen, Howard Eisner, and Thomas McFaul have noted that using this measure several times over half a century has revealed a shrinking social distance between different racial groups.[6] This trend can be seen in a collection of studies documented in Table 3.1. It is a process that illustrates the point of the last chapter—that certain racial minority groups have been moving closer to majority group status.[7] Nevertheless, it is also clear that the social distance between different racial groups has not disappeared, and a fairly consistent racial order seems to have been maintained. For example, European Americans consistently score lower than Native Americans, who in turn score lower than Mexican Americans, who in turn score lower than African Americans. The only exception to this pattern occurred in 1977, when African Americans scored slightly lower than Mexican Americans. The literature on race/ethnicity has suggested that overt expressions of racism are less acceptable today,[8] which can account for the trend toward less social distance between racial groups. But the continued existence of social gaps between different racial groups, and the maintenance of a given racial order in terms of who is more acceptable, indicate that there is a weaker, but still persistent, racial hierarchy within American society.

Despite the progressive changes in civil rights legislation, the existence of a social racial hierarchy that is enforced through informal preferences and customs still exists in the United States. This argument is reinforced by a study undertaken by Carolyn Fang, Jim Sidanius, and Felicia Pratto, which finds opposition to interracial marriage between perceived high-status and low-status group mem-

Table 3.1   Social Distance of Selected Groups, 1926–1991

	1926	1966	1977	1991
Whites	1.10	1.07	1.25	1.00
Native Americans	2.38	2.12	1.84	1.70
Mexican Americans	2.67	2.37	2.17	1.84
Blacks	3.28	2.56	2.03	1.94

Sources: Bogardus 1968; Owen, Eisner, and McFaul 1981; Song 1991.

bers among individuals who possess a high level of social dominance orientation.[9] Social dominance orientation is defined as the desire to establish and maintain hierarchical relationships between socially constructed social groups.[10] While the findings of this study only pertain to individuals with high social dominance orientation, they do suggest that there may be a general understanding of the relative status of different races.

Most of the current understanding of social distance is obtained by knowing whom one is willing to live next to and whom one is willing to allow one's child to marry. Thus I will assess two important measures of this theoretical tool—interracial marriage and residential integration—to evaluate the degree of marital and residential assimilation that exists between racial groups.

Theories About America's Informal Racial Hierarchy

Robert Merton suggests that the hierarchy of racial status prevalent within American society resembles a caste system.[11] In this system African Americans are considered to occupy the lowest social position, while European Americans occupy the highest. This caste system is precisely what the alienation thesis would predict, since both concepts rely upon the idea that blacks will be left behind as all other significant racial groups obtain majority status. Yet James Geschwender advocates a multilayered system of "color-grading," whereby discrimination against members of darker-skinned groups is more intense than discrimination against members of lighter-skinned groups.[12] If this is the case, then European Americans should be more easily accepted than Asian Americans. If Asian Americans are perceived to be of lighter skin color than Hispanic Americans, they should be more easily accepted than Hispanic Americans, who in turn should be more easily accepted than African Americans. Empirical evidence indicates that skin-color discrimination is still common in American society,[13] which is consistent with the notion of Anglo-conformity—the idea that groups who most closely physically resemble the dominant group are more likely to be accepted. Since they remind majority group members of themselves, those with lighter skin color would find more favor in a society controlled by light-skinned dominant group members.

Cedric Herring and Charles Amissah posit two alternate theories regarding the construction of an informal social racial hierarchy.[14]

They first propose a possible "cultural pluralist" model, whereby all the racial minority groups feel favorably toward the dominant culture, but hostilities between different groups remain because they maintain their own cultural values. In this model one should expect European Americans to occupy the top social position, with no clear hierarchical preference structure among minority groups. This model predicts that African Americans, Hispanic Americans, and Asian Americans would generally prefer to marry or live near European Americans than near members of the other minority groups. There will be a bilevel social structure wherein whites occupy the top position and all other racial groups occupy the bottom position. This is the classical white/nonwhite hierarchy that has been useful for understanding previous American race relations.

Second, Herring and Amissah discuss a "conflict theory" model, whereby non-Western groups will prefer other non-Western groups over dominant group individuals. There would be less social distance between different minority groups than between minority groups and whites, which would reflect a larger Western/non-Western division within American society. Under such a theory, one would predict that there might be dual systems of hierarchical social preference—one for European Americans and another for racial minorities. European Americans would clearly reject racial minorities as marriage partners and neighbors without differentiating among the three minority racial groups. Racial minorities would show a greater reluctance to intermarry or live next to European Americans than to live near or marry other racial minorities. For example, it would be expected that Asian Americans would prefer both African Americans and Hispanic Americans as potential neighbors over European Americans. Possible resentment toward European Americans can be the driving force behind the social distance preferences of racial minorities.

Racial Intermarriage

Empirical research that has documented the acceptance of racial exogamy tends to focus on black/white pairings. This work illustrates that majority group members have a relatively greater reluctance toward marrying African Americans than toward marrying members of other racial groups,[15] and that the European American members of black/white unions face more pressure to end the relationship than do African American members.[16] These findings suggest that African

Americans are the least acceptable marriage partners for European Americans,[17] and that black/white interracial marriage is accepted more easily by African Americans than by European Americans.[18]

While social distance in racial intermarriage may be the greatest between European Americans and African Americans, there has been little work on attitudes toward other racial combinations that would validate this assertion. An exception to this is Herring and Amissah's study. They use the 1990 General Social Survey (GSS) data to examine varying amounts of acceptance of exogamy between different racial groups. Their work is valuable because it is the most comprehensive recent attempt to examine resistance to exogamy among several races. Nevertheless, their study has several shortcomings. First, they separate European Americans into Western and Eastern Europeans, as well as Jewish Americans. While early in the twentieth century a great deal of resentment was directed toward Eastern Europeans and Jewish Americans, it is hard to argue that today those with Eastern European or Jewish ancestry face much large-scale resistance toward dominant group exogamy. Second, the answers of the respondents were dichotomized into objecting, or not objecting, to a relative marrying someone of another race. This created a response that cannot capture the subtleties of the differing degrees of opposition that interracial couples may face, since individuals with slight hesitations about racial outmarrying are grouped with those who are unflinching in their opposition to racial exogamy. The third shortcoming of this research concerns the relatively low number of minorities that Herring and Amissah must have used to examine social distance. They did not indicate the number of respondents used in their research, but a rough estimate of the number of their subjects can be obtained. I calculated that the highest number of racial minorities they could have used is seventy-eight Latino Americans, ninety-one Native Americans, and twenty Asian Americans.[19] Based on these low numbers, I do not have confidence that the study accurately portrays the social attitudes of Hispanic Americans and Asian Americans.

In contrast, in the 1999–2000 Lilly Survey of American Attitudes and Friendships (LSAF), respondents were asked if they agreed or disagreed with the following statement: "I would be upset if I had a child who wanted to marry a {blank}." In the blank, one of four races was identified—white, black, Hispanic, or Asian—but not the respondent's own race.[20] The respondent was then asked if he or she strongly, moderately, or slightly agreed/disagreed with this statement. From this question, a seven-point scale was devised. Those who agreed strongly were given a score of 1, those who agreed moderately scored 2, and those who agreed slightly scored 3. Likewise, those who disagreed strongly are scored 7, those who disagreed moderately scored 6, and those who disagreed slightly scored 5. Individuals who neither agreed nor disagreed were given a midpoint score of 4. I will use the LSAF measurement in this chapter and the next to create a seven-point scale that gauges the attitudes of the respondents to different statements; higher scores indicate more disagreement with a given statement.

By asking whether the respondent would allow his or her child to intermarry, the possible effect of personal tastes is eliminated and I get a more complete understanding of how accepting the respondent is toward racial exogamy. If the respondents were asked whether they would personally be willing to outmarry, then their aesthetic perceptions of whether light skin is physically more attractive than dark skin would be captured, regardless of their desire to resist or accept racial exogamy. Asking about a respondent's attitude toward his or her child outmarrying eliminates this concern.

Table 3.2 reveals the mean scores of each of the four racial groups' acceptance of racial exogamy with other racial groups. Lower means indicate less support for racial exogamy. Racial exogamy is significantly less acceptable for European Americans if their children were to marry African Americans, but European Americans are not as concerned about their children marrying either Hispanic Americans or Asian Americans. For Hispanic Americans, African Americans are also the least desirable marriage partners for their children, although there is a significant difference only when Hispanic Americans' acceptance of African Americans is compared to their acceptance of Asian Americans. The pattern of rejecting African Americans continues with the Asian American respondents, as they accept potential African American in-laws less than European American or Hispanic American in-laws. Given the comparatively low number of Asian Americans in the sample, the difference in scores is not large enough to generate a statistically significant finding; nevertheless, this research still supports the notion that African Americans are seen as the least desirable marriage partners among the other three groups.[21] It is only among African Americans that there is not a clear preferred marriage racial partner, with African

Table 3.2   Willingness of European Americans, African Americans, Hispanic Americans, and Asian Americans to Have Their Children Outmarry, by Mean Score

Groups Listed	European Americans	African Americans	Hispanic Americans	Asian Americans
Whites		6.192	5.906	5.486
	—	(109)	(98)	(64)
		1.509	*1.908*	*1.957*
Blacks	4.703		5.406	5.192
	(550)	—	(111)	(68)
	2.377		*2.228*	*2.264*
Hispanics	5.602[b]	6.279		5.562
	(523)	(91)	—	(64)
	1.940	*1.501*		*2.065*
Asians	5.587[b]	6.436	6.368[a]	
	(545)	(96)	(96)	—
	1.931	*1.380*	*1.220*	

Source: LSAF.
Notes: Means are main entries. Numbers of respondents are in parentheses. Standard deviations are in italics.

a. Group asked about mean is significantly different from African Americans with 99 percent confidence.

b. Group asked about mean is significantly different from African Americans with 99.9 percent confidence.

Americans being more accepting of interracial marriage than members of the other three races.[22]

These models clearly affirm that nonblack racial groups are more likely to reject African Americans as potential marriage partners than any other racial group. Furthermore, I do not find a hierarchy of marriage partners once I eliminate African Americans as potential in-laws. It is not only that members of all races feel positively toward their children wanting to marry European Americans, but it is also true that all groups consider Asian Americans and Hispanic Americans acceptable partners. There are twin findings: first, European Americans are not accepted any more than Asian Americans or Hispanic Americans; and second, African Americans face the highest levels of rejection. Both of these findings hold up after the appropriate controls have been utilized, as illustrated in Table A.2 (see appendix). Furthermore, the fact that African Americans are the most supportive group of intermarriage counters the argument that they marry endogamously because they do not want to outmarry. It is the African Americans who are rejected by other races rather than the other way around.

These twin findings have important implications in our understanding of social distance and African American alienation. They suggest that it is rejection of African Americans rather than acceptance of European Americans that shapes this hierarchical structure.[23] Nevertheless, I have only examined one dimension of social distance to arrive at my findings. The next section will examine the tendency of Americans to accept individuals of different races as residential neighbors.

Residential Integration

An illustration of racial rejection in the United States is the phenomenon of "white flight," or the tendency of European Americans to leave neighborhoods as African Americans move into them. Segregation between African Americans and European Americans is more intense than between majority group members and other minority groups,[24] and this segregation persists regardless of the socioeconomic resources of African Americans.[25] This phenomenon has produced a great deal of scholarly debate. William Frey asks whether racial considerations or economic/ecological factors motivate white flight,[26] as it has been argued that in addition to class, a central factor in racial residential segregation is a preference for one's own race.[27] Accordingly, ethnocentrism and racism toward African Americans are viable explanations for white flight. On the other hand, race may be a proxy for the social dysfunctions European Americans expect to find in African American communities.[28] According to this argument, European Americans do not want to discriminate against African Americans but are realistic in their assessments of the social problems (e.g., crime, lower property values) within African American communities. It is not direct rejection of African Americans that fuels segregation but the social conditions that most blacks live within. If majority group members believed that African Americans lived in safe and economically viable neighborhoods, then they would accept living with blacks as they would with any other racial group, but because European Americans perceive African Americans as living in less desirable neighborhoods, they have a powerful incentive to avoid living near blacks. Whether European Americans are correct in their assessment of the living conditions of African Americans is not as important as their beliefs about those conditions. This "race versus race-as-a-proxy" debate dominates much of the current research into why European Americans are hesitant to live in neighborhoods with significant numbers of African Americans. One way to investigate why white flight occurs is to examine the behavior of European Americans—when and under what conditions they leave, or move into, integrated neighborhoods. However, these studies examine what is, rather than what could be. They do not study what people want, but rather reflect the limited choices that whites already have. A person may want to live in a racially balanced neighborhood, but there are few such neighborhoods in the United States. Since these neighborhoods are difficult to find, but same-race neighborhoods are common, the person is basically forced to live in a segregated neighborhood. Furthermore, individuals may encounter factors such as racial steering or lack of housing availability, which prevent them from living in multiracial neighborhoods.

While it is important to ask respondents questions about what sort of neighborhood they want to live in, in contemporary America there are few people, especially dominant group members, who want to be seen as racially intolerant. There is a potential social desirability effect that may prevent whites from honestly exhibiting their preferences to avoid racial minorities, and so it is important to ask questions in such a way that the respondents can express socially acceptable support for segregation. To deal with this issue, I will rely on LSAF research I have conducted with Michael Emerson and Karen Chai.[29] To accomplish this task, we built into the LSAF socially relevant reasons for rejecting an integrated neighborhood using an experimental design called the "factorial survey method."[30] Important changes were incorporated to suit the interests of this study. The analysis of attitudes toward residential integration begins with the following statement from the survey:

> Imagine that you are looking for a new house and that you have two school-aged children. You find a house that you like much better than any other house—it has everything that you'd been looking for, it is close to work, and it is within your price range.

With this opening statement, we have fixed certain variables that are uncontrolled in other research. The respondents are told that they are house-hunting, that they have two children in school, and that they have found a house far better than any other house. What is more, this house is both affordable and conveniently located near work. Relying on the status quo bias—people will prefer what they have or what matches their preferences, even if just told in an experimental setting, as identified in the work of cognitive psychologists[31]—respondents should be extremely favorable to buying the house. The question continues by describing the neighborhood, selecting variables most frequently suggested as the underlying causes for racial segregation. Research has suggested that the two most important variables seem to be crime in the neighborhood and the home's property value.[32] The quality of education in the area, a predominant concern for adults with children, and the value of the house relative to others in the neighborhood, are also factors that potential homeowners are likely to consider.[33] To complete the question, the values for each of these factors are varied by randomly selecting the terms in brackets in the following statements:

Checking on the neighborhood, you find that

- the public schools are of [low, medium, high] quality,
- the neighborhood is [5–100%] [Black, Hispanic, Asian, White],
- the other homes in the neighborhood are of [lower, equal, higher] value than the home you are considering,
- property values are [declining, stable, increasing],
- and the crime rate is [low, average, high].

How likely or unlikely do you think it is that you would buy this home? (Responses range from "very unlikely" [1] to "very likely" [6].)

These sentences were read to the respondent after the opening statement and each respondent had a single, randomly generated combination of factors. The racial composition always represents a racial group other than the respondent's own, and varies from 5 percent to 100 percent in 5-point intervals.[34] The order of the five context variables was randomly generated, eliminating ordering effects.[35]

By using a question that examines whether the respondents are willing to purchase the hypothesized home, the independent effects of context variables on the likelihood of buying a particular house can be tested. The question is "unrealistic" in the sense that it assumes people first visited the house without knowing anything about the neighborhood—which is usually not the way people seek out housing. But the question is most appropriate for this task—that is, to get beyond limitations that occur in real life, such as people not familiarizing themselves with or considering neighborhoods simply because they do not personally know anyone there. By telling respondents about the neighborhood *after* they have found the house, we are in position to know what neighborhood factors shape their subsequent decision to purchase a home.

Because the situation for each respondent is randomly varied by crime rate, quality of schools, and whether property values are increasing, decreasing, or staying the same, over time these nonracial factors will offset each other. For example, if a European American respondent is asked about a neighborhood that has a high percentage of Asian Americans and a high crime rate, then that respondent may be unlikely to move into that neighborhood because of a fear of crime rather than an aversion to Asian Americans. However, since crime rates are randomly selected, European American respondents who are asked about moving into a neighborhood with high percentages of Asian Americans will roughly one-third of the time be told that the neighborhood has a high crime rate, roughly one-third of the time be told that it has an average crime rate, and roughly one-third of the time be told that it has a low crime rate. Over time, respondents' concerns about crime should not discount the ability of this research to assess the willingness of European Americans to live with Asian Americans.

Because of the statistical complexity of this study, I cannot use means to report its results, since I cannot guarantee that the general means of each racial group will represent similar levels of the other factors that determine whether a home will be bought. To get around this problem, regression models are constructed. With these models, the possible effects of crime, education, property value, and the value of the other homes in the neighborhood are controlled. The results of these models are technical and can be seen in Table A.3 (see appendix).[36] Nevertheless, the major findings of these models indicate that European Americans become more unlikely to accept African Americans as the hypothetical percentage of African American neighbors increases. This relationship remained even though "proxy" factors predicted to influence home purchase were controlled. The same was not true regarding whites' acceptance of Hispanic

Americans and Asian Americans. As the percentage stated for those minorities increased, there was no effect on the likelihood of European Americans to purchase a home. Regardless of the characteristics of the neighborhood, European Americans do not want to live with African Americans. Even if the property values are increasing, crime is low, and the quality of education is good, European Americans still are unlikely to move into a neighborhood if the percentage of African Americans is high. The notion that race is merely used as a proxy may be true concerning Hispanic Americans and Asian Americans, since the reluctance of European Americans to live with nonblack racial minorities declines once these those proxy variables are controlled, but it is clear that these variables do not explain the residential segregation of European Americans from African Americans.

The results of this research are conclusive as they concern the residential preferences of majority group members—they do not want to live next to blacks but are willing to live next to nonblack minorities. The number of European Americans interviewed in the LSAF provides enough respondents so that I have confidence in the accuracy of this finding.[37] However, fewer minority group members were interviewed in the LSAF. Because of this small number, there is no assurance that all of the categories of independent variables are sufficiently covered.[38] The problem of dealing with racial minorities is compounded by the fact that I have to divide these groups into smaller categories in order to analyze them. For example, to look at the attitudes of African Americans toward living in the same neighborhood as Asian Americans, one needs a regression model that only includes the one-third of African Americans who were asked about Asian Americans. This left only about 100 respondents for each model of African Americans or Hispanic Americans and about 70 respondents for each model of Asian Americans. Given the number of independent variables needed in the regression models, this is not a sufficient number of respondents to have confidence in the results. Although there was an attempt to use the LSAF to analyze the residential preferences of racial minorities, I discovered that there are an insufficient number of minorities available to accomplish this task and had to look elsewhere to see if there was a multiracial study that examined minorities' social attitudes toward residential segregation.

Fortunately, there is such research in the work of Camille Zubrinsky-Charles.[39] She examined a large multiracial sample of adults in Los Angeles and explored the residential preferences of these respondents with a modification of the showcard method of Reynolds Farley and others, and Howard Schuman and others.[40] In the original sample there were 863 European Americans, 1,119 African Americans, 988 Hispanic Americans, and 1,055 Asian Americans.[41] With the showcard method, the respondents were given a blank neighborhood showcard similar to that in Figure 3.1. They were instructed to fill in the blank houses so that they could create the racial makeup of their ideal neighborhood, indicating *W* for a white family, *B* for a black family, *H* for a Hispanic family, and *A* for an Asian family. This enables the researcher to gain an understanding of what the respondent believes is the ideal racial makeup of his or her neighborhood, regardless of the actual racial residential choices of the respondent.

The strengths of Zubrinsky-Charles's study lie in the large number of racial minorities who were interviewed and the fact that we can look at the respondents' notion of an ideal neighborhood, without

Figure 3.1   Multiethnic Neighborhood Experiment Showcard Used in Zubrinsky-Charles Study

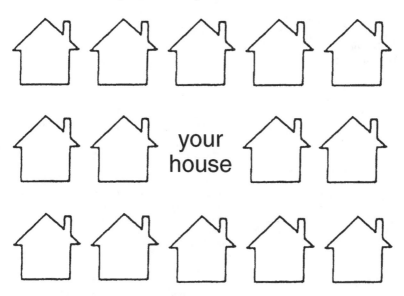

Source: Zubrinsky-Charles 2000.

the constraints of the real options facing a home purchaser. The drawback of this research is that it does not control for social desirability effects. Furthermore, the study is localized in the Los Angeles area, which is more multiracial than most cities of the United States. Yet because of the large number of racial minorities Zubrinsky-Charles included in the study, her research is a wonderful complement to the LSAF and it is better able to assess the residential preferences of racial minorities. Using her data, she calculates the average percentage of each group in a respondent's ideal racial neighborhood and also notes whether the respondent wants to exclude members of a particular race. The results of these calculations can be seen in Table 3.3.

Table 3.3   Summary Statistics of Zubrinsky-Charles Showcard Experiment

Target Group	European Americans	African Americans	Hispanic Americans	Asian Americans
European Americans				
Mean %	49.21	23.67	28.42	32.98
% None	0.24	10.10	12.39	7.24
African Americans				
Mean %	16.15	37.41	13.76[a]	11.05[a]
% None	18.91	0.72	31.66[a]	39.94[a]
Hispanic Americans				
Mean %	17.07	21.32	41.23	15.57[ac]
% None	17.05	8.55	2.76	26.42[ad]
Asian Americans				
Mean %	18.04	17.77[ae]	17.06[ab]	40.98
% None	15.88	15.57[af]	22.43[af]	0.54
N	818	1,082	982	1,027

Source: Zubrinsky-Charles 2000.
Notes: The percentage of each racial group in a respondent's "ideal" neighborhood is the sum of each race included in the experiment in Figure 3.1. The sum of all houses of each racial group, except for the respondents ("your house"), is divided by the sum of all homes. Thus if a respondent includes 4 European American neighbors in his/her "ideal" neighborhood, this would equal 4/14 = 28.57%.
a. Significantly different from European Americans at the 0.001 level.
b. Significantly different from African Americans at the 0.05 level.
c. Significantly different from African Americans at the 0.01 level.
d. Significantly different from African Americans at the 0.001 level.
e. Significantly different from Hispanic Americans at the 0.05 level.
f. Significantly different from Hispanic Americans at the 0.001 level.

The 16.15 mean percentage of African Americans whom European Americans want in their "ideal' neighborhood is not significantly different than the 17.07 mean percentage of Hispanic Americans whom they desire in their ideal neighborhood. However, the 21.32 mean percentage of Hispanic Americans whom African Americans desire in their ideal neighborhood is significantly higher at the 0.05 level than the 17.77 mean percentage of Asian Americans whom African Americans want in their ideal neighborhood. I would argue that this difference reflects a stronger desire for Hispanic American neighbors, as opposed to Asian American neighbors, on the part of African Americans.[42] Not surprisingly, people always have a higher preference for members of their own racial groups, and this difference is reflected in higher in-group means. It is a given that individuals, on average, will desire to live with members of their own race, and the reader can assume that there are significantly strong differences between the desired percentages of the in-group race of the respondent and all other races.[43] Zubrinsky-Charles also records the percentage of respondents who do not want any members of a given race in their ideal neighborhood, indicated in the "% None" rows.

It is worth noting that the means of the target groups for European American respondents do not significantly differ from each other. European Americans are not significantly more likely to avoid listing African Americans in their ideal neighborhood than they are to avoid listing Hispanic Americans or Asian Americans. This is surprising given the results of the LSAF study. To explain this discrepancy I assert that there is a social desirability effect that likely shapes the scores of majority group members more than racial minorities. It is more socially acceptable for racial minorities to desire racially segregated neighborhoods than for European Americans to desire such communities, as certain advocates of minority group members have argued for a policy of pluralism that implies the existence of racially separate communities.[44] Because these individuals are respected in minority communities, as opposed to the chastisement faced by European Americans who propose racial separation, it is easier for racial minorities to advocate for racially separate neighborhoods, thereby negating the social desirability effect for racial minorities. While a social desirability bias has likely affected the responses of European American respondents, it is less likely to have affected the responses of racial minorities, making Zubrinsky-

Charles's study more useful for assessing the attitudes of racial minorities, precisely the groups for whom the LSAF lacks sufficient numbers of respondents for in-depth analysis.

When one compares the mean percentages of desirable races for every racial group except African Americans, blacks are the target group with the lowest score. Furthermore, again with the exception of African Americans, all respondents reject African Americans more than members of other racial groups, which is evident in the higher percentages in each group who desire to have no African Americans in their neighborhoods compared to having no members of other racial groups. While she does not document attitudes that support white flight from African American neighborhoods, Zubrinsky-Charles does illustrate that there may be problems of "brown" or "yellow" flight.[45] The higher levels of avoidance toward African Americans that Latino Americans and Asian Americans exhibit represent a common understanding in American society, even among nonblack minority groups, about the low social place of African Americans, and so Zubrinsky-Charles illustrates the alienation that African Americans are experiencing in the United States from nonblack minorities.

The differences in Zubrinsky-Charles's study are significant, and these results give evidence that African Americans are at the bottom of the social hierarchy in the United States. Both her study and the LSAF explode the myth that the failure of blacks to assimilate is due to their own efforts. African Americans are more accepting of living in integrated neighborhoods than members of other races, as they have a lower desirable same-race mean (37.41) than European Americans (49.21), Hispanic Americans (41.23), or Asian Americans (40.98). The lack of structural assimilation experienced by blacks is much more likely due to external rejection than to any internal preference for segregation.

Residential and Marital Alienation in the United States

The results from these studies of exogamy are robust, but both the LSAF study of residential segregation and Zubrinsky-Charles's research into residential segregation have serious shortcomings that should be addressed in future research. Work that uses either of these methods, which is both national in scope and contains a sufficient number of racial minorities to conduct analysis, will greatly aid researchers in developing future knowledge about residential segregation. However, the research design in the LSAF has the advantage of dealing with problems of social desirability bias, and perhaps such a national survey would be better accomplished with the factorial method instead of the showcard technique. Because of the weaknesses inherent in the current LSAF data, I make my conclusions about the theories of social distance cautiously as it pertains to residential segregation, but more confidently as it relates to racial exogamy.

Based upon this analysis, there is little or no support for the cultural pluralism or conflict theory models. Hispanic Americans and Asian Americans do not show the hostility toward intermarriage and residential integration with one another that the cultural pluralist model predicts. Because these groups do not favor whites over other nonblack racial minority groups, the white/nonwhite dichotomy predicted by the cultural pluralism model does not materialize. The conflict model hypothesized that Hispanic Americans and Asian Americans would have hostility toward European Americans, but I did not find this to be the case. In fact, there is some evidence of a preference for European Americans by Hispanic and Asian Americans in Zubrinsky-Charles's research, while there is less evidence of this preference among African Americans. Color-grading as a possible explanation garners a bit of support, since the perceived darkest-colored group—blacks—face the highest level of rejection. Nevertheless, since Asian Americans are traditionally perceived as being "lighter" in skin color than Hispanic Americans, there should be a preference for Asian Americans over Hispanic Americans. Yet neither my research nor Zubrinsky-Charles's work shows evidence of such a preference. The rejection of the color-grading model is reinforced by the fact that racial minorities do not show a higher preference for European Americans over the "darker-colored" races. It is not that other groups want European Americans, and their lighter skin color, but rather that all nonblack groups reject African Americans.

Given the evidence presented in this chapter, a caste ideology seems to be the best way to conceptualize the hierarchical construction of marital and residential preference in the United States. In such an ideology, African Americans can be seen as the socially "polluted" class who face rejection from all other races. This rejection is a hallmark feature of an informal hierarchy that places African Americans at the bottom of a bilevel structure.[46] The alienation thesis gains clear support from this chapter's findings,[47] which predict the residential and marital acceptance of nonblack racial minorities and the rejection of African Americans, since the alienation of African Americans is demonstrated by the social attitudes of both nonblack minorities and European Americans.

However, it can be argued that the results presented in this chapter may be due to an ignorance about African Americans that arises from a lack of contact between blacks and nonblacks. It is true that Hispanic Americans have more social contact with European Americans than with African Americans,[48] yet this lack of social contact is not an accident but rather is the result of the amount of racial aversion prevalent within American society. The LSAF data do not allow me to assert whether resistance to contact with African Americans is a result of the social inexperience of other races with blacks or an intrinsic devaluing of the worth of social contact with blacks. Yet other research asserts that there is a conscious depreciation of social contact with African Americans on the issues of intermarriage and residential segregation.[49] To the degree that a lack of social contact accounts for the results presented in this chapter, it is just as likely, if not more likely, that this contact is due to a predisposition on the part of nonblacks to avoid blacks rather than due to an innocent ignorance that has happened accidentally. Based on previous research and my current study, I assert that African Americans marry and live with other African Americans because they face alienation and rejection from other races rather than because of the mere ignorance of members of those races about relating to African Americans.

The rejection of African Americans, rather than the acceptance of European Americans, is the best explanation of social distance in the United States. This tendency can be seen in the high level of acceptance African Americans have for racial exogamy and residential integration with all races, indicating a stronger desire for social acceptance compared to other racial groups, which may denote a realization among African Americans that they are a universally unwanted group. If Afro-Anglo culture is meant to imply that there is an acceptance of African Americans by dominant group members, but that blacks value cultural distinctness and therefore avoid assimilation, then the findings of this chapter refute this idea. European American respondents do not seem to have an aversion for marrying or living next to nonblack minority group members, indicating that social interaction with African Americans is particularly undesirable and unique compared to how European Americans treat other racial minorities. Finally, while nonblack minorities do not show a systematic preference for marrying majority group members, they do show hostility toward outmarriage when African Americans are involved, which reinforces the idea that the informal racial hierarchy in the United States is determined more by the rejection of African Americans than by the acceptance of majority group members.

This research supports the contention that social relationships between African Americans and other racial groups are qualitatively different than racial relationships between other racial groups,[50] as the social rejection African Americans experience is more intense than that faced by other racial minority groups. Future research in this area must recognize this distinction and forgo assumptions that issues of social distance involving African Americans only differ in degree, but not in kind, from other types of racial exogamy. Furthermore, because they face less social rejection, I would contend that the possibility of assimilation, or a thinning of their racial identity, is stronger for Hispanic Americans and Asian Americans than for African Americans. This process of assimilation can eventually leave African Americans even more alienated, and this will especially be the case if nonblack minority groups continue to engage in marital assimilation on a large scale so that in time they become part of the majority group. This can leave African Americans as an unassimilable subculture within the larger American society.

The evidence presented in this chapter indicates that there seems to be a consensus among the American racial groups as to the bottom social position African Americans possess,[51] and that African Americans fail to assimilate because of rejection by nonblack groups—not because of choices made by African Americans. But racial alienation has deeper implications than marital and residential segregation. It also implies that African Americans will eventually be ideologically segregated as nonblack racial minority groups begin to accept the privileges of dominant status and to exhibit less concern for racial disenfranchisement. If nonblack racial minorities are experiencing identificational assimilation, then members of those groups should be willing to possess social attitudes that support the social privilege of their perceived majority group status, rather than attitudes that favor the empowerment of disenfranchised racial groups. The next chapter is crucial, as I begin to move beyond the well-documented evidence of marital and residential segregation of blacks into studying the relatively undocumented existence of the ideological segregation of African Americans from members of other racial minorities.

Notes

The research reported in the second section of this chapter is drawn from the presentation of data in two academic articles: Emerson, Yancey, and Chai 2001; and Zubrinsky-Charles 2000.

1. Gitlin 1995; Steele 1996.
2. Buttny 1999; Tatum 1999; Lee 1996.
3. Spencer 1994; Hoskins 1968.
4. McAdam 1982; Frady 1996; Perry 1995.
5. Bogardus 1968.
6. Owen, Eisner, and McFaul 1981.
7. Imagine if we were to devise social distance scales in 1900. At that time, southern and eastern European ethnic groups such as Italian Americans and Polish Americans would certainly be included, as these groups would not be seen as part of the majority. It is impossible for me to speculate what the scores of the members of these groups would be, but I am comfortable in arguing that they would be significantly higher than the scores of English or French Americans. But today all European ethnic groups would likely have similar scores on social distance scales, illustrating how European ethnic groups have undergone a process of assimilation into dominant group status.
8. McConahay 1986; Bobo, Kluegel, and Smith 1997; Firebaugh and Davis 1988; Schuman et al. 1997.
9. Fang, Sidanius, and Pratto 1998.
10. Pratto et al. 1994.
11. Merton 1941.
12. Geschwender 1978.
13. Russell, Wilson, and Hall 1992; Hughes and Hertel 1990; Keith and Herring 1991.
14. Herring and Amissah 1997.
15. Spickard 1989; Lewis 1994; Lewis and Yancey 1995; Gallagher 2002b.
16. Tucker and Mitchell-Kernan 1990; Aldridge 1978; Lewis and Yancey 1995.
17. Spickard 1989; Lewis and Yancey 1995; Gallagher 2002b.
18. Lewis and Yancey 1995.
19. Herring and Amissah reported using ethnic identifications to classify the respondents. In the GSS, respondents were allowed to give up to three ethnicities. I went back to the 1990 GSS to calculate the number of minorities who can be included in Herring and Amissah's research. Ideally, one can argue that only the first ethnicity mentioned should be used, since it is likely that these first ethnicities are the ones wherein a respondent's identity is

most powerfully anchored. If Herring and Amissah only used these designations, then they would have but sixty-three Latino Americans, fifty-one Native Americans, and thirteen Asian Americans available for their study. But if they used those who named a minority ethnicity in any of the three categories, then (assuming that there is no overlap with individuals naming more than one minority ethnicity) Herring and Amissah could have used up to seventy-eight Latino Americans, ninety-one Native Americans, and twenty Asian Americans.

20. The various races were rotated in this question so that a European American had as much of a chance of being asked about a black as he or she had of being asked about either a Hispanic or an Asian, an African American had just as much of a chance of being asked about a white as he or she had of being asked about either a Hispanic or an Asian, and so forth.

21. A researcher should show concern for the fact that not all of the findings were significant in this bivariant analysis. However, in Table A.2 (see appendix) I controlled for other factors that may explain a reluctance to accept exogamy. The results suggested that European Americans, Hispanic Americans, and Asian Americans are all significantly more likely to reject African Americans than other racial groups. Thus regression analysis strengthens my findings that other racial groups universally reject African Americans.

22. The overall mean scores for each group, regardless of the group asked about, were 5.290 for European Americans, 6.300 for African Americans, 5.870 for Hispanic Americans, and 5.063 for Asian Americans. African Americans' scores are statistically significantly higher than those of the other three races.

23. However, it can be argued that even limiting the analysis to attitudes toward exogamy produces important information about the alienation of blacks. Charles Gallagher (2002b) uses qualitative interviews to illustrate how European Americans' hesitation to marry African Americans is linked to larger issues of racial stereotyping and social rejection.

24. Massey and Denton 1996.

25. Kain 1986; Massey and Denton 1996.

26. Frey 1979.

27. Clark 1989.

28. Harris 1999; Taub, Taylor, and Dunham 1984.

29. Emerson, Yancey, and Chai 2001.

30. Rossi and Nock 1982.

31. See, for example, Samuelson and Zeckhauser 1988; and Tversky and Kahneman 1990.

32. Frey 1979; Harris 1999; St. John and Bates 1990.

33. Others variables could, and perhaps should, be included. But because the interviews were conducted using a quantitative phone survey, the number of context variables had to be limited. Future work should include variables found important in this work as well as incorporate others that were not tested for.

34. We did not include a description of the remaining racial composi-

tion of the neighborhood because survey pretests suggested that respondents assumed that the unstated portion was composed of their own racial group.

35. An example of the question with randomly generated values can be read like this to a Hispanic American respondent: "Checking on the neighborhood, you find that property values are stable, the other homes in the neighborhood are of equal value to the home you are considering, the crime rate is low, the neighborhood is 20 percent Asian, and the public schools are of high quality. How likely or unlikely do you think it is that you would buy this home?"

36. For a more complete report of this research, see Emerson, Yancey, and Chai 2001.

37. For example, among European American respondents, 34.5 percent were told that the schools had low quality, 31.5 percent were told that the schools had acceptable quality, and 34.0 percent were told that the schools had high quality. The other independent variables demonstrated similar levels of randomness.

38. The potential number of subcells that can emerge from this work is nearly overwhelming. Just from the question about the percentage of individuals from another race, one can obtain twenty categories, which does not take into consideration the other five variables that can be used to create subcells. If a researcher collapsed the possible responses of the percentage of racial minorities in the potential neighborhood from twenty (5 percent to 100 percent) to three (e.g., under 20 percent, 25 to 50 percent, and over 50 percent), there is a potential of 3^6 or 729 different subcells. This is calculated by multiplying the potential categories of percentage of race (3) by the potential categories of school quality (3) by the potential race of minority group (3) by the potential categories of property values (3) by the potential categories of value of other homes in the neighborhood (3) by the potential categories of crime rate (3). Given such a large number of possible subcells, it becomes important to have a sufficient number of respondents to represent most of the possible residential conditions that will be asked about.

39. Zubrinsky-Charles 2000.

40. Farley et al. 1993; Schuman et al. 1978.

41. These numbers do not match the data in Table 3.3. From my reading of Zubrinsky-Charles 2000, I was unable to determine why this discrepancy occurred, but my guess is that missing data or incomplete responses to this question in the overall survey account for this difference.

42. Because of the recent level of hostility between African Americans and Korean Americans in the Los Angeles area, this is not a surprising result. This local dynamic makes it unwise to be too quick to generalize this particular result to the rest of the nation.

43. This in-group preference has been documented in the work of William Clark (1986, 1991).

44. Jackson and Solis 1995; Sleeter and McLaren 1995; Carr 1997.

45. Zubrinsky-Charles does speculate that much of the effect she documents from nonblack minorities is due to the immigrant status of many Hispanics and Asians, which leads to a high degree of stereotyping of

African Americans by nonblack minorities. Due to the geographical location of Los Angeles, the majority of Hispanic and Asian Americans in her study are first-generation immigrants. Yet despite the nonrandomness of the sample, this research is vital because it is the first multiracial assessment of the social attitudes that lead to residential segregation.

46. Or, as Derrick Bell (1992) describes in the title of his book, African Americans are "faces at the bottom of the well."

47. Of course there is other evidence that supports the notion that African Americans face a qualitatively different level of social alienation than other racial groups. For example, Marlee Taylor (1998) notes that concentrations of African Americans in the local population are correlated with an increased level of traditional prejudice, and a reduced support for race-targeting and government policies related to alleviate the effects of racism. Yet a similar statistical relationship was not found for the presence of Asian or Latino Americans in the local population.

48. Welch and Sigelman 2000.

49. Lewis and Yancey 1995; Gallagher 2002b; Massey and Denton 1996.

50. Lewis and Yancey 1995; Moskos and Butler 1996.

51. My assertion about the alienation of African Americans represents general attitudes across the United States and may not be relevant in certain regions in the United States. Clearly there are areas in the United States where other racial minorities face more alienation than do African Americans. For example, my experience in southern Wisconsin informed me that Native Americans face more racial discrimination, and likely alienation, than African Americans in northern Wisconsin. Such pockets of alienation toward nonblack minorities must not be overlooked. Yet I still contend that blacks generally are the racial group who experience the greatest level of alienation.

·

4

The End of the Rainbow Coalition

It was the day after the 2000 vice presidential debate between Dick Cheney and Joseph Lieberman. I was working in the office and listening to a radio talk show. Callers were discussing who won the debate and how they planned to vote. A European American woman called and said that she was going to vote for George W. Bush, but that her husband, who was African American, supported Al Gore. She went on to remark that she knew other white/black interracial couples for whom the European American partners supported Republicans, but their African American spouses favored Democrats. She did not understand why African Americans supported Democrats even though her spouse was black.

Political pundits often talk about a "gender gap," or the stronger tendency for females to support progressive political candidates.[1] Yet this illustration indicates there is a "racial gap," and that racial differences are much stronger than gender differences.[2] These racial differences are so powerful that apparently even marriage does not always produce political consensus between members of distinct racial groups. Differential racial realities in the United States are one of the most significant shapers of political conflict. While examining political attitudes can be useful for observing how racial aspects in the United States shape contrasting perspectives between racial groups, politics is not the only way by which these racial cleavages become apparent, as nonpolitical social issues also produce contrasting social attitudes. For example, Michael Emerson and Christian Smith note that European Americans, particularly evangelicals, tend to conceptualize freewill individualism as more important to social outcomes than do African Americans.[3] They do not argue that blacks disregard the responsibility of individuals, but that they are more likely to take into consideration structural, as well as individualistic, attributions than are majority group members. Their argument reveals that racial differences can manifest themselves in nonpolitical social attitudes, as well as through measurements of political issues.

Generally, social attitudes, whether political or nonpolitical, where racial distinctions are the greatest, tend to be those that include a racial component. A classical example is affirmative action. The obvious racial nature of this public policy makes it easy to perceive why European and African Americans would have contrasting attitudes about it. African Americans who have experienced the powerful effects of racial alienation are likely to desire the relief that affirmative action promises. European Americans, who often are ignorant of the racism in American society and have a vested interest in protecting the status quo, are less likely to perceive the need for this program. These different life experiences at least partially account for the higher support by blacks for affirmative action programs.[4]

When we look at social attitudes that are affected by the racialized nature of American society[5]—whether those attitudes are political or not—it becomes easy to predict the attitudes of European and African Americans. Because blacks have a lower racialized social position, they will be more likely to adopt attitudes that are supportive of their desires to change the racial status quo. On the other hand, as I will demonstrate, there is a white identity that encourages the adoption of attitudes that support the current racial hierarchy. It can be argued that affirmative action may represent a program that challenges the racial structure that supports the privileges of majority group members. It is in the group interest of blacks to challenge those privileges, but in the interest of whites to support this structure—which explains each group's attitude toward affirmative action.

Historical and contemporary racial reality indicates that European Americans have the dominant social position in the United States while African Americans have a subordinate position. The question this book is addressing is the position of Hispanic and Asian Americans. If these nonblack minority groups are beginning to identify with having majority group status, then it can be expected that they will have social attitudes that are at least as closely aligned with

European Americans as they are with African Americans. In other words, these racial groups may have begun to develop a vested interest in the maintenance of the status quo. If the racial identities of these nonblack minority groups have thinned to the point that those identities lack relevance to their lives, then they may perceive advantages from protecting the racial status quo. This can be true even though these groups have not yet reached majority group status. However, if identificational assimilation is not taking place, then these nonblack minority groups would have a vested interest in overturning the status quo and should have racial attitudes that are closer to the established subordinate group in the United States—African Americans.

Unfortunately, there is limited research that assesses the social and political attitudes of nonblack minority groups. Most of the studies that have examined political attitudes only look at African American and European American attitudes toward a variety of issues.[6] While there are a few national examinations of Hispanic American political and social attitudes,[7] there are virtually no national studies of the political attitudes of Asian Americans.[8] Scholarly examinations of the political attitudes of Asians Americans tend to be limited to analyzing their political behavior as one of several dimensions of study within a particular Asian American ethnicity.[9] Research into nonpolitical social attitudes also tends to focus upon European Americans and African Americans rather than nonblack racial minorities.[10] However, data from the 1999–2000 Lilly Survey of American Attitudes and Friendships (LSAF) allow me to account for the possible racial perspectives of Hispanic and Asian Americans.[11]

Identificational Assimilation

Milton Gordon's theoretical assimilation process supports the prediction that the social attitudes of nonblack minority groups assimilating into the dominant culture are closer to the attitudes of European Americans than to those of African Americans. If these groups have undergone cultural, structural, and marital assimilation, then the next step for them is identificational assimilation. This assimilation occurs when the racial attitudes of minority group members becomes so thin that they start to perceive themselves as part of the majority group. Identificational assimilation does not mean that minority group members no longer remember their previous identity, but rather that this previous identity is no longer very salient in how they understand their social position. To empirically capture this process a researcher must assess the centrality of minority group identity on social attitudes.

Producing evidence of identificational assimilation is difficult. It is tempting to merely use direct racial identity questions to measure the presence of this assimilation. But since nonblack minority groups have not yet completely undergone civic assimilation, direct questions about their racial or ethnic identity are not likely to be useful. No matter how thin an Asian American's racial identity may be, or how much he or she perceives having majority group status, that person is extremely unlikely to answer a racial identity question by stating that he or she is "white." American culture practically demands that individuals with Asian American parents answer such questions with "Asian." It is important to find ways to indirectly assess the degree of majority group identity that a particular racial group has accumulated, as well as how little of the minority group identity they may possess.

At some point in American history, southern/eastern Europeans stopped thinking of themselves as minority group members and began to identify with majority group members. They still recognized their ethnic ancestries, but those identities were no longer very important in shaping their social outlook. Their ethnic identities were surpassed by the master identity of "white," which brought with it majority group status. As these European ethnic groups begin to develop a white identity, it became easier for them to perceive themselves as whites—which in turn minimized the importance of minority identity. This is in contrast to the period in American history when ethnic identities were a critical source of social identification for these groups, due to the discrimination and subordination they faced. But as their identities thinned, these southern/eastern Europeans developed the ability to ignore the relevance of racial/ethnic discrimination and could develop attitudes that were consistent with their new majority group position. Thus they began to accept the attitudes of majority group status as they experienced movement into that status. I argue that Hispanic and Asian Americans are in a somewhat similar social place today—still accessing their Hispanic and Asian identities but moving toward an acceptance of some of the majority group attitudes prevalent in the United States.

Yet evidence of assimilation does not have to mean that members of the minority group have to totally accept the perspectives of members of the majority group. It is possible that majority group members will alter their racial attitudes in response to their interaction with nonblack minorities, just as it is possible that Hispanic and Asian Americans will conform to many of the social attitudes of European Americans. Such a result would be consistent with Gordon Allport's classical notion of the contact hypothesis, which postulates that interracial contact will bring about more racial acceptance by the majority group.[12] If majority group acceptance of nonblack minorities' social attitudes is a more accurate way to conceptualize race relations than the alienation thesis, then we would expect Hispanic and Asian Americans to still maintain racialized attitudes that are similar to those of a minority group. But I will point out in this chapter that the racialized attitudes of nonblack racial minorities are at least as likely to match those of European Americans as they are to match those of African Americans. Therefore, it is unlikely that the interracial contact between Europeans and Hispanics/Asians alters the attitudes of majority group members more than the attitudes of racial minorities—and the attitudes of majority group members may be less affected by this contact.

Social attitudes can become important proxies for discovering the degree of assimilation that members of minority groups have undergone. To the degree that these racial minorities possess the social attitudes of majority group members, distinct from alienated minority groups, it can be argued that certain minority group members have begun to experience identificational assimilation. This is a significant level of assimilation, since it means not only that nonblack minorities are living with and marrying majority group members, but also that they are beginning to think like the dominant group. Since no one would argue that Hispanic or Asian Americans are indistinguishable from majority group members, it is not realistic to believe that either of these groups will agree with majority group members on all racialized issues. But racial groups with an unambiguous minority racial identity should have more sympathy for the concerns of racial minorities in general than for the position of the dominant group. I will show that this is not the case for Latino and Asian Americans.

It is impossible to conclusively demonstrate a longitudinal process with data that are static. But if we assume that Hispanic and

Asian Americans were at one time in American history more likely to have racialized attitudes that are more supportive of minority group members than of majority group members—a realistic assumption given the history of racial abuse that these groups have suffered—then demonstrating that today their attitudes are as close, or even closer, to those of European Americans than to those of African Americans has value in detecting the possibility of identificational assimilation.

White Racial Identity

Our social identities help us to distinguish ourselves from others in the society and inform us of what our place in society is. This social identity is entangled with our personal perceptions of self,[13] and so represents powerful forces that help to shape an individual's perception of social reality. In a racialized society, Americans generally understand that their racial place is generally established for them through their racial identity. Eduardo Bonilla-Silva contends that our racial identity is part of our sense of self—whether we are aware of this identity or not.[14] Despite the protestations of European Americans who claim that they have no racial identity, it is vital to examine the racial identities of both majority and minority group members in order to fully understand how Americans tend to place themselves within the current racial hierarchy. Research in studies of race and ethnicity has typically concentrated upon trying to understand how American racial reality affects the lives of racial minorities. But to understand whether Hispanic and Asian Americans are developing the perspective of majority group members, it has to be established what the perspective of majority group members is. To accomplish this task I am deeply indebted to the emerging field of "whiteness studies," which concentrate upon the importance of understanding how majority group members comprehend racial reality.

Americans develop racial identities so that they can meet important psychological and social needs. These bonds can be important for helping minority group members to weather the racial hostilities they face. For example, it can be argued that racial minorities develop an overt racial identity so that they can find common bonds with others who share their life experiences. Likewise, majority group members develop racial identities that serve their group interests. The research in whiteness studies suggests that, unlike racial minorities, majority group members tend to downplay the importance of racial identity.[15] One of the hallmarks of majority group status is the ability to ignore the importance of race,[16] and empirical studies indicate that European Americans tend to dismiss the presence of racism in American society.[17] The deemphasis of racial identity meets an important need for dominant group members, since by ignoring the presence of race and the effects of racism, majority group members are able to ideologically maintain a system that continues to give them racial privileges.[18] In this way, majority group members can philosophically justify the racial status quo. Many majority group members adopt a "color-blind" ideology that theoretically values the treating of members of all races as equals.[19] Yet dominant group members discourage the reforms necessary for ending racially hierarchical social structures by utilizing this color-blind argument.[20] Thus the notion of color blindness, which is conceptualized as a goal of eradicating all indications that race is significant in the United States, is a key component of white racial identity and aids dominant group members in their quest to maintain racial privilege.

Related to this attempt to ignore race, white racial identity includes the perception that European American culture is normative.[21] All other racial cultures are seen as deviant to the assumed "natural" state of majority group culture. This position of normalcy is a presumed state that European Americans tend to adopt without even recognizing how it degrades the values and priorities of nonwhites. It is similar to an Anglo-conformist perspective whereby members of all racial groups value cultural, phenotypic, and social proximity to European Americans, and under such a social condition, European Americans would not be challenged to adapt to the presence of other racial groups. While majority group members attempt to deny the importance of race within their lives, they simultaneously push aside the perspectives and values of those within other races.

A final aspect of this cursory exploration of white racial identity that deserves comment is individualism. While individualism is a value within a variety of American racial groups, it is particularly strong among European Americans.[22] It is a good philosophical fit for an identity that desires to maintain the status quo, because it allows dominant group members to blame the failures of racial minorities squarely on the individual racial minority, instead of on the social structures that buttress Eurocentrism.[23] At its most extreme level, individualism places all of the responsibility for one's life upon the individual—ignoring environmental and societal effects upon that individual. However, structural analysis allows a social critic to perceive how people of color suffer, at least in part, because of the way that social institutions have been set up to aid European Americans. It has been documented that the racial attitudes of Europeans inhibit their ability to challenge the social structures that harm African Americans, even though these individuals do not show high levels of overt racial hatred or prejudice.[24] By focusing only upon individual overt racism, the emphasis upon individualism among European Americans allows them to escape accusations of racism, while they continue to protect the racial structures in the United States that work to their benefit.

All of these aspects of white racial identity point to a common goal of maintaining the racial advantages of majority group members. These advantages have been conceptualized by the term "white privilege."[25] It is logical for an individual to protect this privilege as long as he or she believes that he or she will receive the benefits of it. Thus it is understandable that European Americans tend to accept the qualities of a white racial identity that help them to gain from white privilege. However, protecting white privilege make little sense if people do not perceive that this privilege is available to them, and so for African Americans it is not logical for them to ignore the effects of racialized social structures within their lives or to blindly endorse an individualist philosophy. France Winndance Twine has done interesting work with biracial black/white women who grew up in predominantly middle- to upper-class white neighborhoods.[26] She found that these women, as high school girls, developed the same traits of white identity as do most European Americans. She documents that they accepted color blindness, race neutrality, whiteness as a position of middle-class privilege, and individualism. She attributes this identity development to the ability of these girls to find acceptance in the dominant culture. Yet as these young women entered the University of California at Berkeley, they found that they were no longer easily accepted into the dominant culture and that African Americans demanded their racial loyalty. This led to the women developing a black identity to meet the new social needs that developed at Berkeley. As they lost the potential benefits of whiteness in college, a white racial identity was no longer plausible for them.

Two points are worth taking from Twine's work. First, I must point out the powerful alienation she documents. Twine observes that one of the reasons that these women affiliated themselves with African Americans, instead of European Americans, is that majority group college men would not romantically pursue them. To have access to romantic encounters, they turned their back upon some of the dominant culture they grew up in and often were resocialized by their black boyfriends. If these women found majority group romantic partners, then many of them chose to retain much of their white racial identity and experienced some degree of identificational assimilation. Twine's work helps to deeply illustrate the powerful result of the lack of marital assimilation that African Americans experience. Second, these women were free to adopt dominant group values as long as they were able to experience acceptance from the majority group. In their middle-class neighborhoods they experienced the benefits from a societal status quo where their wealth likely gave them status regardless of their race. When they entered an atmosphere where that acceptance was no longer available, these women began to reject this dominant identity, finding that a "black" identity would better meet their social and psychological needs. Likewise, nonblack racial minorities who experience acceptance have the ability to acknowledge a "white" identity. But if they experience rejection from dominant group members, then such an identity is no longer available.

The concept of a white racial identity is an abstract concept, but it is one that can be used to enable a researcher to understand why European Americans have certain perspectives about social and political issues. If we compare the attitudes of majority group members to those of a group recognized as alienated—African Americans—then these social and political issues will be valuable proxies for measuring the possible presence of white racial identity. Since a test for identificational assimilation requires an attempt to measure the presence of a white racial identity within nonblack racial minorities, using social and political issues is theoretically justified for accomplishing this purpose.

Using the LSAF to Assess Racial
Alienation and Identificational Assimilation

Structuralist theories of racism imply that the examination of racialized social structures, and the ideologies that perpetuate those structures, is the best way to assess contemporary racism.[27] As I stated in Chapter 1, I am not opposed to the argument that understanding contemporary social structures is a key to comprehending why social and economic advantages are disproportionally given to those in the majority group. Yet social attitudes are not unimportant in the assessment of how the United States has maintained its racialized nature. Racialized social attitudes and racialized social structures are not unrelated. These social attitudes reflect attempts of majority group members to maintain the racial status quo and attempts of alienated minority group members to alter the racial economy. They can also indicate whether certain minority groups are more likely to accept the perceptions of the dominant group than other minority groups who are suffering from more extreme forms of alienation.

The LSAF offers survey research that can shed light upon the possibility that African Americans suffer from a degree of alienation that escapes other minority groups. Yet doubt has been cast upon whether survey work is useful for assessing the racialized nature of American society. Perhaps the strongest critique of using such survey work has been done by Bonilla-Silva.[28] Beyond the general assertion that social desirability effects tend to conceal the true racial division between majority and minority group members, Bonilla-Silva puts forth two more critiques of using survey research. First, he argues that surveys tend to utilize outdated questions that may have been useful when a Jim Crow type of racism was prevalent in American society, but are not useful for capturing the more subtle types of "color-blind" racism that currently dominate American society. Second, he contends that surveys are limited by their quantitative nature, which leads to problems of how to interpret their results. Instead of relying upon surveys, Bonilla-Silva advocates the assessment of racial ideologies with qualitative interviews, which can produce a more nuanced and in-depth assessment.

Let me first answer his second objection. Survey work should certainly not be the only assessment of racial attitudes. The quantitative results reported in this book must be followed up with qualitative work that either supports or refutes the basic findings that I assert. Yet the alienation thesis makes assertions about the general state of the different racial groups in the United States. This requires empirical evidence that is not limited by regional or subcultural influences.[29] Qualitative work by its very nature is difficult to generalize out to the larger society, since the subjects are not picked through a probability sample. To use a national probability sample to discover if there is a basis for my claims is valuable, since such work will indicate whether there is a general tendency of nonblack racial groups to accept the racial ideas of majority group members. If this tendency is established, then future qualitative work will be necessary for learning more specifically how nonblack groups such as Latino and Asian Americans conform to white racial identity as well as how they may differ from majority group members. Such work can also prove insightful for determining which Hispanic and Asian ethnic groups are more likely to assimilate in the near future and which are still fairly alienated from the larger society. But survey data are necessary for establishing whether attitudinal difference generally exists between the distinct racial groups.

Issues of social desirability and outdated questions also challenge the advisability of using survey research to assess racial attitudes. While social desirability can also affect the accuracy of interviews, clearly it is easier for majority group members to disguise their potential racial insensitivity when they answer a survey, since they do not have to have a face-to-face encounter with the researcher. Research into contemporary racism has illustrated that it is supposedly racially neutral attempts to maintain the racial status quo, rather than overt racial hatred, that power the current social system of racial inequality.[30] Interestingly, these proponents often use measurements of social attitudes to demonstrate how the social positions of European and African Americans help to determine differing solutions to the problem of racism.[31] Survey work does not have to be limited to outdated questions, or by the power of social desirability effects. As I will argue, cross-racial differences in social attitudes can be expected regarding racialized issues that reflect the relative power of distinct racial groups in the current racialized hierarchy. When it is found that blacks and whites significantly differ on racialized social issues, a researcher can be fairly confident that neither the forces of social desirability nor the probability that the question is outdated is powerful enough to prevent that question from indicating the desire of majority group members to maintain the racial status quo. Such questions are also theoretically useful for assessing the degree that Hispanic and Asian Americans also accept the maintenance of the status quo, and thus white racial identity.

Finally, Bonilla-Silva has questioned the ability of researchers to correctly interpret the results of survey work. He is correct in pointing out this limitation. Because the researcher is unable to follow up on respondents' answers with probes that can provide further enlightenment to the researcher, interpretations of survey research should always be carefully done. Yet given the reality of the contrasting social positions of European and African Americans within the United States and, as Bonilla-Silva would himself assert, the differential incentive of majority and minority group members to maintain the racial status quo, it is reasonable to argue that on racialized issues the responses of whites and blacks are largely shaped by their own racial interests. If this reasonable assumption can be accepted, then it can be further postulated that the racial attitudes of nonblack groups should reflect the desire to change the racial status quo, and thus be more consistent with the attitudes of African Americans. However, if this is not the case, if Latino and Asian Americans generally possess racialized attitudes that are more consistent with European Americans than with African Americans, then the basic premise that blacks are suffering from an alienation that escapes these racial groups can be supported.

Racialized Issues

The LSAF asks respondents to indicate whether they agree or disagree with a series of statements. Some of these statements can be seen in the questionnaire in this book's appendix. For my purposes, it is important to use statements that are indications of the possible effects of racial alienation. These are issues on which the answers of majority group members are likely to reflect aspects of white racial identity: color blindness, individualism, and Eurocentrism as normalcy. It is with such issues that I can begin to determine the degree of adherence that Hispanic and Asian Americans have toward either a majority or a minority group perspective.

To determine which statements I would use for this examination, I established two criteria. First, the statement had to have produced a statistically significant difference of opinion between whites and blacks. If European Americans are the group with the dominant position, and thus the most likely to adopt a majority group perspective, and African Americans suffer from racial alienation, and thus are the group most likely to adopt a minority group perspective, then issues on which these two groups do not significantly differ fail to exhibit racial alienation. After all, if these two groups are in agreement, then how can an argument be made that opinion on this issue is driven by racial alienation? Thus, when the data in the LSAF study indicate that European and African Americans do not significantly differ on their attitudes toward environmental issues, I conclude that environmental issues are not issues that contain a component of racial alienation.[32] Second, there had to have been a theoretical racial component in the statement. I did find significant differences between European and African Americans on issues such as abortion, gun control, and homosexuality, but there is no theoretical way to understand these issues through a perspective of differing racial power. I assert that these differences were more likely due to internal aspects within the African American culture that led blacks to understand these social and moral issues in a contrasting manner compared to majority group members.[33]

I found seven sociopolitical issues that met these two criteria. These racialized issues are support for affirmative action, whether we should have tax cuts, whether there is too much talk about race, whether churches should integrate, whether we should spend more money on prisons, whether able-bodied people should receive welfare, and whether we should have school choice. African Americans are significantly more supportive of affirmative action, talking about race, integration of churches, allowing able-bodied people to receive welfare, and school choice than are European Americans. African Americans are significantly less supportive of tax cuts and spending money on prisons than majority group members. The statements used to measure these issues can be seen in Table 4.1. I have already discussed how affirmative action illustrates how a racialized political issue can develop. Whether there is too much talk about race and

Table 4.1   Selected Statements Given to Respondents of the LSAF for Agreement or Disagreement

1. I support affirmative action policies.
2. The federal income tax should be cut.
3. There is too much talk today in the United States about racial issues.
4. Religious congregations should actively seek to become racially integrated.
5. We should spend more money on prisons so that we can put criminals away for a long time.
6. Able-bodied people should not receive welfare.
7. We need a program of parental school choice.

whether churches should integrate are issues for which the racialized component is evident.[34] However, the other four issues deserve further explanation.

On the surface it may seem that tax cuts are a class issue, rather than a race issue. But this assertion is based on the assumption that the issue of tax cuts only represents who will receive a direct monetary benefit from a tax cut. Tax cuts also represent attitudes toward the size and scope of the federal government.[35] A disenfranchised racial group is likely to desire a powerful government that can aid them in their struggle to overcome racial alienation. Yet for majority group members, the individualism within their racial identity provides an ideological justification to downplay the need for government intervention. Other studies have also demonstrated that African Americans are more likely to support an interventionist government than are dominant group members.[36] Since there are no cultural reasons that explain why African Americans are less likely than majority group members to support tax cuts, the greater desire of African Americans to obtain an advocate for racial justice in the government, and to have more racial power in society, is the best explanation of this significant difference.

Spending money on prisons is another issue that appears to have a nonracial nature, but is in fact driven by racial perspectives. One of the racialized aspects in the United States is the tendency to stereotype, and it has been documented that Americans tend to stereotype African Americans as being criminals.[37] It is argued that these stereotypes produce a fear among majority group members that creates a desire for them to "get tough on crime."[38] Because of their values of color blindness and individualism, European Americans are less responsive to understanding how the social structures created by racism may lead individuals into criminal acts—making them less likely to support alternatives to harsh punishment. On the other hand, African Americans disproportionally receive the results of efforts to punish criminals,[39] enabling blacks to be less desirous of a "get tough on crime" approach and of spending money on prisons.

The desire of African Americans to oppose a tax cut so that they may gain a governmental ally can be the same desire that motivates greater support for governmental programs such as welfare. For a disenfranchised racial group, welfare offers a hope of economic salvation. However, because white racial identity is built upon a perspective of middle-class normalcy,[40] European Americans are less likely to be supportive of individuals who receive welfare. This middle-class normalcy is built upon the myth that any able-bodied American who works will be able to at least obtain a middle-class style of living. For many dominant group members, welfare indicates an unfair taking of resources from "hard workers," which are then given to "lazy bums." This perception is likely exacerbated by the stereotypical image of lazy minorities receiving welfare, which produces a racialized element to the subject of welfare and shapes the perspectives of majority group members.[41] While white racial identity demands that such a program should be opposed, other research has documented the greater tendency of African Americans to support welfare programs.[42]

Finally, the issue of school choice is tricky. It is possible to make a cultural argument for a higher level of black support for school choice. Perhaps African American culture is more likely to support a voucher plan because of values connected to academic freedom. This seems unlikely given the higher tendency of European Americans to adhere to individualism, but the possibility cannot be completely dismissed. Yet there are also structural reasons for African Americans to support school choice. Historical racial discrimination and residential segregation have led blacks to send their children to schools that are educationally inadequate.[43] Many African Americans are locked into economically depressed neighborhoods that deprive their children of a quality education. Given this situation, such individuals likely want an opportunity to send their children to higher-quality schools. Theoretically, school choice or voucher programs offer them that opportunity,[44] even as such programs threaten the educational status quo that has benefited majority group members. Thus school choice can be conceptualized as an issue shaped by racial alienation.

Clearly these seven issues do not adequately cover all potential racialized differences between alienated minority and majority group members. For example, it can be argued that school spending, rather than school choice, may be a more racialized educational issue. Perhaps a question about residential integration or open housing, rather than about church integration, would be a better way to understand primary racial acceptance. Who is to say that questions about reverse discrimination, police brutality, racial profiling, busing, the death penalty, or electoral reform could not better capture racialized attitudes? But in conducting this analysis, I am limited to the issues asked about in the LSAF. The weaknesses of other studies pointed out in Chapter 1 also prevent me from pursuing those issues. Given such a limitation, I found that the two criteria enunciated earlier present the best and least arbitrary way to discover which issues in the LSAF are most likely to be racialized.

It can be debated that some of these seven issues are not adequately racialized for measuring the possible effects of alienation. But given the dearth of previous work into the racial attitudes of nonblack minorities, these seven issues can serve as an adequate initial examination of whether Latino and Asian Americans are more likely to have majority or minority group attitudes. I make no assertion that these issues will encompass all of the possible dimensions of American racialized attitudes,[45] and in fact I know that they do not accomplish this task. But they will provide a guidepost to which future cross-racial assessments of racialized attitudes can be compared. Future studies, with more racial measures, can be used to illustrate which racial dimensions are more conducive to Hispanic and Asian Americans accepting the perspectives of dominant group members as well as which perspectives indicate a greater willingness to accept the stances of an alienated minority group.

The LSAF data indicate that European Americans and African Americans differ on these seven issues. The alienation thesis suggests that nonblack minority groups are more likely to differentiate themselves from African Americans than from European Americans. I do not argue that they will agree with majority group members on all of these racialized issues, since if they did, then there would be a strong case that Hispanic and Asian Americans have already adopted majority group identity and have experienced an extremely high degree of assimilation. No one who is aware of the degree of discrimination and prejudice that these nonblack groups still face would make such a claim. Rather, my hypothesis is that these racial groups are about as, or even more, likely to agree with European Americans than they are with African Americans. Given the fact that both Hispanic and Asian Americans are racial minorities who still experience racial discrimination, evidence that they may adhere to some of the attitudes of the majority would be surprising—unless these groups are in the process of identifying with the dominant culture.

Comparing the Attitudes of
the Four Major Racial Groups

Previous research has suggested that Hispanic Americans tend to adopt a progressive political agenda based upon concerns of immigration, urban issues, and affirmative action,[46] which can serve as a baseline for this study. While I do not claim that the LSAF can capture a trend toward more conservative attitudes, it will be noteworthy to find out whether, given their historical acceptance of a progressive ideology, Hispanic Americans have attitudes that are similar to those of majority group members. No such assertions can be made about Asian Americans, since there is little, if any, research into their previous social or political attitudes.

In Table 4.2, I document measures of the sociopolitical attitudes of the four major racial groups using the seven questions discussed above. Each measure is the mean on the seven-point agreement/disagreement scale (higher scores indicate more disagreement). These measures indicate that Hispanic Americans are almost as supportive of affirmative action as African Americans, are more supportive of welfare than African Americans, and are just as likely to support school choice as African Americans—with none of the differences being significant. Hispanic Americans are significantly different from European Americans in their higher support for affirmative action, an even lower willingness to discuss race, a higher support for welfare, and a higher support for school choice. Thus on the issues of affirmative action, welfare, and school choice, Hispanics are more likely to adhere to the perspectives of African Americans than to those of European Americans. Yet Hispanic Americans are significantly more supportive of tax cuts, less willing to discuss racial issues, less likely to support church integration, and more willing to spend money on prisons than are African Americans. The fact that Hispanic Americans are even less supportive of talking about race than European Americans may indicate a greater support for color blindness on this issue. On these latter four issues Hispanic Americans are more supportive of the majority group perspective than the perspective of African Americans. Given the economic depravation and institutional discrimination that Latino Americans still face in the United States, this relative tendency to side with majority group members is insightful.

Arguably the issues that are most overt in their racial interpreta-

Table 4.2   Social Attitude Variables Among European Americans, African Americans, Hispanic Americans, and Asian Americans, by Mean Score

	European Americans	African Americans	Hispanic Americans	Asian Americans
Support for affirmative action	3.303	2.233[c]	2.466[c]	2.898[afg]
	(1,479)	(277)	(264)	(187)
	2.204	*1.727*	*1.878*	*2.062*
Income tax should be cut	2.564	3.257[c]	2.525[f]	2.640[e]
	(1,616)	(286)	(298)	(199)
	1.953	*2.519*	*1.986*	*2.061*
Too much talk about race	2.808	3.369[c]	2.470[af]	2.717[e]
	(1,621)	(293)	(301)	(199)
	2.179	*2.627*	*2.072*	*2.074*
Churches should integrate	3.208	2.884[a]	3.476[e]	3.463[e]
	(1,584)	(292)	(296)	(190)
	2.244	*2.386*	*2.343*	*2.234*
Spend money on prisons	3.818	4.471[c]	3.747[f]	4.117
	(1,613)	(292)	(301)	(201)
	2.393	*2.598*	*2.431*	*2.380*
Able-bodied should not receive welfare	2.168	2.532[b]	2.818[c]	2.863[c]
	(1,640)	(292)	(300)	(202)
	1.869	*2.216*	*2.318*	*2.272*
School choice	2.508	2.110[b]	2.186[b]	2.500[d]
	(1,563)	(285)	(289)	(195)
	1.839	*1.755*	*1.707*	*2.500*

Source: LSAF.
Notes: Means are main entries. Numbers of respondents are in parentheses. Standard deviations are in italics.
   a. Significantly different from European Americans at the 0.05 level.
   b. Significantly different from European Americans at the 0.01 level.
   c. Significantly different from European Americans at the 0.001 level.
   d. Significantly different from African Americans at the 0.05 level.
   e. Significantly different from African Americans at the 0.01 level.
   f. Significantly different from African Americans at the 0.001 level.
   g. Significantly different from Hispanic Americans at the 0.05 level.

tion—talking about race and whether to have integrated churches—are the issues on which Hispanics are most likely to adhere to a dominant group perspective. This can indicate that Hispanics are highly likely to accept a notion of color blindness, which is a strong feature of majority group identity. The three issues on which Hispanic Americans are more likely to adhere to the perspectives of African Americans—affirmative action, welfare, and school choice—are issues that are related to the lower economic standing of Hispanic Americans. It appears that one of the greatest barriers to the identificational assimilation of Hispanic Americans is their lower socioeconomic standard. This possibility will be examined later.

Asian Americans are significantly more likely to reject affirmative action, accept tax cuts, reject talking about race, and reject the integration of churches, and less likely to support school choice than African Americans. Asian Americans only significantly differed from European Americans in their stronger support for affirmative action and welfare. The data in Table 4.2 indicate a stronger adherence by Asians to the perspective of majority group members than by Hispanic Americans. It can be argued that the higher socioeconomic status of Asian Americans may enable them to accept a dominant group perspective more easily than Latino Americans.

The relative economic standing of the racial groups can influence their social attitudes, leading to a potential critique that the contrasting economic status, rather than the differential racial status, of European Americans is why they have distinct social attitudes compared to racial minorities.[47] This implies that it is European Americans' greater financial success, instead of their superior racial standing, over other racial groups that leads them to protect the status quo. Determining whether it is economic or racial distinctions that drive these social attitudes is important, since if these distinctions are driven by economic differences, then class-based programs are the best way to handle American racial problems.

To address this potential problem I eliminated all the respondents who made under $30,000 dollars a year,[48] leaving only Americans who are at least in the lower middle class in the comparison. Such a limitation removes the possibility that it is the higher percentage of lower-income African Americans who are driving the attitudinal differences between blacks and other racial groups,[49] and I will be able to control whether these income distinctions account for the tendency of Hispanic and Asian Americans to differ in their attitudes from African Americans. The results of this comparison can be seen in Table 4.3.

Respondents in the higher income bracket show many of the same differences in social attitudes as those in the lower income bracket. Hispanic Americans are still significantly more likely to support spending money on prisons and less likely to talk about race than African Americans. The significant difference in their lack of support for integrated churches disappears, yet now they are also significantly more likely to resist affirmative action, at the 0.1 level, than African Americans, and they are no longer significantly different in their support of school choice and welfare from European Americans. It appears that Hispanic Americans at these higher income levels are just as, or even more, likely to adopt majority group attitudes than those who live in poverty, while higher income African Americans maintain their ideological distinctness from Europeans Americans.

A similar argument can be made for Asian Americans at the higher income levels. They are significantly more likely to resist affirmative action, support tax cuts, resist school choice, and avoid talking about race than African Americans. Asian Americans also show a significantly higher propensity, at the 0.1 level, to accept prison spending than African Americans, although they also are significantly less likely to support such spending than European Americans. There is no evidence that eliminating lower-income respondents reduces the tendency of Asian Americans to agree with majority group members over African Americans, and the possibility that the results of Table 4.2 reflect class differences only is unlikely.

Socioeconomic status is not the only variable by which African Americans can differ from other racial groups. Perhaps there is another social or demographic difference between blacks and other racial groups that accounts for some of the results of Tables 4.2 and 4.3. Yet when I controlled for other social and demographic variables, the strength of the alienation thesis does not wane. In the book's appendix are regression models that control for a variety of social and demographic variables by which blacks may differ from other racial groups. After these controls I found that Hispanic Americans were significantly more likely to not support integrated churches, not want to talk about race, spend money on prisons, and

Table 4.3   Social Attitude Variables Among European Americans, African Americans, Hispanic Americans, and Asian Americans Making over $30,000 Annually, by Mean Score

	European Americans	African Americans	Hispanic Americans	Asian Americans
Support for affirmative action	3.320 (921) *2.218*	2.168[c] (116) *1.742*	2.662[hb] (94) *2.006*	2.991[f] (122) *2.021*
Income tax should be cut	2.469 (987) *1.883*	3.065[b] (115) *2.496*	2.758 (98) *2.131*	2.466[d] (130) *1.890*
Too much talk about race	2.937 (988) *2.201*	3.926[c] (115) *2.648*	3.155[d] (99) *2.385*	2.775[f] (128) *1.996*
Churches should integrate	3.238 (974) *2.245*	2.984 (116) *2.395*	3.299 (96) *2.413*	3.497 (123) *2.336*
Spend money on prisons	3.813 (988) *2.366*	4.916[c] (116) *2.441*	3.944[e] (98) *2.577*	4.322[ah] (130) *2.399*
Able-bodied should not receive welfare	2.113[h] (997) *1.793*	2.462[b] (116) *2.130*	2.359 (98) *2.119*	2.579[b] (131) *2.087*
School choice	2.638 (955) *1.888*	1.969[c] (112) *1.499*	2.316 (97) *1.759*	2.514[e] (126) *1.820*

Source: LSAF.
Notes: Means are main entries. Numbers of respondents are in parentheses. Standard deviations are in italics.
   a. Significantly different from European Americans at the 0.05 level.
   b. Significantly different from European Americans at the 0.01 level.
   c. Significantly different from European Americans at the 0.001 level.
   d. Significantly different from African Americans at the 0.05 level.
   e. Significantly different from African Americans at the 0.01 level.
   f. Significantly different from African Americans at the 0.001 level.
   g. Significantly different from Hispanic Americans at the 0.05 level.
   h. Significantly different from African Americans at the 0.1 level.

not support school vouchers than African Americans. Asian Americans were significantly more likely to avoid talking about race, not support affirmative action, and spend money on prisons than African Americans. In these regression models there was no situation where the nonblack minority groups differed significantly in a direction opposite from that by which European Americans differed from African Americans. For example, if European Americans were more supportive of tax cuts than blacks, then neither Latino nor Asian Americans were significantly less supportive of tax cuts than African Americans.[50] The regression models solidify, rather than challenge, the predictions of the alienation thesis.

Generally, when Americans talk about people of color, they are referring to any group who are not considered "white." Historically this has been an accurate way to conceptualize minority groups, because racial minority groups have developed an identity that reflects their devalued position in American society. This is not to state that minorities from different racial groups will develop identical social attitudes, because there are quantitative and qualitative differences in the disenfranchisement each group faces. Furthermore, cultural differences—such as the tendency of Hispanics to adhere to a Catholic faith,[51] as opposed to the Protestant beliefs of African Americans[52]—will determine some of the differences in social attitudes. Yet when it comes to issues about changing the racial status quo, it should be expected that these groups would generally enjoy similar social attitudes, especially when we compare their attitudes to those of dominant group members. My research challenges this assumption. At the very least, these results indicate that Latino and Asian Americans are as likely to disagree with African Americans as they are with European Americans on a variety of racialized issues.[53] In fact, on the issues that are arguably most overtly racialized (talking about race, whether to have integrated churches), they have an even greater tendency to develop a dominant group perspective. Furthermore, it is possible that the limited number of variables in the LSAF has forced me to potentially understate my argument for the alienation thesis. With more racialized variables I might be able to detect other ways by which nonblack racial groups have adopted the perspective of majority group members. Regardless, the evidence here suggests that nonblack minorities are in fact slightly more likely to agree with European Americans than with African Americans on racialized issues. If these social attitudes are at least partially shaped by the racial identity of the respondents, then Latino and Asian Americans are more likely to adopt the racial identity of dominant group members than to adhere to a minority racial identity. In such a manner these groups show evidence of a beginning progression toward identificational assimilation.

Criticisms of the Alienation Thesis

It would be foolhardy for me to claim that the evidence from the LSAF is the final word on the alienation thesis. Indeed there are several criticisms that can be leveled at my assertions. But I do not believe any of these criticisms to be fatal, and at best they only point out the need for further research to either refute or confirm this hypothesis. Regardless, I shall endeavor to address them.

The first and perhaps most obvious criticism is that this evidence is incapable of detecting any trends in social attitudes because the data are static. I can determine the attitudes of these racial groups as of the year 2000, but this says nothing about what the racial attitudes of these groups were ten years ago—much less what they will be ten years from now. It is always impossible to use data from a single point in time to demonstrate a general trend. Furthermore, because of the weaknesses of other data sets discussed in Chapter 1, it will be almost impossible to use earlier data that verify a trend in the attitudes of Hispanic and Asian Americans.

Yet these data do show that Hispanic and Asian Americans differ from African Americans on several racialized dimensions and suggest that these differences will remain as all racial groups improve their socioeconomic status, even as the attitudinal differences between European Americans and these nonwhite minority groups begin to shrink. Thus in Table 4.3, Latino Americans who earned over $30,000 a year only significantly differed from European Americans in measures of affirmative action, while they continued to significantly differ from blacks on affirmative action, talking about race, and spending money on prisons. Likewise, Asian Americans in this income bracket only significantly differed from European Americans on spending money in prisons and welfare policy. But they significantly differed from blacks in every category except welfare policy and integrated churches. If these nonblack minority groups continue to improve their economic standing, relative to European Americans, then it seems likely that more of them will adopt many of the social attitudes of majority group members.

Since these are not dynamic data, I cannot offer conclusive proof that the attitudes of nonblack racial minorities were different in the past and that they are changing as these groups move into the future. Yet it is important to remember the unlikelihood that these nonminority groups would historically have social attitudes that are supportive of a majority group ideology. The activism of these groups in the 1960s,[54] and the growth of Chicano and Asian studies in academia that developed from this activism,[55] seem to suggest that these groups have historically been more sympathetic to the plight of racial minorities than to the protection of the racial status quo. Yet my research indicates that the members of these groups are today just as likely to protect that status quo as they are to be sympathetic to the plight of alienated racial minorities. Future studies must be implemented to examine the possible longitudinal changes in the racialized attitudes of nonblack minorities.

A second noteworthy criticism is that the questions used in the LSAF are not good measures of a possible dominant group racial identity. As I noted earlier, it is very tricky to measure racial identity. Individuals clearly "know" what racial identity they are supposed to state when a researcher overtly asks them about race. But this does not mean that such measures capture their intrinsic racial identity. To demonstrate what I mean, let me use a real-life example. I have a friend who is a second-generation Mexican American. She cannot speak Spanish, she is Protestant, her best friends are European Americans, she generally dates European American men, and she lives in a predominately European American neighborhood. Her lifestyle indicates a high degree of assimilation into the dominant society and a considerable thinning of her Mexican identity. Furthermore, she also exhibits the acceptance of many of the ideological constructions of dominant group ideology (e.g., individualism). If a researcher were to ask her directly what her racial identity is, she would state that she is a Hispanic American, yet this women is an excellent example of a racial minority who is exhibiting identificational assimilation and a thinning of her minority identity.

The only way to assess the degree to which Hispanics are adapting to majority group ideology is to speculate about what a majority group identity may resemble and then measure how much each

Hispanic American adapts to the social attitudes that theoretically flow out of a majority group ideology. This methodology is open to criticism, since it can always be claimed that the questions used are not adequate for assessing racial identity. For example, perhaps assessing how money is spent on prisons is not an adequate measure of a racialized difference between European and African Americans. This difference may be due to cultural distinctions between these two groups that have little to do with racial power, in the similar manner that blacks have distinct attitudes from whites toward abortion.[56] It is very possible that the attitudinal distinctions documented in this chapter are due to cultural differences rather than the alienation of African Americans. This possibility must be taken seriously. However, it is instructive to note that in Table 4.2 the two variables that are most distinctly overt by racial attitudes—talking about race and support for interracial churches—are the variables on which blacks significantly differ from the other three racial groups, suggesting that the more clearly a variable is racialized, the more likely it is that blacks attitudinally stand apart from other racial groups. Cultural differences seem to ameliorate, rather than explain, the alienation effect.

There is definitely a need for future multiracial comparisons on other racialized measures that may also help to determine how much of the dominant group identity Latino and Asian Americans have accepted. But this research suggests that they are more defensive of the racial status quo than African Americans. I speculate that, given the findings in Table 4.2, future research that utilizes racialized variables will be more, not less, likely to find evidence of this acceptance.

These data can also be criticized because they fail to indicate an alienation effect in all of the variables used. For example, in Table 4.2 the measurement of welfare indicates that racial minorities share a similar level of support distinct from that of European Americans. This difference remains even when I look only at those who earn more than $30,000 a year and when I introduce other social/demographic controls.[57] Critics can point at this variable to argue that the case for alienation is overstated. If blacks were alienated to the degree that I am suggesting, then Hispanic and Asian Americans should differ from African Americans, and should adopt attitudes similar to majority group members, in all racialized variables.

Yet as I have stated before, it has never been my claim that these nonblack minorities would differ from African Americans on all racialized variables. This would only be true if these minority groups had already undergone complete identificational assimilation, and I have never claimed that this has occurred (my contention is that by 2050 significant portions these groups will have become "white"). My argument is that these groups are in the process of reaching this state of assimilation, but have not yet achieved it. While my findings clearly support this, they also indicate that Hispanic and Asian Americans do not possess the racial thickness of African Americans—the group who clearly inhabit an alienated minority racial position in the United States. This suggests that these nonblack minority groups occupy a position between that of an extremely alienated minority group and that of a majority group. Furthermore, although it is not clear from the comparisons I have made in this chapter, there is statistical evidence that the racial attitudes of these nonblack minority groups are actually closer to the perspectives of European Americans than to those of African Americans.[58] This implies that the assimilative tendencies of Latino and Asian Americans have more influence on their attitudes toward racialized issues than does their racial minority stance, even though they have not yet completely adopted the attitudes of the dominant group.

It should be pointed out that this research might underestimate possible attitudinal differences between African Americans and nonblack minorities. There is at least antidotal evidence that some individuals with Latino heritage already identify themselves as "white." This propensity might be especially likely for suburban, affluent Hispanics.[59] If this trend is significant, then Latinos who have already undergone identificational assimilation are not registered as "Hispanic" in this current research effort. This can create a self-selection effect whereby I exclude Latinos who have already taken on white racial identity and thus underestimate alienation effects.

Finally, some have questioned the measuring of social attitudes as a means for assessing the degree of racism in the United States, since it can be argued that people may not always express racism through their social statements.[60] It can be argued that a better way to assess the racial order in the United States is through an assessment of racialized social structure. In Chapter 1, I briefly touched upon a few of the structural theories of racism. It would be a mistake to ignore the institutional/structural ways that racism is manifested in our society. Too much of an emphasis on social attitudes places too high of a priority on an individualist perspective on race relations. Given these concerns it is fair to argue that the evidence presented in this chapter is necessary, but it is not sufficient proof of a developing black/nonblack division in our country.

Yet this is not the only evidence of this developing racial chasm. There are also important structural indicators of the alienation that African Americans experience in the United States. For example, both Latino and Asian Americans have higher outmarriage rates than African Americans,[61] even though these three groups date exogamously at similar levels.[62] These higher rates of exogamy indicate that members of these racial groups experience more acceptance from majority group members than do African Americans. Furthermore, it was noted in Chapter 3 that African Americans are less likely to live in an integrated neighborhood, even if they possess middle- or upper-class socioeconomic status, than are nonblack minority groups.[63] While there is some research that indicates exceptions to this general tendency,[64] clearly Latino and Asian Americans are more structurally integrated into majority group neighborhoods than are African Americans.

The different ways that marital and residential social structures impact African Americans, as opposed to most other racial minority groups, provide evidence beyond the social attitudes that have been documented in this chapter. Thus it is not my claim that the evidence in this chapter is sufficient by itself to document the alienation that African Americans have experienced and the emergence of white identity among Hispanic and Asian Americans, but rather that the findings in this chapter, in conjunction with other evidence, provide a powerful basis by which I can claim that a black/nonblack reality is developing within American society.

Conclusion

In 1984 Jesse Jackson attempted to run for the presidency of the United States based upon the idea that he could build a "Rainbow Coalition."[65] The idea of this coalition is that various disenfranchised groups would find a common purpose in opposing the status quo and thus would be motivated with a radical vision of empowerment. This strategy was not successful enough for Jackson to win the presidency, and now we might be able to understand why he failed. Jackson assumed that most, if not all, minority racial groups would be part of his coalition. Being an African American who knows what it is like to be alienated from the larger society, he likely presumed that other racial minorities perceived the same degree of alienation he felt. For some racial minorities this is undoubtedly true. He ran for president only forty years after the internment of Japanese Americans, and at a time when the hysteria against Hispanic illegal aliens was strong. There were members of these specific racial groups who had experienced an alienation similar to, or even greater than, that perceived by many African Americans.

Yet as the data from my research suggest, this alienation experience is less commonplace among nonblack minorities than one might expect. On social attitudes of racialized issues, nonblack minorities are at least as likely to match the attitudes of European Americans as they are to match the attitudes of African Americans. Whether this was true in 1984 cannot be determined by the LSAF. However, if the process of identificational assimilation was occurring among nonblack minorities at that time, then it is no surprise that Jackson's political strategy was unsound. The idea of a Rainbow Coalition would not be possible because a significant proportion of nonblack minority racial groups would fight against, rather than for, social change. Even if such a coalition had been possible in 1984, the data in this book indicate that it is not possible today. African Americans will occupy a bottom position in society as other minority groups accept the perspective of majority group members. Unless the attitudes of the members within these minority groups change, any Rainbow Coalition of alienated racial groups that anyone attempts to create will have one dominant color—black.

Jackson is not alone in his belief that it is vital to gather together a coalition of minority groups to effect the changes necessary to empower racial minorities. The social and political orientations of those who engage in Chicano, Asian, or Native American studies tend to exhibit a similar concern about the disenfranchisement of people of color. Yet I have reason to believe that these nonblack voices, important as they may be, do not represent the general direction of these nonblack minorities. That general direction is movement toward the majority community—just like the Irish, Polish, and Germans before them. Proponents of segmented assimilation may be correct when they assert that the process of assimilation today differs from the assimilation of European ethnic groups, but the difference in the assimilative experience is much greater between blacks and

European ethnic groups than between Hispanics/Asians and European ethnic groups.[66] In whatever manner the assimilative, or identificational thinning, process is unique for Hispanic/Asians, it is my prediction that the conclusion of this process for European ethnic and Hispanic/Asians is the same—the incorporation of both groups into the dominant power structure. This means that a coalition of various racial minority groups will not occur, but instead that African Americans will eventually be left to fend for themselves as certain racial minorities of today become part of the dominant culture of tomorrow.

The Rainbow Coalition does not crumble merely because of marital and residential assimilation. That integration is important because of the social barriers that break down due to the relationships developing in integrated families and neighborhoods. However, Latino and Asian Americans can live next to and marry European Americans without losing their racial minority identity. The evidence presented in this chapter indicates that this minority identity is breaking down as these nonblack minorities begin to accept the social attitudes that reflect the values of color blindness and individualism—hallmarks of a white racial identity. If these nonblack racial minorities begin to completely accept these and other dominant group values, then the only barrier that will remain between them and majority group status is whether European Americans will begin to see them as "white." Given the racial history of southern/eastern Europeans and the already high occurrence of intermarriage of Hispanic/Asian Americans with European Americans, this acceptance is likely to come soon. Once again I challenge the predictions that whites will be a numerical minority in fifty years. These nonblack minorities already freely live and marry with whites. They are learning to think like whites. In a reasonable amount of time many of them will become "white."

Historically we have thought about race relations along a white/nonwhite dichotomy. As a result, any group that was not considered white faced varying degrees of oppression and racism. Yet if nonblack minority groups are becoming part of the dominant structure, then we have to reconceptualize modern race relations. Having a white/nonwhite dichotomy will not be viable, since so few racial groups will be considered nonwhite. The one group who will consistently be considered nonwhite will be African Americans, and the alienation of this group will dramatically shape the racial hierarchy in the United States. Instead of having the European Americans on top and a variety of racial groups possessing lower levels of status below them, an alternate racial hierarchy will develop, with African Americans on the bottom and all other racial groups above them. If this transformation takes place, then a black/nonblack dichotomy will be more meaningful for understanding American race relations than the white/nonwhite dichotomy used today.

Notes

1. Mueller 1988; Norrander 1999.
2. According to Matt Bai and Michael Isikoff (2000), 90 percent of all African Americans voted for Gore in the 2000 presidential election, compared to only 54 percent of all women. Clearly there is much more political polarization along racial lines than along gender boundaries.
3. Emerson and Smith 2000.
4. Schuman et al. 1997; Steeh and Krysan 1996; Edsall and Edsall 1991; Hacker 1992.
5. Eduardo Bonilla-Silva (1997: 44) has defined a racialized society as "a society that allocates differential economic, political, social and even psychological rewards to groups along racial lines; lines that are socially constructed."
6. See, for example, Welch and Sigelman 1989; Davis and Davenport 1997; Zilber and Niven 1995; Bobo and Gilliam 1990; Weakliem 1997; Danigelis 1977; and Kinder and Sanders 1996.
7. On political attitudes, see, for example, Welch and Sigelman 1992; Welch and Sigelman 1993; and Arvizu and Garcia 1996). On social attitudes, see, for example, Valenzuela and Dornbusch 1996; and Southwest Voter Registration Project 1984.
8. The exception is the work of Myrtle Bell, David Harrison, and Mary McLaughlin (1997), which examines the attitudes of Asian American students toward affirmative action. However, this study may not be easily generalizable to the rest of the Asian American population. Additionally, there are a few studies that examine the breakdown of general elections across a variety of racial groups (e.g., Quirk 1989; Pomper 1997; Flanigan and Zingale 1998). While such studies are useful, they do not produce sufficient data for sophisticated analysis of intergroup differences.
9. Examples of such work can be seen in Fugita and O'Brien 1991 and San Juan (1998). Furthermore, while there are few, if any, sophisticated examinations of the political attitudes of Asian Americans, there have been some general political polls of how Asian American groups tend to vote, generally conducted by the major political parties or news services. The purpose of these polls is not to obtain scientific knowledge but to help push a particular political agenda or promote a certain news story. As a result of

this potential bias, these polls cannot be relied upon to deliver relatively objective analysis on what fuels Asian American political behavior.

10. For example, studies of religiosity tend to examine the social attitudes of blacks instead of nonblack racial minorities (e.g., Taylor et al. 1996; Jacobson, Heaton, and Dennis 1990; Hunt and Hunt 1999; Lincoln and Mamiya 1990). Yet assessments of Hispanic religiosity are generally limited to analysis of Hispanic Catholics (Doyle and Scarpetta 1982; Gonzales and La Velle 1985; de la Garza et al. 1992: 37), and Rudy Busto (1999) argues that there is little systematic analysis of the effects of religion in Asian American communities. Research into other types of social attitudes shows a similar neglect of the perceptions of nonblack minorities.

11. Howard Schuman and others (1997) argue that it is impossible to do a longitudinal study of Hispanic attitudes due to the fact that the definitions of "Hispanic" have shifted over time. Furthermore, they note that because of the tendency of some survey organizations to exclude the Spanish-speakers who could not conduct an English interview, Hispanic Americans are vastly underrepresented in survey research. So Schuman and others do what most researchers do when confronted with Hispanic Americans in their sample—they include most of them in the "white" category, which excluded the attitudes of Hispanics from any type of analysis because of the flawed assumption that the attitudes of Hispanics will be roughly similar to the attitudes of majority group members. Myrtle Bell, David Harrison, and Mary McLaughlin (1997) argue that although research into the attitudes of Hispanic Americans has improved over the past decade, the social attitudes of Asian Americans are still generally ignored in academic research.

12. Allport 1958.

13. Jenkins 1996.

14. Bonilla-Silva 2001.

15. Dyer 1997; Wildman and Davis 2002.

16. Dalton 1996; Dyer 1997.

17. Emerson and Smith 2000; Blauner 1989; Gallup Organization 1997.

18. Wildman and Davis 2002; Lipsitz 1998; McIntosh 2002.

19. Carr 1997; Cose 1997; Ansell 1997; Bonilla-Silva 2001.

20. Bonilla-Silva 2001; Kovel 1984.

21. Twine 1997.

22. Kluegel 1990; Bonilla-Silva and Lewis 1997; Bellah et al. 1985.

23. Emerson and Smith 2000; Klugel 1990; Virtanen and Huddy 1998.

24. Emerson and Smith 2000; Klugel 1990; Pettigrew 1985.

25. McIntosh 2002.

26. Twine 1997.

27. Bonilla-Silva 2001.

28. Ibid.

29. In fact, one of the problems with much of the work that buttresses notions of segmented assimilation is that it tends to concentrate upon racial subcultures who are the most alienated from the dominant group. Thus some of the work that demonstrates that assimilation is not linked to social mobil-

ity uses case studies of Sikh immigrants (Gibson 1989), Central American immigrants (Suarez-Orozco 1987), and first-generation Mexican immigrants (Matute-Bianchi 1991). None of these subgroups are likely to be easily incorporated into the dominant culture, since they have been in the country a relatively short period of time and thus are not a good test of straight-line assimilation. However, the LSAF uses general racial groupings as the unit of analysis, and it can be argued that African Americans, Latino Americans, and Asian Americans have generally been in the country for at least four generations—making this unit of analysis more viable for capturing any potential assimilation or racial identity thinning that may be occurring. The LSAF also gathers data about these general racial groups with a probability technique that better assesses the attitudes of these groups in general than ethnographic studies.

30. Bonilla-Silva 2001; Carr 1997; Kluegel 1990; Bobo, Kluegel, and Smith 1997.

31. Even Eduardo Bonilla-Silva himself (2001: 76–77) uses measurements of the general attitudes of whites and blacks to illustrate how African Americans have been able to develop an oppositional viewpoint in contrast to the dominant ideology of European Americans.

32. It can be theoretically argued that African Americans should be more likely to support efforts to clean up the environment, since they are more likely to suffer the consequences of a polluted atmosphere. Yet my data do not indicate that environmental racism has influenced African Americans to be significantly more likely than European Americans to accept a progressive environmental philosophy. Despite the theoretical argument for a racial effect on attitudes toward the environment, there are no empirical data that support this contention, and nonracialized social attitudes are more likely to shape the preceptions of whites and blacks toward the environment.

33. The one exception to these criteria is my decision to eliminate a statement about immigration from future analysis. Blacks and whites did significantly differ on this issue, and immigration is definitely an issue shaped by contrasting racial power. However, it is an issue that is of particular concern to groups containing large numbers of recent immigrants. The racialized effects of immigration do not theoretically shape the lives of disenfranchised minorities who have been in the country for several generations, such as African Americans. Furthermore, there is no theoretical reason to believe that nonblack minorities may adopt a dominant group perspective on issues of immigration, since they are more likely to be negatively affected by a majority perspective than African Americans. Immigration is a political issue whereby African Americans are clearly less likely to face racial alienation than Hispanic or Asian Americans.

34. Michael Emerson and Christian Smith (2000) document that African Americans tend to be more supportive of integrated churches than European Americans. They do not analyze nonblack minorities.

35. There is a common argument in the Republican Party about using tax relief to "defund" the federal government (Feder 1996). According to

this argument, in order to reduce the size of the government, it is important to reduce its funding. Those who make such an argument often have philosophical reasons for desiring a smaller government (e.g., less centralized power in the public sector), and a smaller tax bill is a happy side effect of this desire. Their ideological tie of tax relief and governmental size indicates that the linking of taxes and government size is not limited to African Americans. It is logical to argue that the willingness of individuals in all races to accept a tax cut is related to a person's preference for a small government.

36. Schuman et al. 1997; Sears et al. 2000.
37. Anti-Defamation League 1993.
38. Skogan 1995.
39. Tonry 1996; Walker, Spohn, and DeLonc 1996.
40. Barthes 1976; Twine 1997.
41. Sniderman and Piazza 1993; Gilens 1998.
42. Kinder and Sanders 1996.
43. Massey and Denton 1996; Yinger 1995.
44. Opponents of school choice programs have argued that these initiatives threaten to drain resources from the current public school system (Cobb 2001; Buzbee 1995) and that in the long run such a reform will damage members of the lower class, who thus might be more likely to oppose school choice. Yet such an argument fails to take into account the degree of general mistrust that blacks have for the public school system. Lower-class African Americans who do not have confidence in the current public school system are more willing to risk its deterioration if it means gaining a chance that their children will be able to go to a better, private school. Clearly it is far easier for middle-class whites, who tend to send their children to better schools, to oppose a voucher program in favor of preserving the educational status quo of complete funding for public schools. It may also be relatively easy for lower-class whites to support the public school system, since within the American system of racial educational segregation, such individuals may, more easily than African Americans, be able to send their children to schools with members of the middle class.
45. If I asserted that these issues could cover all of the different racialized dimensions of social attitudes, then it would be advisable to assign each issue into the appropriate dimensions. In a previous paper (Yancey 1999) I developed several dimensions for the racial attitudes of European Americans. Yet for that paper I had thirty-one racial variables to work with, instead of the seven in the LSAF. Furthermore, I only had the task of determining the racial dimensions for one racial group (European Americans), not four. It seems likely that the racial dimensions I discovered for European Americans are not always relevant to non-Europeans, and that even more than thirty-one racial variables might be necessary for discovering the racialized dimensions of social attitudes for these four racial groups. I cannot replicate in the present study the factor analysis conducted in that earlier paper. Until a data source can be found that adequately addresses the methodological concerns raised in Chapter 1, and that contains enough

racialized variables to discover the appropriate racial dimensions for these four groups, researchers will be unable to assess them.

46. On a progressive political agenda, see Garcia 1996. On concerns of immigration, see Blinder and Polinard 1997; and McLemore and Romo 1998: 430. On urban issues, see Browning, Marshall, and Tabb 1984. On affirmative action, see Browing, Marshall, and Tabb 1990.

47. This argument would be similar to that put forth by William Wilson (1980) in that class differences are argued to be more important in contemporary America than racial differences.

48. Ideally, I would like to move the income cutoff point even higher, but to do so would dramatically reduce the number of respondents in the three minority groups, making t-test comparisons less feasible.

49. This bivariant comparison cannot account for all income effects, since the groups can have varying percentages of wealthy individuals. This sort of outlier effect can distort the true findings of bivariant comparisons. However, regression in Table A.4 (see appendix) controls for this possibility.

50. I constructed models that had Hispanic and Asian Americans as the reference groups. The models indicated that these two racial groups did not significantly differ from other racial groups in adopting attitudes opposite to European Americans. Unlike African Americans, who significantly differed from whites in six of the seven variables even after the controls were applied, Hispanic Americans only differed from whites in their stronger support for affirmative action and welfare, while Asian Americans only differed from majority group members in being less willing to talk about race and more supportive of affirmative action. This offers more evidence that these nonblack groups have racial attitudes similar to those of whites.

51. Gonzales and La Velle 1985; de la Garza 1992.

52. Lincoln and Mamiya 1990.

53. Of course, this research looks at generalized differences between these racial groups. It is possible that certain Hispanic and Asian ethnic groups are more likely to experience racial alienation than others and to adhere to the racial attitudes of African Americans. In Chapter 2, I argued that nonblack racial ethnic groups who have been in the country longer than other ethnic groups of their own race should be more likely to have accepted a majority group identity. The Hispanic and Asian groups who are most likely to have achieved such a position in the United States are Mexican, Japanese, and Chinese Americans. I conducted a t-test comparing the scores of Mexican Americans (n = 190) to other Hispanics (n = 117), and a combined group of Japanese and Chinese Americans (n = 102) to other Asian ethnicities (n = 108), on the seven racialized issues under discussion. Of the fourteen comparisons, I discovered a significant difference only when comparing Mexican Americans to other Hispanics on the welfare question (Mexicans were more supportive of welfare than other Hispanics at the 0.05 level), a question on which Hispanics already tend to agree more with blacks than with whites. Mexican Americans were less likely, at the 0.1 level, to support interracial congregations than were other Hispanics, but in four of the remaining five measures their probability scores were over 0.4. For

Asian Americans, five of the probability scores were over 0.4, and the lowest score was 0.218, in the measurement of affirmative action.

54. Delgado and Stefancic 2000; Gutierrez 1995; Wei 1993.

55. Gutierrez 1995.

56. Scott and Schuman 1988; Smith 1998.

57. See Table A.4 in the book's appendix.

58. In the appendix I use a technique called discriminate analysis to assess whether the racialized attitudes of Hispanic and Asian Americans are more closely correlated to the attitudes of whites or to the attitudes of blacks. The results of this analysis can be seen in Table A.5 and indicate that generally the racialized attitudes of nonblack minorities are more similar to those of European Americans than to those of African Americans. A white/nonwhite dichotomy suggests that European Americans will be attitudinally separate from minority racial groups, since they alone occupy the top position in society, while a black/nonblack hierarchical structure suggests that African Americans will be attitudinally separate from other racial groups, since they suffer from a racial alienation that escapes other groups. The results in the appendix do not completely vindicate the alienation thesis, but do show that a black/nonblack structure is superior to a white/nonwhite structure in explaining racialized attitudes. If future research indicates persistence, or even strengthening, of this black/nonblack dichotomy, then the alienation thesis will gain even more support.

59. Moore and Fields 2002.

60. Bonilla-Silva 2001; Emerson and Sikkink 1997; Kuklinski et al. 1997.

61. Edward Murguia (1982) argues that Mexican Americans are slowly moving toward marital assimilation, and Mario Barrera (1988) concludes that a considerable amount of intermarriage is taking place among Hispanics. For evidence about Asian Americans, see Takaki 1989. Charles Gallagher (2002b) provides some evidence for both Latino and Asian Americans having a higher propensity to outmarry.

62. Yancey 2002.

63. Saporito Salvatore and Annette Lareau (1999) provide a possible answer to some of the fears that nonblack racial groups may have about living among African Americans. Their study qualitatively documents that European Americans cite a desire to avoid African Americans as their main criterion for choosing a school for their children. Salvatore and Lareau's study indicates that it is fear of blacks, and not other racial minorities, that drives this desire among majority group members, suggesting that blacks face a degree of alienation that escapes other racial groups. This research is limited to European American respondents; it would be of interest to see whether Hispanics and Asians are also likely to cite the desire to avoid African Americans as their main criterion for choosing a school for their children.

64. See Orfield et al. 1996: 58–60 for one such example.

65. Pierce 1988.

66. Portes and Zhou 1993.

5

The Changing Significance of "Latino" and "Asian"

The degree of racialization in the United States has been historically assessed by a standard of "whiteness." If a group was considered white, then that group was accepted in mainstream American society. The more white a group was considered, the more social prestige and legal rights members of this group would gain. Over time, minority groups have fought for "racial equality." One of the ways to perceive this equality is the ability to obtain the same rights and privileges that majority group members have. It can be argued that the various civil rights organizations have been fighting for the right to be treated the same way that whites are treated—and thus to become "white" as it concerns racial power.[1] Conceptualized in this manner, the success of the civil rights movement can be measured by the relatively stronger likelihood that these groups enjoy the privileges of being "white." It is ironic that the racial group who largely began the modern civil rights movement—African Americans—is the group least likely to enjoy the privileges of white status. The civil rights movement may be deemed a success in that blacks theoretically enjoy the same legal rights as all other racial groups, but when it comes to social acceptance and prestige, African Americans seem destined to lag behind the rest of the population in the United States.

The possible assimilation of nonblack racial minorities and the alienation of blacks in the formation of the future racial structure in the United States have largely been neglected in social research. While social theorists have concentrated upon the white/nonwhite society that has accurately characterized America's past, the implications of the persistent alienation of African Americans have not been

125

fully explored. There has been a great deal of work on how European ethnic groups have become part of the majority group,[2] and important work on the discrimination faced by Hispanics and Asians.[3] Yet none of this research is adequate for dealing with the unique position of African Americans. In the coming black/nonblack social reality, most racial/ethnic groups who are not African American will become "white." This will bring up new research questions to be explored. In this chapter I will engage in some speculation about what the process of Hispanics and Asians becoming part of the dominant culture may look like, as well as examine the presuppositions embedded in my assertion about this transformation and the coming alienation that blacks will experience.

The Coming Black/Nonblack Society

While I have challenged the argument that whites will soon be a numerical minority in the United States, it is important that I further clarify my predictions about the coming racial reality. I have stated that large nonblack racial groups, Latino and Asian Americans to be specific, will soon merge into the dominant culture. For all practical purposes, they will become "white"—just like the southern/eastern Europeans before them. But how will this assimilative process take place, and in what sort of time frame will it occur? I will attempt to predict how these groups might thin their racial identities and thus become part of the dominant culture. This analysis is highly speculative, but such conjecture is useful for understanding the forces behind the assimilative process of Hispanic and Asian Americans. While my prediction about the timing is speculative, and subject to inaccuracy, the principles that I have outlined in this book give me confidence in the ultimate outcome of this process—the incorporation of Latino and Asian Americans into the dominant power structure.

It is my belief that Latino Americans will lose their racial identity before Asian Americans. They have the advantage of a closer phenotypic similarity to European Americans, although not all Hispanic ethnic groups have significant degrees of European ancestry, and they have been in North America for a longer period of time. These characteristics will outweigh the assimilative tendencies that Asian Americans possess due to their higher socioeconomic standing. Given the relatively high degree of marital assimilation that is already taking place between Hispanic and European Americans as well as the loss of the Spanish language that many third- and successive-generation Latinos have experienced, assimilation into dominant group status is already occurring. In fact, given the results presented in Chapter 4, it is likely that most third- and many second-generation Hispanics have already undergone a certain degree of identificational assimilation, and if this is true, then it is only the influx of immigrants that maintains a powerful Hispanic cultural presence in the United States.[4]

A huge barrier to the ability of a minority group to join the majority group is their perceived biological distinctness. Most Hispanic Americans are, to differing degrees, already partially European, as attested to by the fact that the U.S. census does not record Hispanic Americans as a separate racial group, but rather as a distinct ethnic group.[5] So while Latinos are currently treated in the United States as a separate racial group socially, the bureaucratic instruments are already in place to identify them as a white ethnic group. These instruments are important in shaping perceptions about Latino Americans. With the emergence of the terms "non-Hispanic whites" and "Hispanic whites," there has been an increase in the "whitening" of Latino Americans. In the 1990 census more than half of the Hispanic population identified themselves as white,[6] and in 1992 about 95 percent of Latinos self-identified as white.[7] There is little doubt that many Hispanics are ready to accept majority group status. The key for Latinos is whether the majority group will accept them as whites, unlike the situation for Asian Americans, who still have a barrier of a perceived biological difference.

A major reason today that Latinos are not seen as white is the high percentage of this population who are unacculturated. As long as the number of Hispanics who are first or second generation is greater than the number of Hispanics who are third generation or later, cultural differences between most of the Latinos and the majority culture will hinder the perception of Hispanics as white. It is likely that Latinos who are new immigrants will always be perceived as different and will face certain social barriers from the dominant culture. But as more Latinos assimilate into the dominant society, the concept of Hispanics becoming white will gain acceptance. The key for this group will come when the number of later-generation Latinos is sufficiently high compared to the number of first-generation Hispanics.[8] How much higher this number must become to counter

the perception of Latinos being a mostly immigrant group is a subjective question, but for the sake of argument, let me assume that
when the number of native-born Hispanics is at least three times the
number of immigrant Hispanics, then the acceptance of Latinos as
whites is likely to occur. This is a reasonable assertion, since when
the later-generation Hispanics outnumber the newer Hispanics by
such an amount, Americans will be much more likely to repeatedly
encounter later-generation, and thus acculturated, Hispanics than
those who are new to the country. At that point it will be relatively
easy for dominant group members to accept Hispanics into the dominant culture and perceive the newer generation as exceptional to the
typical Latino American

According to the 2000 census, there are slightly more than 35
million Hispanics in the United States.[9] The 2000 supplemental census survey indicates that about 15 million Hispanics in the United
States are foreign born,[10] meaning that almost half of all self-
recognized Hispanics were not born in the country. All other things
being equal, if a non-Hispanic meets a Hispanic, then that person has
about as much of a chance of encountering a Hispanic who was born
in another country, and thus is not acculturated to American society,
as meeting a Hispanic who has undergone a certain amount of acculturation.[11] As long as so many foreign-born Hispanics are present in
American society, it is not surprising that an image of Hispanics as a
foreign entity will be prevalent.

But most of the Hispanics in the United States today will have
children who are a step closer to assimilation than their parents.
These children will not have the degree of exposure to Latino culture
as their parents, and since they are less likely to exhibit foreign customs or to have an accent, they will learn the advantages of experiencing more social acceptance than did their parents. There is
evidence that native-born Latinos have a stronger likelihood to comprehend European culture than Latino culture.[12] Second-generation
Hispanics are closer to becoming incorporated into the dominant culture than their first-generation parents, even if the individuals in that
second generation are not racially mixed. Yet census data have indicated that foreign-born Hispanics have higher rates of outmarriage
than native-born blacks or whites.[13] The emergence of these Hispanic
multiracial children will make acceptance of Hispanics into the dominant culture easier, since they will exhibit more European phenotypic features, and since they will receive greater exposure to majority

culture and dominant values than their monoracial counterparts.[14] While second-generation Hispanics, multiracial or not, will not automatically become "white," these individuals will grow up in a society that accepts them residentially and maritally. The racial identity of such individuals will greatly thin. According to Milton Gordon's hypothesis, the next step of identificational assimilation will not be far behind. Just as European ethnic groups have dismissed the importance of their ethnic identities, Latino Americans will begin to treat their racial identities in a similar manner. Charles Gallagher has noted that many European ethnics regard their identity as symbolic, meaningful only on holidays or during other special circumstances, or as "name-only," whereby such individuals perceive themselves as ethnic only because of the ethnicity of their last name.[15] It is not unrealistic to predict that by 2050 the majority of Latino Americans will treat their Hispanic heritage as either symbolic or "name-only."

The percentage of Latinos who have not been born into the country is declining. Barring some unforeseen event, immigration is not likely to dramatically increase over the next few decades. Non-Hispanic Americans will become more likely to encounter Hispanics who are at least partially more assimilated than they are today, and in time the image of Hispanics as foreigners will be replaced by images of Latinos as an integral part of American society. The lessening of the image of Hispanics as foreigners is likely to soon be followed by the societal acknowledgment of Hispanics as being "white."

How soon will this occur? We have been told that whites will be close to being a numerical minority by 2050, and that there will be about 95 million Hispanics in the United States at that time, about 24 percent of the population.[16] Yet projections from the census indicate that while the number of individuals who have a Latino heritage will increase, the percentage of those individuals who are first-generation Hispanics will steadily decline. According to those projections, first-generation Latino Americans will make up 27.7 percent of the Hispanic population by 2025, and 20.0 percent of the Hispanic population by 2050.[17] If these projections are correct, then by 2050 the number of native-born Hispanics in the United States will be about four times higher than the number of foreign-born Hispanics, a great enough difference that the typical Hispanic will be seen as one who is acculturated. Americans who encounter Latinos will be much more likely to encounter a Latino who exhibits the cultural aspects of the

United States than the cultural aspects of Latin America. At that point, majority group members will find it much easier to accept Hispanics as "white," especially given my predictions that Hispanics will largely adopt majority group attitudes. This means that other projections concerning the number of Hispanics in the United States will have been overstated, as many of the individuals projected to be Hispanic will in fact be accepted as dominant group members.

The fate of Asian Americans will slightly differ from that of Hispanic Americans. As a group Asians enjoy more economic success than Latinos, but have more phenotypic differences from European Americans. Asian Americans also have a relatively high-percentage immigrant population.[18] Their novelty to American culture means that dominant group members have not had sufficient time to accept them into the majority society. Yet because of their economic success, Asian Americans will enjoy a relatively high degree of social acceptance when compared to blacks or Hispanics. But while Asians are now perceived as a different biological race from whites, they will not face the same degree of social rejection that blacks and Hispanics experience, because of their status as a "model minority." In time, Asian Americans will lose even the notion of physical distinctness. It is important to remember that this is a group who are outmarrying at a rapid rate. This racial exogamy will allow Asian Americans to lessen their phenotypic distinctions from majority group members. As more Asian Americans begin to marry European Americans and many more multiracial individuals with partial Asian ancestry emerge in American society, notions of Asians being a physically different race than whites will lessen. Like the Irish and the Italians before them, Asian Americans will be seen as an ethnic group rather than as a racial group. New Asian immigrants may be treated as a different race, but not Asians who will have been in the United States for multiple generations. With sufficient time and a sufficiently high outmarriage rate, Asian Americans will lose the social perception that they belong to a different race.

James W. Loewen's research indicates the power of Asian Americans to overcome phenotypical differences.[19] He examines Chinese who immigrated into the Mississippi Delta. These Asians were at first seen as a third race—distinct from blacks and whites. But over time it became cumbersome to maintain this tri-tiered hierarchy and these Chinese Americans began to develop a majority group identity. This identity was not merely an internal perception by the Chinese Americans, since their European Mississippi neighbors accepted them as part of the majority. The European Americans in the Mississippi Delta began to see the Chinese as "white" and granted them the privileges of majority group status. Much of the integration of the Chinese that occurred—into white-dominated schools, into white-dominated employment, into white-dominated neighborhoods—happened early in the 1900s, well before the prominence of the modern civil rights movement. If such acceptance of Asians into the dominant society can occur in the pre–civil rights South, then given their high outmarriage rates, Asian Americans can surely experience a movement toward "whiteness" in the postmodern United States.

Because of their relatively high socioeconomic position in the United States, Asian Americans will be more likely to adopt the attitudes of dominant group members than Latino Americans. If they had brought with them partial European ancestry, then I would predict a more rapid acceptance as a white ethnic group. However, because of their phenotypic differences from European Americans, Asian Americans will be more slowly accepted as "whites" by majority group members than will Hispanics. The physical distinctions between Asian Americans and European Americans make interracial marriage necessary for Asian Americans to lose their racial distinctness. There is empirical evidence that interracial marriage does have sufficient power to alter the racial identity of Asian Americans in ways that it cannot for African Americans, as a 2000 study by the National Health Interview Surveys indicated that over 46 percent of multiracial individuals who marked both "white" and "Asian" as their racial identity chose "white" as their "main" race, while this occurred for only 25 percent of those who marked both "white" and "black" as their racial identity.[20] Although Asians will begin to think more like majority group members, this assimilative process will occur over the next two or three generations, as opposed to the next few decades. My speculation about the assimilation of Asian Americans is that it will probably take about 100 years before they are commonly accepted as a different ethnic group, as opposed to a distinct racial group.

Even though I predict that it will take longer for Asian Americans to become "white" in the United States, as a group they are likely to accept certain aspects of white racial identity before Latinos. In the short term the relatively higher socioeconomic status and relative acceptance Asians experience in the United States make it easier for them to accept concepts such as individualism and color blindness than for Hispanics. This ideological transition implicates that although it may take longer for Asians to fully obtain majority group status, their social attitudes will resemble those of the dominant group long before they are considered "white." It is likely a mistake for African Americans to hope to utilize Asian Americans as a political and social ally. As it concerns social power, a black/nonblack dichotomy may form even before Asian Americans fully become an accepted into the dominant group culture.

This speculation concerns the general prospects of assimilation, or identity thinning, of Latino and Asian Americans. Naturally, not all ethnic divisions within these two racial groups will experience entrance into the dominant structure at the conjectured rates. Among Hispanic Americans, groups who have a significant percentage of African ancestry, such as Puerto Ricans, may find it difficult to enter into the dominant culture because of the social "pollution" that comes with that black ancestry. Asian American groups who do not enjoy relative economic and educational success, such as the Hmong, may not be as quick in adopting the social attitudes of the dominant group and thus will lag behind the assimilative process of other Asian American ethnics. Other characteristics of distinct ethnic groups may work to help them retain a thick racial/ethnic identity for some time to come. Yet the largest Hispanic and Asian groups— Mexican Americans and Chinese Americans—tend to have the characteristics that are important for assimilation, and my speculations are appropriate for the vast majority of second-generation Latino and Asian Americans in this country.

The Assumptions Necessary
for a Black/Nonblack America

I have challenged the assumptions embedded in the belief of many about the coming numerical minority of whites. Yet I would be remiss if I did not also examine the assumptions that I have made myself in the formulations of the alienation thesis. My prediction that African Americans will remain a rejected minority group while Latino and Asian Americans become some version of "white" is based upon presuppositions I wish to clarify. I assert that they are solid presuppositions, but others may argue that these assumptions are faulty. Ultimately it is up to the reader to decide whether or not my predictions are built upon a solid foundation.

The Assumption of Normal Immigration

My first assumption is the assertion that the rate of immigration will remain relatively normal. To be specific, I am assuming that immigration will not dramatically increase over the expected projections in the next 50 to 100 years. If for some reason nonblack minorities immigrate in extremely large numbers, then it is very possible that they will remain estranged from the dominant group. Under such a circumstance the majority group may perceive a racial threat from this immigration, and the resentment that the dominant group feels toward the new immigrants may be transferred to racial members of that group who have been in the country for many generations. The ensuing conflict could force them to retain their subordinate status for many years to come.

Given the importance of this assumption, it is useful to speculate about why immigration may dramatically increase. Immigration increases dramatically when events in the country of origin influence people to leave their home. Because there are about 285 million individuals in the United States, it would take a catastrophic event in another country to send enough immigrants to the United States that a racial threat would be perceived by majority group members. For example, the United States experiences a significant amount of immigration from Mexico because of the stronger U.S. economy. If this relatively stronger economy remains the only powerful incentive for Mexicans to immigrate into the United States, then it seems unlikely that immigration will dramatically increase. But what if Mexico were to suffer a civil war or famine? Such events might create a stream of refugees in the tens of millions. The high number of unacculturated immigrants would likely engender notions of racial threat and thus delay, or possibly even derail, the future assimilation of Latino Americans. These unacculturated immigrants would also serve to thicken the racial identities of Mexican Americans, who would experience more discrimination under the racial threat this immigration would bring.

Clearly Mexico is a country that could generate enough immigrants to create a sense of racial threat. An extremely high rate of immigration is less likely from Asian countries for several reasons.

First, many Asian countries are smaller than Mexico (e.g., Vietnam, Korea). Thus it would take dramatic events in multiple Asian countries to significantly increase Asian immigration into the United States. Second, Asian countries tend to be developed, rather than underdeveloped, nations. This makes it less likely that a catastrophic event will occur in those countries, since they tend to have more stable economies. Third, immigrants from Asian countries, as opposed to immigrants from Central and South America, have a greater choice of destinations. If tragedy occurs within one Asian nation, citizens may immigrate into other Asian nations or Europe. Yet because of proximity, the easiest country for Hispanics to immigrate into continues to be the United States. However, even given all these reasons, it is still possible that a large and relatively underdeveloped Asian nation, such as China, may experience a catastrophic event that could produce abnormally high immigration into the United States. So while I argue that the possibility of high immigration threatening the assimilation of racial minorities is more likely for Latinos, I do not completely dismiss the possibility of rapid Asian American immigration.

Of all of the assumptions that I make, this is the one that is the hardest to defend, since it is always possible that events such as war, famine, disease, or some other Mathusian tragedy may change world events and affect the racial climate in the United States. Yet as the population in the United States continues to grow, it will take even more immigrants for the notion of racial threat to develop within the United States. Over time, rapid immigration movements will be less likely to upset America's racial atmosphere.

The Assumption That Minorities Want to Become White

Another assumption within my analysis is that certain racial minorities want to assimilate into the dominant culture. It can be argued that Hispanic and Asian Americans will become "white" only if they desire to become part of the majority group. Advocates for cultural pluralism contend that this assimilative process would destroy the unique cultures of these minority groups and should be avoided.[21] If these advocates have correctly captured the attitudes of racial minorities, then Hispanic and Asian Americans will not allow assimilation to occur.

Cultural pluralists assert that assimilation means the end of the native culture of racial minority groups.[22] This may be true, and I am not advocating assimilation as a desirable goal for racial minorities. Whether the disappearance of these cultures is desirable or detrimental is a value judgment. However, I have presented evidence that the ability of nonblack groups to maintain racial attitudes distinct from those of majority group members is waning, and so the assimilative process may be happening regardless of whether social activists find it desirable. The reality of this assimilation should not be a surprise, since other former minority groups—such as southern/eastern Europeans—have also been incorporated into the dominant culture once they received sufficient societal acceptance. I agree with Mary Waters, who suggests that the debate over immigration is misplaced in its emphasis on asking whether new immigrants want to be American.[23] She argues that immigrants come to the United States because they want a better life for themselves, and that becoming American is a way to achieve that life—making acculturation an economic decision. Likewise, I would suggest that it is misguided to ask whether racial minorities want to integrate into the power and economic structure of the United States, since racial minority groups will usually attempt to assimilate when the majority group accepts them to a sufficient extent. Such assimilation means an increase in cultural status, economic standing, and social power.

The desirability of cultural pluralism tends to be a goal for certain leaders of racial minority groups.[24] I believe that some of these leaders criticize the inevitability of assimilation because they value cultural pluralism, instead of reacting to evidence that assimilation is not taking place.[25] As a social scientist, I do not believe that I have the luxury to ignore this evidence, and believe that even as certain minority group leaders fight against the loss of their racial identity, this process is still highly likely to occur for Hispanic and Asian Americans.

Finally, let me touch upon the idea of segmented assimilation.[26] This theory postulates that there are diverse possible outcomes for the process of adaptation of different racial groups. Certain minorities, most notably European ethnic groups, can move progressively from the lower to the higher economic classes. Other minorities, generally nonwhite ethnic groups, do not have this sort of mobility open to them and thus develop an adversarial stance toward the majority culture. I am not opposed to this theory, but believe that the advocates of this theory are too optimistic about the ability of minorities

to succeed without accommodating majority group culture. This ability may exist for immigrant groups who have only recently come into
American society, yet I am not convinced that such a trend will
maintain itself over time for a given group—unless that group faces a
level of alienation that fosters the maintenance of an adversarial
stance. While I have my doubts that over several generations
Hispanic and Asian minority ethnic groups will materially benefit by
rejecting acculturation into the dominant society, persistent alienation is precisely the situation that blacks face in the United States.
The strength of segmented assimilation lies in its contention that the
manner by which a group has historically entered into the dominant
society influences the ability of the members of that group to become
part of the dominant group—and even influences whether members
of that group will want to become part of the dominant group. The
1999–2000 Lilly Survey of American Attitudes and Friendships
(LSAF) indicates that Latino and Asian American racial groups,
broadly defined, do have attitudes that are at least as representative
of the dominant culture as they are of an alienated minority racial
group. The implications of segmented assimilation are that certain
nonblack minority groups will eventually undergo a similar path that
European ethnic groups have experienced, while African Americans
may be more likely to find success by rejecting the dominant culture
that alienates them. It is unlikely for nonblack minority groups that
there will be a positive correlation between an adversarial stance and
economic success after they have been in the United States for more
than a couple of generations.[27]

The Assumption of Shared Experiences

Significant debate has developed over the nature of former European
ethnic minority groups.[28] It has been suggested that southern/eastern
Europeans were not considered to be of a different race from other
Europeans, even though they clearly were treated as a minority group
in the United States.[29] Instead they were seen as being an inferior
type of "white" person. If this assessment is accurate, then the argument can be made that it has been relatively easy for the dominant
group to accept these Europeans, since they were never seen as being
racially distinct. It can then be argued that because Latino and Asian
Americans are seen as being biologically distinct from those who are

today called "white," it will be much more difficult for them to gain acceptance into the majority group.

This problematic assumption is necessary to make the argument that these nonblack groups will become "white." Whether or not this transition happens as fast as I suggest it might, does not mean that I am inaccurate in describing the process by which these groups are assimilating into the dominant culture. In Chapter 1, I pointed out that even those who challenge the notion that minority groups will assimilate into the dominant culture must still admit that over time some minority groups experience a thinning of their racial/ethnic attitude, which becomes less central to social standing. Even if members of those groups are able to maintain a distinctness from the majority group, this distinctness becomes less important in shaping the perceptions of those minority group members or in determining the level of discrimination they face from the dominant group. For all practical purposes, those with a thin racial/ethnic attitude are part of the dominant culture and their inclusion will leave an alienated group at the bottom of a racial/ethnic hierarchy. The evidence in this book suggests that such a thinning exists for Latino and Asian Americans, and that soon they may be part of the dominant culture, regardless of whether they ever completely assimilate.

There is no guarantee that an ethnic or racial group's social identity will thin over time. But there is evidence that this is what may be happening to Hispanic and Asian Americans. The evidence provided in Chapter 4 shows that these nonblack minority groups have perspectives on racialized issues that are at least as close to the perspectives of the dominant group as they are to the perspectives of the alienated group—African Americans. If the social position of these nonblack racial groups is that of an alienated group, then members of these groups should be more willing to challenge the racial status quo than the data from the LSAF suggest. The fact that they are just as, or more, willing to accept the positions predictive of white racial identity on racialized issues as they are to challenge the racial status quo suggests that they experience much more acceptance than African Americans. Since the evidence in this book suggests that these nonblack minority groups enjoy a level of acceptance that is qualitatively greater than that enjoyed by African Americans, that this acceptance is likely much greater than it has been in the past, and that this acceptance is likely to grow in the future as residential integration and interracial marriage between these groups and the dominant group remain high, there is strong support for the assimilation, or the thinning of racial attitudes, of these groups. Whether this assimilation will occur as fast as it has for European ethnic groups may be challenged, but there are solid empirical grounds for the acceptance of nonblack minority groups and the alienation of African Americans.

The Assumption of Unaltered Racialized Perspectives

Throughout the book I have discussed the perspective of European Americans as being the dominant outlook that protects the status quo, and the perspective of African Americans as the outlook of the alienated class. Consequently, I have argued that the perspectives of Hispanic and Asian Americans are closer to the dominant perspective of the majority group than to the alienated perspective of a racial minority. This may give the reader the impression that I am arguing that the perspectives of European and African Americans are unalterable, and only the racialized attitudes of nonblack minorities may change. For simplicity, it has been useful to avoid discussing this impression, but now I wish to further clarify my thesis.

Gordon's theory of assimilation uses an Anglo-conformist model, which predicts that minority groups eventually conform to the majority group. Such a model implies that the majority group does not change at all. While I find many aspects of his model theoretically useful, I reject the Anglo-conformist perspective. It is more likely that assimilation occurs in a situation whereby both majority and minority groups undergo some cultural and attitudinal adjustments. As a novel racial culture emerges, the new dominant group will contain most of the elements of the old "white" racial group but also elements of the Latinos and Asians it has assimilated. So majority group members will have to make some cultural adjustments, just like the minority group members must do.

While extended interracial contact between majority and minority group members is very likely to help alter the attitudes of minority group members, majority group identity will also change over time to help accommodate the new groups who have, or will, become part of the majority. For example, white supremacy ideology has historically included Catholics, along with racial minorities and Jews, among the groups that were perceived as inferior to the "white" race.

This discrimination was linked to the fact that European Catholics tended to come from southern and eastern Europe. As these Europeans became part of the majority group, this anti-Catholicism largely diminished. Contemporary ideologies used to maintain the racial status quo generally do not have elements of this religious prejudice. Movement away from anti-Catholicism is at least partially the result of the movement of "white" Catholics into the majority group. The dominant group altered its perspective on Catholicism in reaction to the interchange of northern and western Europeans with the former minority groups of southern and eastern Europeans. Likewise, European Americans will alter their perspectives because of their interaction with Hispanic and Asian Americans, and change to accommodate these groups. It is my prediction that ideological components separating Hispanic/Asian Americans from European Americans will either disappear or grow much weaker over time.

Yet the majority group will not make the ideological adjustments necessary to accommodate African Americans. No matter how white racial identity may be conceptualized, 100 years from now it will contain components that separate the majority group from African Americans. Furthermore, it is also unimportant whether the attitudes and racial identity of African Americans change. As long as blacks maintain their alienated status in the United States, their racialized attitudes will be the result of the alienation they continue to face. Any alterations of their attitudes and perspectives will likely be shaped by the different ways that this alienation has manifested itself. While it may be argued that the alienation thesis requires static social positions of dominant group members and black Americans, this is not the case. The alienation thesis only requires that blacks' social position remain alienated from the dominant group. How the ideology of the majority group changes over time to keep African Americans in this alienated position, and the corresponding changes in the ideology of African Americans, are topics that future researchers should explore.

The Assumption That Racial Conflict Will Not Escalate

The assimilation of nonblack minorities assumes that there will not be a social event that dramatically increases the amount of racial tension between those groups and the majority group. Sometimes external world events affect the way that racial groups are treated in the

United States. For example, World War II dramatically changed the way that European Americans dealt with Japanese Americans, and majority-Japanese relations deteriorated during that time.[30] Likewise, internal events can change the relations between European Americans and nonblack minority groups. The Zoot Suit riots have poisoned race relations between Latinos and majority group members in the Los Angeles area for some time to come. These events may lessen the acceptance of nonblack racial minorities by majority group members, and minority groups will retain a disenfranchised status—sharing a similar place in the social racial hierarchy as African Americans.

However, given the degree of acceptance that Latino and Asian Americans already experience, I contend that such events would have a limited effect. Middle-class Hispanic and Asian Americans live among and marry dominant group members. If a precipitating incident to intergroup conflict takes place, then European Americans will not be socially isolated from Hispanic and Asian Americans, allowing these nonblack minority groups to have an opportunity to influence the perspectives of majority group members. However, because of the social isolation and alienation that African Americans continue to experience, if a racial incident incites racial tension between them and European Americans, then it will be much more difficult to subdue racial hostilities.[31] Thus the potential for tensions to worsen due to a racial incident is much greater for blacks than for Latinos and Asians.

It is possible that some unforeseen racial incident may alter the relations between majority group members and Hispanics or Asians. But given the growing numbers and power of such groups, I believe that it would take a major, national incident to alter relations with any degree of permanency. As I write this book, a test case for the power of such an incident to worsen race relations has developed among Americans of Middle Eastern ancestry. The events of September 11, 2001, have brought the United States to war, and fears of Arab terrorists continue to plague Americans. Furthermore, the Middle Eastern community in the United States is small enough that its leaders may not have sufficient power to shield Middle Eastern Americans from a social backlash. It is too early to assess how much damage the September 11 attacks have done to relations between majority group members and Middle Eastern Americans. If future empirical evidence shows that Americans of Middle Eastern ancestry are able to move into the dominant society despite the enormous fear caused by these terrorist attacks, then the power of other nonblack minorities to assimilate should not be underestimated. Yet even if future tests show an inability of Middle Easterners to find social acceptance, their alienation can hasten the assimilation of Latinos and Asian Americans, as Middle Easterners might become a new scapegoat by which Americans can ignore previous racial differences and against whom they can unite. Since Middle Easterners are likely to numerically remain a very small group, African Americans cannot take much solace in the fact that this possible ally for racial justice will share in their alienation.

The Assumption That African Americans Will Not Assimilate

The black/nonblack dichotomy can only develop if African Americans remain an alienated group in the United States. Perhaps in the creation of a new out-group, such as Middle Easterners, blacks will gain an acceptance that invalidates predictions about their alienation. It is also notable that while racial exogamy is low among African Americans, outmarriage does occur. Over time it may be possible that the small number of exogamous unions will increase and blacks will start to undergo the type of identificational assimilation seen in other racial groups. However, the continuing alienation of blacks is an assumption that I have great confidence in, even more so than the inevitable assimilation of nonblack minority groups.

In the United States, with the exception of Native Americans, Africans and African Americans have had a longer period of contact with Europeans and European Americans than any other racial group. Yet the rejection of African Americans remains a powerful influence in our society. If blacks have not assimilated in the past several hundred years, why would we think that they would assimilate in the next hundred years? If somehow the present war against terrorism escalates and the hostilities toward immigrants from Middle Eastern countries persist, then it is very possible that a new out-group may face a level of rejection equivalent to, or even greater than, the rejection that blacks experience. But the development of a new out-group will not alter the racial reality of a group that suffers from such a level of alienation. African Americans may have company on the bottom rung of the racial hierarchy in the United States, but they will not be lifted from that rung. Unfortunately, American history teaches that majority group members have the ability to temporary vilify a group more than blacks, such as Japanese Americans during World War II, and still maintain a relationship of estrangement and disenfranchisement with blacks.

Neither will outmarriage lift African Americans from that rung. Interracial sexuality is not new to the United States. The persistence of the one-drop rule has been used to negate the potential assimilative effects of such sexuality among African Americans as well as to prevent any thinning of black racial identity. The only way that African Americans have been able to assimilate historically is if they have enough European phenotypic characteristics to "pass" as white. Of course this passing has been available only to a limited number of blacks, greatly reducing the number of African Americans who can assimilate. While this rule no longer has the legal power that it once did,[32] a one-drop understanding of African Americans still has strong informal persuasive power even to the point that today African Americans police this rule by pressuring biracial individuals with black ancestry to identify themselves as fully black.[33] Intermarriage may allow certain individuals to assimilate, but because of the persistence of the one-drop rule, African Americans as a group will not be allowed to assimilate.

Finally, it can be argued that if blacks are able to improve their economic status relative to majority group members, then they will experience a degree of acceptance that is linked to economic gains. This claim can be substantiated by the relative acceptance of Asian Americans, a racial minority group who have enjoyed relative economic success, by European Americans. But an increase in the economic prosperity of African Americans will not create a favorable circumstance for them to gain social acceptance. Unlike Hispanic or Asian Americans, the socioeconomic status of African Americans is not correlated with their having a higher propensity to live in an integrated neighborhood, and thus that higher socioeconomic status will not allow African Americans to easily residentially integrate. Furthermore, the evidence presented in Chapter 4 indicates that attitudinal differences between African Americans and other racial groups did not disappear when only respondents who earned over $30,000 a year were examined. It seems that blacks with higher incomes are no more likely to move closer to the racial attitudes of majority group members than are other African Americans. Even if African Americans are able to economically improve their economic success relative to European Americans in the coming years—a shaky assumption indeed—this improvement will not move them into full-fledged majority group status.

No matter what happens with other racial groups, it is clear that African Americans will not soon become "white." The length of the racial alienation that blacks have suffered makes it reasonable to argue that the lower status of blacks is a core staple of American culture. Such an underlying cultural expectation will not disappear merely because of the development of another racial out-group or because a few members of that group can outmarry and residentially integrate.

Conclusion

Despite the assumptions that have to be made about the alienation thesis, there is empirical evidence that some degree of assimilation of Latino and Asian Americans and the alienation of African Americans are significant elements of American race relations. Based upon these assertions, it can be predicted that over time these nonblack racial groups will eventually become part of the mainstream society. Of course not all of the Hispanic and Asian ethnic groups will be able to assimilate at the same rate, and some of these ethnic groups are likely to find themselves left behind in the racial hierarchy for some time to come. But it is reasonable to argue that the majority of later-generation Latino and Asian Americans will soon find their way into the dominant society. In this chapter I have speculated more specifically how this process may take place. While speculation of course cannot be conclusive, the underlying process of incorporation of these nonblack minority groups is built on solid theoretical and empirical evidence; and while the details of the assimilation of nonblack minorities may be uncertain, the evidence in this book suggests that there are solid reasons to believe in the eventual inclusion of these nonblack minority groups into the majority society and their obtaining of "white privilege."

In this chapter I have not speculated about what will happen to African Americans over time. Obviously if the alienation thesis is correct, then the devalued social position of blacks will remain the same as it is today. What will change is that there will be fewer members of other racial groups who share this position in the United States. This social fact has important implications for how scholars should approach the study of race/ethnicity, the fate of African Americans, and public policy in the United States, subjects I will address in the final chapter.

Notes

1. The flip side of such an assertion is the argument that these civil rights organizations have been fighting to remove all vestiges of whiteness in American society, which would theoretically put all citizens of the United States on the same racial footing—the end result being the same as allowing everyone to have the privilege of white status. Either goal—abolishing whiteness for everyone, or giving whiteness to everyone—would have the same result of eliminating racial stratification.

2. Waters 1990; Gans 1979; Alba 1990.

3. Kitano and Daniels 1988; Moore and Pachon 1975; U.S. Commission on Civil Rights 1992; de la Garza et al. 1992; Martinez 1994; McWilliams 1968; Noble 1995; Zinsmeister 1987.

4. It is useful to see whether first-generation Hispanics interviewed for the LSAF had different racialized attitudes compared to other Hispanics. But even though the LSAF was conducted in Spanish, it is likely that illegal aliens are still undersampled in this research. Hispanic immigrants in the LSAF are likely to be more educated and have a higher socioeconomic status than Hispanic immigrants in general. Since the LSAF is only likely to capture the attitudes of immigrants who have attitudes similar to nonimmigrant Hispanics, it is of little use for this comparison. Given this expectation, it was not surprising that I found inconsistent evidence that Hispanic immigrants had more alienated attitudes than nonimmigrants (Hispanic immigrants were significantly more likely to believe that there is too much talk about race, more likely to desire school choice, and less likely to support integrated congregations). While the inclusion of illegal aliens may have produced racialized attitudes that reflected a racially alienated reality, this is not evident in the LSAF.

5. It is noteworthy that in 1993 the U.S. Office of Management and Budget considered a proposition to make "Hispanic" an official race, instead of an ethnic group. Clara Rodriguez (2000) argues that, despite the potential of such a category to reinforce a Latino identity, there was little relative support for such a category among Hispanics. Furthermore, she contends that this proposal was dropped when it became clear that the inclusion of such a category would result in fewer Hispanics and whites being counted. This episode indicates that majority group members are already beginning to see value in granting Latinos majority group status and that Hispanics are not enthusiastic about fighting against this inclusion.

6. U.S. Bureau of the Census 1993.

7. U.S. Bureau of the Census 1992: B-1.

8. An important question that I cannot address with the LSAF data is how many generations it takes for most of Hispanics to become incorporated

into the dominant power structure. While some have suggested that this process takes about three generations (Spickard 1989; Gordon 1964; Glazer and Moynihan 1963), it may not take this long for some Latinos to partially assimilate into American culture. Isis Artze (2000) cites a study from the *Washington Post* indicating that only 10 percent of all second-generation Hispanics rely mainly on Spanish to communicate. While merely speaking English is not a sufficient standard for assessing assimilation, Artze's study does suggest that the notion of large numbers of Latinos who rely heavily upon Spanish and who are embedded in Latino culture is only accurate as it concerns first-generation Hispanics. It should be remembered that modern social pressures against overt expressions of racism might enable second-generation Hispanic Americans to experience social acceptance faster than earlier immigrant groups. While it is not reasonable to argue that second-generation Hispanics are likely to experience full assimilation, it is not illogical to assert that such Latinos might experience a partial degree of assimilation through freedom to intermarry and residentially integrate into the dominant culture. The tendency of second-generation Hispanics to experience partial assimilation is especially likely for middle- or upper-class Latinos.

9. U.S. Census Bureau, Census 2000 Summary File, Matrices P#, P$, PCT4, PCT5, PCT8, and PCT11.

10. Census 2000 Supplementary Survey, tab. P039.

11. Of course in real life it is not this simple. We do not have a random chance of running into any given person in the United States. Whom we meet depends on social environmental factors such as our socioeconomic status, where we live, where we work, and many other variables. The professional who works in Chicago is much more likely to encounter Hispanics who have undergone more assimilation than is the construction worker in southern Texas. Certain majority group members will always have constant exposure to foreign-born Hispanics and will maintain a perception of Latinos as illegal aliens. But the general point of this argument is still significant. The higher the percentage of foreign-born Hispanics, the more likely non-Hispanics are to be exposed to such individuals and thus to develop a perspective about Hispanics that prevents their acceptance into the dominant group. The percentage of majority group members who routinely encounter unacculturated Hispanics will dramatically decline as the percentage of unacculturated Hispanics begins to shrink.

12. For example, according to Rodolfo de la Garza and others (1992) only 11.5 percent of foreign-born Puerto Ricans, 6.7 percent of foreign-born Mexicans, and 9.4 percent of foreign-born Cubans solely speak English or speak English better than they speak Spanish. Yet 67.7 percent of native-born Puerto Ricans, 67.5 percent of native-born Mexicans, and 67.6 percent of native-born Cubans solely speak English or speak English better than they speak Spanish. Given the importance that the Spanish language has for communicating Hispanic cultural identity, pride, and cultural maintenance (Torrecilha, Cantu, and Nguyen 1999), the fact that most native-born Latinos understand English better than Spanish indicates that most Hispanic

Americans likely possess a deeper understanding of North American culture than Latino culture.

13. Artze 2000.

14. Of course the census challenges the notion that Latino/white children can even be considered multiracial, since Hispanics can be considered a different ethnic group, but not a different racial group, than European Americans. This sort of confusion is linked to the social construction of race and the permeability of white status. The fact that Latino/white individuals may not even be considered multiracial is even further evidence of the growing ability of Hispanics to adopt majority status.

15. Gallagher 2002a.

16. U.S. Department of Commerce 1997: 19.

17. Population Projections Program 2000.

18. Barringer, Gardener, and Levin 1993: 44.

19. Loewen 1988.

20. See "Using New Racial Categories in the 2000 Census" at www.aecf.org/kidscount/categories/bridging/htm.

21. Hilliard 1988; Bash 1979; Hirschman 1983; Newman 1973.

22. It is clear that attempts in the late nineteenth century to assimilate Native Americans have worked to eliminate aspects of their culture. Native American children in the boarding schools were not allowed to practice their religion, wear long hair, or speak their native language. The forcing of Native American children into boarding schools left many tribes with few or no individuals who were still acculturated in their heritage culture. This phenomenon illustrates the fear among cultural pluralists that minority cultures will be destroyed by attempts to assimilate racial minorities.

23. Waters 1999.

24. Choi, Callaghan, and Murphy 1995; Spencer 1994.

25. But this may not be the case for racial minorities who are not leaders, as Douglas George (2001) finds that racial minorities are generally no more likely to advocate for cultural pluralism than are European Americans.

26. Portes and Zhou 1993.

27. Because I use general racial designations as the unit of analysis, my conclusions should be limited to these racial groups in general. Whereas I challenge the idea within segmented assimilation that the adversarial stance and economic success of Hispanics and Asians are generally positively correlated, this challenge may not be accurate as it concerns certain Hispanic and Asian ethnic groups. Since some of these groups have only recently immigrated into the United States and might practice social customs that make assimilation more difficult, they may develop a degree of alienation that keeps them from becoming "white" for some time to come. While the general acceptance of Hispanic and Asian Americans means that most of these groups will gain entrance into majority group status, the possibility of certain Hispanic and Asian ethnic groups retaining their minority status in the foreseeable future should not be overlooked.

28. An excellent example of this debate can be found in a dialogue in *International Labor and Working Class History* 60 (fall).

29. Arnesen 2001.

30. Weglyn 1976; Ignacio 1976; Daniels 1969.

31. This was clearly seen in the continuing hostility in Los Angeles between African and European Americans that was engendered by the Rodney King trial. When I visited this city on another research project, it was clear that the outcome of this trial had a lasting effect on the willingness of the African Americans in that area to trust whites in general and the Los Angeles police department in particular. This mistrust is likely connected to the fact that King was an African American, which led blacks to perceive themselves as having a personal stake in the trial. I did not detect this degree of mistrust among other racial groups in Los Angeles. Given the power of local racial incidents to shape attitudes of estrangement, it is important to monitor potential precipitating events to determine whether African Americans are more likely than other racial groups to be the focus.

32. Davis 1991.

33. Korgen 1998; Twine 1997; Rockquemore and Brunsma 2002.

6

The Black/Nonblack Society

Social scientists have often been accused of living in an ivory tower from where we study society but do not take into consideration the real concerns of human beings. This book could easily become such an exercise. College students often wonder why they have to learn about some of the subjects we professors teach. Those of us who teach race and ethnicity may have an easier time convincing our students about the importance of studying racial issues, since it is clear that racial tension is still prevalent in the United States. But it is important for us to think through the practical implications of theoretical assertions such as the alienation thesis.

Even if I am correct in my predictions about the coming black/nonblack society, the average American may ask, "So what?" This is a fair question. What does it mean to the average person that this black/nonblack society is emerging? How will American racial reality be different under a black/nonblack framework than under the current white/nonwhite framework? Obviously this coming social order means much more to blacks than to nonblacks, but it still has powerful implications for anyone who cares about the racial issues in American society.

In this chapter I will look at the implications of the alienation thesis. I will first discuss what the black/nonblack society should mean to social researchers in general. Then I will speculate about the sort of black/nonblack racial future that I perceive for the United States. As I engage in this speculation it will become clear that the future holds fewer and fewer allies for African Americans. Finally, I will expound upon some of the policy questions that a black/nonblack society brings. While I basically believe that a black/nonblack structure is inevitable, a discussion of public policies in light of this coming racial reality is still necessary.

Implications of a Black/Nonblack Dichotomy for Research in Race and Ethnicity

Despite the potential uncertainty of the assumptions listed in the last chapter, I still contend that my basic assertions surrounding the assimilation, or racial identity thinning, of nonblack minorities and the persisting alienation of African Americans offer the best predictions about the future makeup of the American racial hierarchy—a black/nonblack structure with African Americans at the bottom of society. Previous sociological work in race/ethnicity has generally assumed either a racial hierarchy whereby several racial groups each occupy a given social position or one whereby whites occupy the top position and oppress all other groups. My argument is that there is a new racial reality distinct from both of these models that needs to be evaluated. Since previous work has not considered this new hierarchy, it is important that future research into race and ethnicity assess the implications of a black/nonblack perspective.

The Persistence of the White Majority

American society has been constructed for the benefit of European Americans. This dominant group possesses the ability to adjust to changes in society so that they will continue to receive the lion's share of benefits. For example, the basis of previous racial discrimination was notions of racial superiority. As white supremacy has lost its legitimization in American society, this justification has been replaced with a philosophy of color blindness,[1] which serves to negate contemporary efforts to overturn the effects of centuries of racism.[2] Thus a notion of meritocracy has replaced racial superiority as the prevailing ideology supporting American racial inequality.[3] In this way, the dominant majority are able to adapt to changing social realities so that its members will continue to gain the benefits of white privilege.

Numerical superiority is connected to political and social power in the United States. Given the ability of the majority to adjust to changes to maintain their racial privilege, researchers should not be surprised that this group will adapt to the possibility that they will be a numerical minority in a few decades. This adaptation comes through the expansion of majority group identity to include groups previously perceived as racial minorities. This process has historically been used to deal with the possible numerical threat of minority group members. In Chapter 2, I documented how the inclusion of previous racial minority groups occurred as their numbers grew to such an extent that previous majority group members (i.e., northern/western Europeans) found themselves in danger of losing their numerical superiority. In a similar manner, contemporary majority group members will incorporate first Hispanic Americans, and then Asian Americans, into their own racial group to avoid becoming a numerical minority group.

Future researchers must build upon the understanding that race is a social construct and majority group status is permeable. Those who study issues of race and ethnicity must not make the mistake of perceiving race as a static concept. The majority group will adjust its boundaries in ways that will enable them to hold on to racial power, which periodically means the inclusion of previously rejected groups. Students of race/ethnicity must account for this tendency if they are to understand how racial relations in the United States will evolve over time. Instead of holding on to a perception of a stable majority group who forever work to keep all other racial groups oppressed, a more accurate observation is that there is a majority group that selectively includes certain previously disenfranchised minority groups so that those currently in the majority can maintain racial power. This change of perception means that researchers should pay more attention to the lessening conflict between the dominant group and nonblack minority groups, as well as document how those groups may begin to create alliances with one another. Researchers will also want to explore whether, and how, majority group members are beginning to bestow the benefits of dominant group status upon Hispanic and Asian Americans in exchange for their support in the maintenance of black alienation.

But must the process of assimilation and inclusion always reject African Americans? It can be argued that one day it will be in the interest of majority group members to include African Americans within the dominant group. I disagree with such an argument. As important as it is for the dominant group to maintain its numerical superiority in the United States, it is also important to maintain an out-group against which members of the dominant group can unite. In the foreseeable future African Americans always will be included in that out-group. It is tempting to believe that the Middle Easterners may play the role of out-group for Americans. While it is possible, and perhaps even likely, that Middle Easterners will be an out-group for Americans for some time to come, they will not completely take the place of African Americans. Unlike Middle Easterners, blacks have a numerical size large enough that they can be perceived as a constant threat to majority group members. Because of the lack of visibility of Middle Easterners, outside a few heavily populated communities, it will be easier for other Americans to learn to fear blacks since their presence will be more easily seen. Furthermore, there is a deeper history of racial animosity that provides a more lasting basis for black racial alienation. The stereotypes and prejudices that Middle Easterners face are real, but they are recent. The contemporary nature of this prejudice makes it easier to reeducate individuals about the myths and bias unfairly used against Middle Easterners. Given the level of social desirability most people assign to avoiding appearing racist, I doubt that the overt racism faced by Middle Easterners today will have the permanence of the racism that African American experience.

In short, it is in the interest of dominant group members to include previous minority groups in an effort to maintain their numerical majority, but also to have an out-group to act as a scapegoat against which they can unite. The assimilation of nonblack racial minorities and the alienation of African Americans meet these needs. A great deal of previous work has attempted to comprehend the needs and desires of racial minorities for obtaining racial justice or equality.[4] Yet understanding the desires of majority group members, and what the dominant group needs in order to maintain its racial privilege, is also important for predicting changes in American race relations. Future work in race and ethnicity must not make the mistake of overlooking majority group members' ability to adjust to social changes so that they can maintain racial power.

The Inevitability of Assimilation of Nonblack Racial Minorities

It has been argued that assimilation into American society will eventually wipe out old racial hatreds.[5] But evidence from this research suggests that we can no longer count upon the process of assimilation to bring blacks into the American social environment. It has been suggested that new immigrant groups require about three generations to fully intermarry and assimilate into American society.[6] But the vast majority of African Americans have ancestors who have been in the United States for many generations and have yet to experience assimilation. Assimilation is a plausible solution for the oppression and racism faced by many nonblack racial groups, but it is not a viable option for African Americans.

Some contend that as racial minorities move into the dominant culture, there will be fewer racial misunderstandings, since there will be more interracial interaction with members of other races.[7] This argument implies that such interaction will produce a common agreement on racialized issues that will reduce, or even eliminate, future potential racialized arguments. On the other hand, cultural pluralists have argued that assimilation may dictate conformity to European standards for minority group members.[8] This is a false argument. Minority groups can only assimilate if the dominant group accepts them into the majority culture, and those who can assimilate will do so if they perceive it advantageous. Since assimilation generally means greater acceptance into the power structure of society, minority groups tend to assimilate when offered the chance.

Rather than arguing whether assimilation is beneficial for minority group members, I contend that researchers of race/ethnicity would do well to assume that assimilation, or racial identity thinning, tends to occur when the majority group members allow it. Given this assumption, there is fruitful research among those who assess the effects of assimilation of minority groups. For example, how does the incorporation of only certain groups into the dominant society affect groups who are unable to merge into that culture? What are the precipitating conditions necessary for assimilation? Why do majority group members allow assimilation of certain groups but not others? Are there conditions whereby minority groups will not assimilate, even if the majority group allows such assimilation to take place?[9] While I have touched upon some of these questions in this book, future research should explore them more deeply so that we might better understand how racial groups may react and relate to each other.

The Uniqueness of the African American Experience

The rise of Chicano and Asian studies is in part a reaction to the emphasis of blacks as the focus of study within the field of race/ethnicity. The research that comes out of these venues is a necessary correction to the idea that racial issues in the United States are reducible to blacks and whites only. While studies of American race and ethnicity should avoid neglecting minority groups other than African Americans, I do contend that in the examination of American racial issues, blacks should be treated as a special case. The alienation that blacks face is unique in the United States and extra effort needs to be taken for social scientists to understand the its full effects.

While others have also theoretically argued that racial relations with African Americans deserve special attention,[10] this research offers empirical verification for that attention. Previous research on majority group domination tends to be built upon either the concept that white supremacy is, or was, the dominant ideology among majority group members,[11] or the concept that dominant group members utilize notions of color blindness to protect their racial position of privilege.[12] Both concepts lead to an understanding of an American racial hierarchy formed by a white/nonwhite dichotomy. In such a system all non-European groups face social rejection and theoretically all non-European groups deserve an equal amount of academic attention—even if they have not been receiving it. Yet given the merging of nonblack racial minorities into the dominant culture, this white/nonwhite dichotomy is losing relevance. A black/nonblack dichotomy produces more understanding about contemporary race relations. It suggests that the informal rejection of African Americans, rather than a tendency by the majority to oppress all minority groups in a roughly equal manner, is the linchpin to the American contemporary racial hierarchy. Given the importance that this rejection and alienation of African Americans plays in this new racial reality, a special emphasis upon the racial reality of blacks can be theoretically defended, and resources used to study African Americans can justifiably be greater than the resources used to study other minority groups. Research into the outcomes of racism and discrimination for Hispanic and Asian Americans must continue, but the increased and increasing attention that has been given to the alienation of African Americans is warranted.

The Forging of Alliances
Between Whites and Nonblack Minorities

The alienation thesis predicts that African Americans will lose valuable allies in their struggle to escape racial oppression. Racial minority groups who previously aided blacks will increasingly perceive themselves as being "white" as opposed to having minority status. It is important for social scientists to document this process. To date, most researchers have been using a white/nonwhite dichotomy, which dictates that the important conflict in the United States is between whites and racial minorities. But since certain racial minority groups will be allowed to assimilate into the dominant society, consensus, rather than conflict, may characterize certain types of white/nonwhite relations. Just as Noel Ignatiev records the process by which the Irish developed ideological consensus with the majority group,[13] there is a need for scholarly work to document the contemporary development of majority group consensus with Hispanics and Asians.

If Hispanic and Asian Americans start to more fully adopt the racialized attitudes of majority group members, then it can be predicted that conflict between these groups and African Americans will develop.[14] This conflict can arise as Hispanic and Asian Americans obtain more social power and attempt to distance themselves from African Americans. Documenting the alliances that may develop for Hispanics and Asians with majority group members will provide additional evidence of the assimilation, or racial identity thinning, of these nonblack minority groups, which will help researchers to understand the dynamic nature of intergroup racial relations in the United States.

This final area of study should be of particular importance to activists for racial justice. If the alienation thesis is correct, then African Americans will increasingly find themselves alone in their fight. Progressive social activists would do well to monitor the "whitening" of Hispanic and Asian Americans as well as the persistent alienation that blacks suffer, since these twin developments may indicate a need for activists to redouble their efforts in advocating for African Americans. As African Americans become more isolated from other racial groups, they will need support from individuals in the majority group to deal with the persistence of institutional racism. Some of these majority group individuals will include Hispanic and Asian Americans who have majority group status but are still willing to advocate for African Americans. Yet as they gain more benefits from white privilege, the number of Latinos and Asians who support the empowerment of racial minorities will decline—since members in these groups will have a stake in protecting majority group privilege. As more nonblack minorities are recruited into the dominant group and start to work toward protecting the racial status quo, a racialized society that continues to deprive certain racial groups of full participation seems destined to persist.

The Coming Black/Nonblack World

If the alienation thesis it correct, then eventually the racial status of blacks will be the most inflexible racial designation in American society. Distance from having a black racial status will define all other groups. Just as researchers will have to rethink how to study race and ethnicity, all Americans will have to prepare for this new racial order. While certain nonblack minority ethnic groups (e.g., late-arriving immigrant groups, ethnic groups with a discernible level of African ancestry, Middle Easterners) may remain, at least for some time, at the bottom of the racial hierarchy in the United States, it is useful to speculate about the implications of the coming black/ nonblack society.

One of the most powerful of these implications was alluded to in Chapter 4. The desired "Rainbow Coalition" that many progressives have hoped for is unlikely ever to materialize, particularly as it concerns racial issues. Of course, this is not to say that all Latino and Asian Americans will stop supporting issues that blacks care about. Just as there are progressive European Americans who support the empowering of African Americans, so too will there always be Hispanic and Asian Americans who support blacks. In fact, for some time to come these nonblack racial minorities will generally be more supportive of blacks than are dominant group members, given that it will take time for members of these groups to become completely "white." Furthermore, as I have already noted, some of the ethnic groups within these nonblack minorities will require a much longer time to assimilate, or to have their racial identity thinned, than others. But it is still vital to note that these groups will not support progressive racial causes to the same degree as do African Americans, and that this lower level of support will decrease over time.

An example can be seen in the defeat of affirmative action through Proposition 209 in California and Initiative 200 in Washington. It would be very difficult to pass these referendums with just the support of European Americans. Both states have populations of nonblack racial minorities who can sway a close election.[15] Given the expected high level of resistance that these propositions received from African Americans and progressive European Americans, overwhelming opposition by Latino and Asian Americans should have spelled the defeat of this legislation—at the very least in California.[16] The fact that such antiprogressive measures were passed in states where nonblack minorities possess political power suggests that African Americans will not be able to rely upon other racial minority groups for political support in the coming black/nonblack society. I contend that this pattern of voting, with nonblack minorities siding with European Americans on racial issues, is likely to grow stronger, instead of weaker.[17]

Given this political reality, I predict that the era of using governmental programs to correct historical and contemporary racial injustice is coming to an end. As more Hispanic and Asian Americans adopt a white racial identity, and the notion of color blindness that is a part of that identity, their support for programs that attempt to compensate for racial injustices will begin to wane. Without the support of a majority of these groups, there simply will not be enough votes among African Americans and sympathetic European Americans to sustain the most controversial elements of affirmative action programs. Laws that protect against overt individualistic racism will stay in place, as the color-blind individualism of the dominant culture does not accept overt acts of racism. Such laws, while of course necessary, serve to legitimate the structural forms of racism in American society, since they relieve majority group members of the concern that "Jim Crow" types of racism still legally exist.[18] However, just as Reconstruction, which initially was valuable in helping former slaves, was reversed soon after its implementation, so too will the current governmental attempts to deal with institutional racism eventually be reversed due to lack of political support.

Along with a loss of political power, I also predict that African American culture will continue to be marginalized. Social observers have noted that there is a dichotomous black/white cultural formation in the United States.[19] Of course, the cultures of nonblack racial minorities will continue to exist, but the expression of their cultures will become more symbolic in the coming years as the members of these groups assimilate into the dominant culture.[20] Cultural distinctions between the Hispanic/Asian cultures and the majority culture will become less important in the lives of later-generation minorities, as members of these groups will adopt more elements of the mainstream culture. This will not be a simple adoption of majority group culture, as European Americans will also take on some of the elements of these nonblack minority groups and a new dominant social culture will emerge that incorporates elements of former minority groups even as the distinctions between those minority groups and the new dominant culture will be discounted.

What will happen to African Americans while these groups are culturally merged into the new dominant culture? There will always be a strong cultural presence of blacks in American society, as blacks will not have the ability to assimilate into the dominant society. The key difference between the experience of African Americans and Latino/Asian Americans will be that black culture will remain noticeably distinct from the majority culture. This is not to say that African American culture will be unable to influence the dominant culture. There will always be nonblacks who are heavily influenced by elements of African American culture. Black music, art, television programming, and other expressions of African American culture will enjoy respect within certain progressive and radical subcultures in society. However, unlike what I predict will happen with many elements in Hispanic/Asian culture, while African American culture may be tolerated, it will not be accepted as part of the mainstream in the United States.

I also predict a continuation of the type of social estrangement that currently exists between blacks and the majority group, except that many non-European groups will also participate in that estrangement. By social estrangement, I mean the fact that African Americans are less likely to marry European Americans than other racial groups,[21] and that middle-class blacks are less likely to live in integrated neighborhoods than other racial groups.[22] The evidence in Chapter 3 clearly indicates that it is not just European Americans who reject social relations with African Americans. Latino and Asian Americans are also less likely to desire African Americans as neighbors and in-laws. As these nonblack groups continue to accept white racial identity, their social apathy toward blacks is likely to increase. This level of social estrangement will further harden the barriers between African Americans and other racial groups in the United States. Because relatively few nonblacks will develop close relations with blacks, the common stereotypes that are attached to African Americans (e.g., criminality, living on welfare) will continue to persist even as the racial stereotypes attached to nonblack groups begin to wither away. African Americans will continue to dwell in a semi-caste existence whereby individual blacks will have access to some of the paths to economic success in the United States, but African Americans as a group will be unable to escape racially based social rejection.

In short, the future of American race relations holds the continuing estrangement of African Americans on the political, cultural, and social fronts. There is no evidence that alienation of African Americans will lessen over time. The presence of the current level of alienation that blacks face will make it more difficult for African Americans to become a part of the mainstream. Given the ability of the forces that create alienation for African Americans to sustain this estrangement, I am unable to predict how long it will take for African Americans to overcome their separation from the dominant culture. In fact, a better prediction may be that blacks will never be able to totally overcome the powerful effects of the alienation they experience.

Public Policy Suggestions

I did not write this book in an attempt to shape public policy. I merely wanted to report upon an important racial trend that has been neglected by previous social researchers—the transformation of Latino and Asian Americans into majority group members. But while the main focus of this book is not policy change, I do believe that there are some important implications of this research for the public sector.

Charles Moskos and John Butler have argued that affirmative action programs should concentrate upon aiding African Americans.[23] They argue that the unique history and predicament of blacks justify this special emphasis. It is not that they contend that other minority groups should be excluded from affirmative action aid. I generally agree with them that a special emphasis should be placed upon the needs of African Americans, but rather than using the history of blacks to justify this emphasis, I rely upon the most likely future of blacks—which is one of racial alienation. Because of this alienation, African Americans do not have the same opportunities to escape into the majority culture as do other racial minorities. Public programs that are designed to aid African Americans must be prepared to deliver long-term assistance, rather than act as a short-term fix.

Making this distinction is important, because it is likely that in the coming years Latino and Asian Americans will economically improve relative to African Americans. If this occurs, then many members of these nonblack minority groups will begin to justify their higher status by adopting the concepts of white privilege, just as many European ethnic groups have done before them.[24] Even if these minority group members do not fully adopt white privilege, it is still likely that majority group members will use the relative success of Hispanic and Asian Americans to justify their own social position.[25] It is important for the proponents of affirmative action programs to clarify a different design to address the long-term alienation of African Americans, as opposed to the relative short-term needs of nonblack minority group members.

This persistent alienation also has implications as it concerns attempts to desegregate schools and neighborhoods. Since research has demonstrated that most nonblack minority groups can integrate into dominant group neighborhoods and educational institutions, once they reach middle-class status,[26] the most effective way to improve race relations between such groups and majority group members may be class-based economic programs. For African Americans, such programs will not by themselves dramatically improve race relations, since even middle-class blacks find themselves alienated from the dominant group. It is tempting to merely assert that efforts to integrate African Americans into schools, workplaces, and neighborhoods must be redoubled, yet research into such interracial contact indicates that, by itself, this type of integration will not end racism, since mere interracial contact does not alter racial attitudes.[27] This explains why after decades of attempting to integrate educational institutions, racial alienation between European and African Americans tends to be as high as ever.

To deal with the racial alienation of African Americans will require efforts beyond integration in secondary organizations, to institutions where primary relationships are developed, such as churches and social clubs. I believe that these primary organizations hold important keys for helping majority group members to become more accepting of African Americans and to challenge notions of white privilege. I have spent the last three years conducting research on multiracial churches, one possible location of primary interracial contact. This research has suggested that Americans who attend multiracial churches are more likely to have integrated social networks,[28] and are more likely to accept racial exogamy.[29] Furthermore, there is evidence that being part of a multiracial church is one of the strongest predictors of whether a person has an integrated social network,[30] indicating that integration into primary institutions can have a qualitatively different effect upon the attitudes of Americans than integration into secondary institutions.[31] This work suggests that those who attend interracial churches are more accepting of the presence of African Americans in their intimate social spheres, which allows for the possibility that racial alienation will be lessened. Since there is at least some evidence that racial attitudes that support the maintenance of the racial status quo, or white privilege, are inversely related to the presence of African Americans in multiracial churches,[32] it is plausible to argue that these interracial organizations are part of the solution to racial alienation.

If such interracial organizations are a solution, then an important question is what can the public sector do to encourage the development of such organizations? Once again there is insight from the work of Charles Moskos and John Butler in their suggestion that the military is an organization that can break down walls of racial misunderstanding in ways that have not occurred in educational institutions.[33] Since most Americans will not enter into the military, Moskos and Butler suggest that a National Service Corp can serve the same purpose. Although I am still skeptical about the need to encourage a larger military, even after September 11, 2001, I do concur with much of their argument concerning the importance of a such a corp and believe that it is one of the ways that the U.S. government could encourage fruitful interracial contact. However, beyond this corp and the military, there is little the public sector can do, since the voluntary nature of primary integrated organizations is part of what makes them effective. The public sector should look to support these organizations through applied research,[34] publicly encouraging the development of these groups and even highlighting successful multiracial primary organizations.

However, all of this brings to mind a very fundamental question: How important is it for African Americans to assimilate, or thin their racial identity, rather than to retain their cultural distinctness? I have refrained from attempting to answer such a question and still will not address the relative values of assimilation versus pluralism—such as whether there is a great intrinsic merit in keeping one's culture intact. But from a pragmatic viewpoint, African Americans may have to attempt some steps toward assimilation, even though they live in a society that is currently denying them the opportunity to assimilate. As long as other racial minority groups are merging into the dominant society at a relatively high rate, blacks continue to run the strong risk of being left behind in a black/nonblack society. Cultural pluralism can be justified as a way of protecting African Americans from rejection by the dominant society, yet this pluralism also feeds into a social system that works to ostracize African Americans, since by avoiding interaction that leads to assimilation African Americans help to keep themselves outside the social power structure in the United States. All attempts by blacks to become incorporated are likely to fail due to the powerful forces of alienation, yet resistance to these forces by African Americans is still necessary—if only so that blacks do not fool themselves into believing that the coming black/nonblack society is of their own choosing.

A final important policy issue concerns multiracial identity. The U.S. census recently allowed all Americans to choose as many racial categories as they wanted. This decision was in large part a response to the desire of some multiracial individuals to have a multiracial category. Such a category may theoretically create a new racial group, such as the way the Mexican "race" developed from the Mestizos—the mixed-race group who preceded them. A new race can emerge, which then may become a buffer group between African Americans and majority group members. If this buffer group resists the maintenance of the racial status quo, then African Americans will gain an ally even as they lose the potential aid of Hispanic and Asian Americans. I am skeptical that such a mixed-race buffer group will last, as I believe that they will eventually be assimilated into the dominant group, yet for however long this multiracial group exists there will be a third group in the hierarchy and African Americans will be spared from the full implications of a black/nonblack society.

For this reason I argue that it is a mistake for African American organizations to oppose the recognition of multiracial people.[35] They generally do so out of a fear that the number of African Americans will decrease as more blacks choose to be multiracial. By attempting to make the racial choice dichotomous, these organizations hope to put pressure upon multiracial blacks to conform to an African American identity. My contention is that African Americans who prefer a multiracial identity already have a very thin "black" identity. Forcing them to choose a racial identity that they do not perceive to be socially accurate is a violation of their right to self-determination and may even encourage them to avoid any identification with African Americans.[36] If they have enough phenotypic similarities with European Americans, then they may choose to "pass" instead of fighting African Americans for their right to create their own identification. Aiding instead of fighting multiracial people may enable us to support a buffer group who may still be willing to oppose the racial status quo in American society, instead of driving multiracial individuals away from the African American community. The temptation to exert social pressure so that such individuals will stay "faithful" to their race is understandable, but rather than risk alienating multiracial Americans, I contend that we should embrace their decision to be multiracial and then in friendship, not in intimidation, enlist their aid in dealing with racial alienation. A persistent multiracial community will be a benefit, rather than a cost, to the African American community, and blacks should work with, instead of against, this community.

It is debatable whether these suggestions will make the lives of African Americans easier, and I hope that those who are becoming aware of the coming black/nonblack society will offer their own solutions for overcoming the alienation of blacks. Unfortunately, I believe that there is little that the public sector can do to slow the movement toward a black/nonblack society. Yet this pessimism does not absolve us from the responsibility of doing all we can to reduce the alienation that African Americans continue to experience.

Conclusion

Even if the above adjustments are made, I am doubtful that the coming black/nonblack society can be avoided. It would give me great pleasure to be proven wrong and to not see African Americans by themselves at the bottom of the social ladder. But my reading of the research indicates that the exceptional historical and contemporary experiences of African Americans will relegate them into a lower social status for some time to come. Much of the failure to perceive this coming racial reality is linked to the notion that racial identity is unchanging—an idea that history has been repeatedly shown to be false. Data from the 1999–2000 Lilly Survey of American Attitudes and Friendships (LSAF) and other studies indicate that the special type of alienation African Americans experience will persist and that other racial minority groups are undergoing an incorporation into the dominant society that escapes blacks. It is more responsible to prepare for what the future likely holds than to merely wish that it would be different. It is with that philosophy that this book is a warning to blacks about losing allies, as well as a prediction that the largest nonblack minority groups will soon shed their distinctions from majority group members. Whether the readers of this book agree with my possible solutions to this dilemma, speculations about what a black/nonblack society will look like, or suggestions for alternate paths of research into race/ethnicity, I hope that they accept this warning and prediction so that the debate about solutions and alternate paths of research can develop from realistic assumptions about America's coming racial reality.

Notes

1. Carr 1997; Winant 1994.
2. Carr 1997; Kilson 1995; Mack 1996.
3. Kluegel 1990; Sniderman and Piazza 1993; Sears et al. 2000.
4. Carr 1997; Feagin 2000; Hacker 1992; Robinson 2001; Maki et al. 1999; Munford 1996; Massey and Denton 1996; Thompson 2001.
5. Schlesinger 1992; Hughes 1993. Of course there are those who argue that assimilation has not taken place even for European ethnic groups, but rather that a process of racial identity thinning has occurred. My point throughout this book has been that regardless of whether we want to call it assimilation or identity thinning, the end result of the incorporation of the dominant identity by minority groups still occurs—isolating African Americans from potential allies.
6. Spickard 1989; Gordon 1964; Glazer and Moynihan 1963.
7. Myrdal 1944; Parsons 1965–1966; Patterson 1977.
8. Bash 1979; Hirschman 1983; Newman 1973.
9. Paul Metzger (1971) also asks some of these questions, but there is little evidence that social scientists have adequately followed up on his queries.
10. Moskos and Butler 1996; Lieberson 1980; Bobo and Hutchings 1996.
11. See, for example, Ferber 1998; and Feagin 2000.
12. See, for example, Carr 1997; Kluegel 1990; Emerson and Smith 2000.
13. Ignatiev 1995.
14. There is already evidence of this type of conflict between African

Americans and Asian Americans in many larger U.S. metropolitan areas. For examples of this conflict, see Kim 2000–2001; and Anderson 1992. In these areas African Americans often complain that Asian Americans are invading their neighborhoods and stealing their jobs. Asian Americans often complain that African Americans do not have the initiative to lift themselves out of poverty and are exhibiting racism and jealousy toward them. This type of conflict should be expected from a minority group, in this case Asian Americans, who live among African Americans and who are accepting the perspectives of the white racial identity. The conflict between Hispanics and African Americans is not as well documented, but there is evidence that in some metropolitan areas blacks and Latinos have fought over political turf (Harris 1996; Chavez 1990).

15. According to the 2000 census Latino Americans currently make up 32.4 percent of the population in California and 7.5 percent of the population in Washington. Asian Americans make up 10.9 percent of the population in California and 5.5 percent of the population in Washington.

16. In fact, while there were no data on the racial breakdown of minorities on the Washington vote, the percentage of white voters who supported the measure matched the percentage of all voters who supported the measure—58 percent each (according to the Cable News Network exit poll). This suggests that people of color were just as likely to support the measure as majority group members. If African Americans are less likely to support that measure, then it can be argued that nonblack minorities may be even *more* likely to support it than European Americans. In California's battle, over 209 Latino Americans (70 percent) were about as likely to oppose this measure as African Americans (74 percent). But only 55 percent of all Asian Americans opposed the measure, indicating that almost half of this minority group opposes affirmative action.

17. Charles Gallagher (2002b) also argues that the expansion of the definition of "white" to include Hispanics and Asians can serve to limit support for progressive racial concerns, since these assimilated minorities will be allowed to join the dominant group.

18. Gallagher (2002a) finds that much of the color-blind racism that majority group members tend to exhibit is based upon the fact that overt racism no longer exists. If he is correct, then the prohibitions of blatant racism within civil rights legislation serve not only to protect racial minorities from gross forms of racism, but also to protect majority group members from having a need to challenge the racial status quo.

19. One of the best examples of this can be seen in the tendency of European Americans and African Americans to watch different television programs (Lusane 1999; Schneider 1997). The vast majority of the top shows among European Americans are rarely popular among African Americans, and vice versa. Just as there are distinctively African American styles of music, clothing, and art, there are also television shows and networks that possess a black cultural style.

20. This would be similar to the type of symbolic ethnicity that several scholars have talked about (Gans 1979; Alba 1990).

21. Lewis and Yancey 1995.

22. Alba and Logan 1991; Massey and Fong 1990; Massey and Mullan 1984.

23. Moskos and Butler 1996.

24. Waters 1990.

25. In fact, this is already being done in light of the relative success of Asian Americans. The concept of the model minority myth that has been developed to account for the success of Asian Americans is used to criticize other minority groups (Tachiki 1971; Hurh and Kim 1989). Such critics argue that since Asian Americans overcame racism, other racial groups should be able to succeed as well. Given the existence of such an ideology, it is easy to predict that if Hispanic Americans start to achieve relative economic success, then they will also be used as a "model minority" to justify the higher economic position of majority group members. Such a process would mimic the experiences of European ethnic groups as noted by Mary Waters (1999).

26. Massey and Denton 1988, 1987.

27. St. John 1975; Ford 1986; Smith 1994; Sigelman and Welch 1993.

28. Emerson, Kimbro, and Yancey 2002.

29. Yancey 2001.

30. Personal communication with Michael Emerson.

31. In another paper (Yancey and Emerson, unpublished), primary institutions are defined as the organizations where individuals tend to form primary social relationships (e.g., families, churches, social clubs) and secondary institutions as the organizations where individuals tend to have mostly secondary social relationships (e.g., schools, workplaces, residential neighborhoods).

32. Yancey 1999, 2001.

33. Moskos and Butler 1996.

34. In fact, I am at this time working on a book that can be used to help religious institutions that want to become multiracial by disseminating some of the findings of my research into multiracial congregations. In that book I outline several principles that are used by successful integrated churches to maintain the multiracial nature of their congregations, as well as examine the different types of multiracial churches that exist. While the book will clearly be aimed at aiding religious congregations, I believe that many of these principles might also be used by nonreligious organizations that also want to become multiracial.

35. As an example of this opposition, see Williams 2003; Brown and Douglass 2003; and *San Francisco Chronicle* 1997.

36. For examples of arguments by multiracial people who resent the imposition of the one-drop rule by African American civil rights organizations, see Zack 2001; Cohn 2000; Daniel 1996; and Spickard 1992.

Appendix:
Description of the Study

Although there are a great number of studies that have examined the social attitudes of European Americans,[1] and a smaller but significant number of studies that have examined the attitudes of African Americans,[2] the study of the social attitudes of Hispanic Americans is sparse, and the study of the attitudes of Native Americans, Asian Americans, and multiracial individuals is virtually nonexistent. Although there is a dire need for research into the social attitudes of Hispanic Americans and Asian Americans,[3] little has been done to rectify this need.

The General Social Survey (GSS) is probably the survey most commonly used by social scientists to examine social attitudes. Yet the race question used in the GSS only allows respondents to identify themselves as "white," "black," or "other." Unless a researcher is willing to make the highly problematic assumption that the experiences of all nonblack racial minorities are identical, this design makes analyzing the attitudes of nonblack racial minorities impossible.[4] The GSS is not alone in this measurement problem. Gallup polls, which are useful for monitoring social attitudinal trends, measure the race respondents as "white," "nonwhite/black," or "black,"[5] creating the same measurement difficulties found in the GSS. It is impossible to use these two popular research instruments to assess the social attitudes of nonblack racial minorities.[6]

There are lesser-known survey instruments—such as the Southern Focus Poll, Louis Harris and Associates Polls, and the National Election Survey (NES)—that report more detail about respondents' race. But these survey instruments incorporate samples of Hispanic

Americans and Asian Americans that are generally too small to be useful. None of these three polls typically survey more than 1,300 respondents.[7] For example, the 1998 NES had a sample of 1,281. This sample contained 152 African Americans, 138 Hispanic Americans, and 16 Asian Americans. Numbers this low makes it difficult to conduct the analysis necessary to examine differences in cross-racial social attitudes.

Until recently, nonblack minorities had relatively small national populations. A common method for obtaining information from a small population is oversampling. A survey designed to obtain a sufficient number of Hispanic Americans for a given research project will expend extra energy and financial cost to find Latino individuals. Only researchers who have a strong interest in learning about Latino American culture are willing to pay this price and use oversampling.

Not only do researchers lack understanding of the attitudes of nonblack racial minorities, but we also lack understanding of the attitudes of African Americans and European Americans *toward* nonblack racial minorities. Major national studies regularly assess people's stereotypes of, and social distance from, African Americans, but not for other groups.[8] Charles Jaret notes that much of what we know about the attitudes of whites toward Hispanic Americans is based upon local rather than national surveys.[9] The lack of a national survey on majority group members' attitudes toward Hispanic Americans means that we do not have systematic knowledge about how the dominant group perceives Latino Americans. Only by understanding social attitudes toward nonblack minority groups can social scientists compare their level of acceptance or rejection with that of African Americans. With one exception, my search of the poll surveys mentioned above did not turn up any examples of questions that assessed social attitudes toward Hispanic or Asian Americans.[10]

The Lilly Survey of American Attitudes and Friendships

These serious gaps in understanding call for better data. In response, I have turned to the 1999–2000 Lilly Survey of American Attitudes and Friendships (LSAF) to use for the bulk of the quantitative analysis done in this book. In the design of this survey, steps were taken to avoid the limitations of previous surveys. The LSAF surveyed just over 2,500 Americans, aged eighteen and older, with oversamples of

African, Hispanic, and Asian Americans. A phone survey allows the LSAF researcher to question a large number of respondents, essential for analyzing the attitudes of racial groups. The LSAF is designed to tackle the underrepresentation of nonblack minorities without compromising the advantages of random sampling, namely generalizability.[11] It used random-digit dialing to get an initial sample. Specific racial quotas were set as targets so that once those quotas were reached, members of that race were no longer surveyed. For example, once there were enough European American respondents, interviewers kept dialing random numbers—but when a person identified him- or herself as white, the call was ended. Using this method the LSAF set quotas at 300 African Americans, 300 Hispanic Americans, and 200 Asian Americans, ensuring that there would be enough racial minorities for the sample.[12] Another problem the LSAF addresses is the grouping of all nonblack racial minorities as "other." The race question allows individuals to choose among "white," "black," "Hispanic," "Asian," "Pacific Islander," "American Indian," "mixed," and "other." By giving the respondents such a variety of potential responses, the LSAF is able to more accurately measure the racial diversity among the respondents.[13] The breakdown of the different races can be seen in Table A.1.

A third important improvement incorporated into the LSAF is that questions are asked about the attitude of respondents toward all four major racial groups (i.e., European Americans, African Americans, Asian Americans, and Hispanic Americans).[14] To avoid biasing respondents' answers by asking the same questions about each and every group, an experimental design was used. For many questions,

Table A.1   Racial Makeup of the LSAF Sample

	N	%
European Americans	1,662	64.9
African Americans	298	11.5
Hispanic Americans	307	12.0
Asian Americans	210	8.2
Pacific Islanders	6	0.2
Native Americans	30	1.2
Mixed Race	33	1.3
Other	17	0.7
Total	2,561	100.0

the racial group about which the respondent was asked was randomly assigned. With this method, respondents heard the question only
once and about only one racial group, but the survey of the entire
population can assess the question in response to each racial group.
For example, as noted in Chapter 3, about a third of European
American respondents were asked about how they would feel if
their child wanted to marry an African American, a third were asked
how they would feel if their child wanted to marry a Hispanic
American, and a third were asked how they would feel if their child
wanted to marry an Asian American. I measured the effects of race
by comparing how different individuals within the same race
responded to the same question, except with the mentioned racial
group changed.

Limitations of This Research

Like any research endeavor, this effort has its limitations. Because of
the quantitative nature of this research, I am unable to expound upon
issues that I believe would benefit from in-depth qualitative work.
For example, although this research will document that African
Americans face more social rejection than other racial groups,
Saporito Salvatore and Annette Lareau have been able to use qualitative interviews of majority group members to illustrate the power of
this rejection.[15] Their research shows that whites in a large urban
area use the racial makeup of a school as the first, and most important, factor in helping them to decide where to send their children.
Only after whites have eliminated all predominately black schools do
they then examine other factors such as location and school performance. This sort of rich analysis is only possible through a qualitative examination.[16]

Furthermore, I only examined the attitudes of four racial groups:
European Americans, African Americans, Hispanic Americans, and
Asian Americans. Critics may ask questions such as these: Why not
include smaller racial groups such as Native Americans or individuals of Middle Eastern descent? Why, given the diversity of the ethnic
groups that the "Asian American" category comprises, assume that
all Asian Americans have similar social attitudes? Or for that matter,
why assume that different Hispanic American ethnic groups have
similar social attitudes? Where do the attitudes of mixed-race individuals fit into these issues?

These are legitimate questions. It is impossible to assess all the potential racial groupings in the United States with a single research survey. In this research I attempted to include Hispanic and Asian Americans, which is an upgrade from previous research efforts that concentrate only on European Americans and African Americans. Latino and Asian Americans were included because they are the largest American nonblack minority groups, and documenting the assimilation of these groups provides an assessment of the largest possible effect upon the changing American racial reality. The conclusions that result from this research can only be applied to these two groups, but if, over the next fifty years, only these two groups assimilate to a significant degree into the majority group, then the "whites as minority" thesis will be incorrect no matter what happens with other smaller racial groups. Nevertheless, Middle Easterners, Native Americans, mixed-race individuals, and other smaller racial groups deserve study and future research should include them as subjects.

I appreciate the ethnic diversity found within the Hispanic and Asian American communities. A researcher can argue that, because of the diversity of ethnic groups who are designated as "Asian American," there exists no "Asian" culture by which the social attitudes of that group can be captured. When I assess social attitudes toward Asian Americans, this critique does not have much merit. While there is a diversity of ethnic groups who are considered Asian American, most non-Asian Americans still perceive Asian ethnic groups as similar to each other.[17] However, this critique has relevance when the LSAF assesses the attitudes of Asian Americans. Clearly the perceptions of newer immigrant groups likely differ from those of more established Asian American groups. While I respect this argument, I also contend that the social position of contrasting Asian American groups is similar. I argue that, with some variation, Asian American groups tend to experience a similar level of acceptance in the dominant American culture—perhaps because of the way that non-Asian Americans tend to lump all Asians together. If this is true, then the racialized social attitudes between different Asian American ethnicities may be similar, as the individuals possessing Asian ethnicities undergo similar levels of racial acceptance by other Americans.

As I pointed out in the body of the book, certain later-arriving immigrant minority groups will be less likely to assimilate into the dominant culture. The alienation thesis is not refuted because the different ethnic groups assimilate into the dominant culture at varying speeds. In fact, given the diversity of ethnic groups present in the general "Hispanic" and "Asian" categories, it would be surprising if there was not some variability in these groups' acceptance of majority group racial attitudes. The fact that despite this intraracial diversity I still find evidence of a general movement of Latino and Asian Americans toward white racial identity strengthens the argument that a significant number of these nonblack minorities are rapidly assimilating into the dominant society.

In short, despite these legitimate critiques, this research is a positive step forward in the assessment of relationships between racial identity and social attitudes. The expanded racial classification is a vast improvement over the minimal categories used in the existing literature. The questioning about Latino and Asian Americans allows for an assessment of the informal racial hierarchy that is superior to past efforts, and the LSAF will allow me to test the alienation thesis in ways that were not previously possible.

Design of the LSAF

The LSAF was designed to assess individual attitudes, social networks, and involvement in religious life of congregations, and consists of over 2,500 American respondents.[18] Funded by a grant from the Lilly Endowment, Inc., to study multiracial congregations, the telephone survey was conducted by the University of North Texas Survey Research Center. While the primary purpose of this survey was not to conduct research into the social and racial attitudes of European, African, Hispanic, and Asian Americans, its design makes it a very valuable tool for addressing questions that I wanted to explore. As a member of the research team that organized the LSAF, I was in a unique position to include questions that would allow me to assess the degree of assimilation that Latino and Asian Americans have experienced relative to African Americans.

The survey was performed from October 1999 through March 2000, with the exception of the last three weeks in December. The survey had ambitious aims in terms of content, experimental designs, and oversampling of African Americans, Hispanic Americans, and Asian Americans (300 of first two groups and 200 Asian Americans). Using a random list of prefixes from Survey Sampling, Inc., and random-digit dialing for the last four digits, telephone numbers were called with the goal of speaking to the person eighteen years or older who had the next birthday.

The survey, which was programmed into the CATI (computer-assisted interviewing) system, was also translated into Spanish. In the case of no answer, up to eight callbacks were performed. In the case of refusals, two conversions were attempted. For the completed sample, slightly fewer than 6 percent of respondents (134) were refusal conversions. Approximately one-third of the interviews completed with Hispanic respondents were conducted in Spanish. Due to the variety of Asian languages, the survey represents only English- and Spanish-speaking Asian Americans.

When the European American quota (1,660) was filled, the survey introduction was changed to request to speak to nonwhite respondents only. The African and Hispanic American quotas were filled quickly, but at the time of their completion, less than 100 Asian American interviews had been finished. One more week was spent attempting to identify and interview a random sample of Asian Americans. At the conclusion of the week, 73 interviews had been completed. Due to money and time constraints, the remaining 147 interviews were conducted using a surname phone number list compiled by GENESYS. This method suffers from the obvious bias of missing any Asian Americans with nonidentifiable Asian surnames. It is estimated that approximately 40 percent of Asian Americans are excluded by this method. Because there was a sufficient number of randomly selected English-speaking Asian Americans, the impact of this sampling choice could be estimated and corrections could be made for any resulting bias.

Survey Representativeness and the Response Rate

The LSAF aims to represent the English- and Spanish-speaking adult population who have phones and, due the study's aims in measuring residential issues and attitudes, have lived at their current residence for at least three months. No claims to representation beyond these parameters are made.

The response rate for the LSAF was 53 percent. According to Thomas Mangione, response rates between 50 percent and 60 percent "need some additional information that contributes to confidence about the quality" of the data.[19] Error from nonresponse is a function of how large the nonresponse is, and how different the nonresponders are from the responders. According to the survey research literature, the additional information that can aid in the assessment and, if needed, improvement of sample representativeness includes the following:

1. Comparing the sample to a census or sample with a much higher response rate.
2. Comparing refusal conversions to initial respondents, under the assumption that refusal conversions are similar to other refusers, or at least more similar to them than to initial respondents (those who responded on the first call).
3. Comparing information of nonrespondents with that of respondents, though it is rare (almost by definition) to have such data.

Because the research team wished the LSAF to be representative of the population it desired to cover, a careful analysis of the sample and its representativeness was undertaken. This was done by obtaining another survey for comparison. The U.S. census typically is an excellent choice, but not in this case. The most recent data available were ten years old, and the demographics of the United States had changed since 1990. (The 2000 census was conducted the month after completion of the LSAF, but full results were not released until 2002.) Ideally, it is important to compare the LSAF to a reliable data source representing the midpoint of the LSAF survey period. Fortunately, the U.S. Department of Labor conducts a large, monthly survey called the Current Population Survey (CPS). The January 2000 CPS was selected, which, with its 124,000 cases, 93 percent response rate, and elaborate weighting procedures, was an excellent, contemporary source for comparison.

Based on comparisons of sociodemographic variables, the LSAF, like most telephone surveys, underrepresents the less educated and males. To correct for this, and for the oversamples of nonwhites, weights for each respondent were constructed. A table was generated from the CPS that created cells for each racial group by gender and five categories of education (less than high school, high school, some college or vocational technology, bachelor's degree, and post–bachelor's degree). The same cells were generated for the LSAF. For each cell, a weight is calculated by taking the CPS cell percentage and dividing it by the corresponding LSAF cell percentage. Before analysis on the LSAF is conducted, this weight must be applied to the sample. Doing so produces percentages on race, sex, and education that are nearly identical to those of the CPS. Applying this weight within these categories produces percentages on marital status, income, and age that also closely resemble those of the CPS. Demographically (and only demographically at this point), applying the weight variable renders the LSAF representative of the population.

It would be convenient to assume that, within each subcategory for which the weight corrects, those who did not respond are much like those who did respond. If this assumption were correct, it could be said with confidence that the LSAF now represents the population. However, without additional information, this assumption may not be justified. For this reason, a comparative analysis of initial respondents to refusal conversion respondents was undertaken. The aim was not just to compare these two groups by demographic variables, as was done with the CPS, but also to compare them by a number of attitudinal, religious, and social network variables. Comparisons were tested statistically using independent-sample t-tests and, when the comparison variable was not interval-level, chi-square tests of significance. Statistically comparing initial respondents to refusal conversion respondents on over fifty variables produced three clear patterns.

First, the two groups were statistically identical on about 90 percent of the comparison variables. Second, the refusal conversion respondents are more shy, as measured by the fact that they, compared to initial responders, are more likely to prefer being with people they know as opposed to meeting new people. This explains in part why they initially refused an interview and had to be coaxed into agreement. Third, the four other differences that exist can be attributed almost exclusively to one key difference: the refusal conversion respondents were twice as likely to be over sixty-four years of age as were the initial respondents (31 percent to 15 percent). This led to employment status difference, in that the refusal conversion respondents were also twice as likely to be retired as were the initial respondents (30 percent to 15 percent). All other initial differences—racial makeup of social network, the belief that morality ought to be universal, and the belief that able-bodied people should not receive welfare—disappeared when age was accounted for.

The results are instructive for assessing the representativeness of the LSAF. Nonresponders are more likely to be over sixty-four years of age and retired. This population is typically underrepresented in surveys, which, for the variables of interest in the LSAF, can lead to a slight overstatement on the degree of interracial networks, and slightly more liberal stances on a few selected attitudinal variables. Based on the fact that when age is accounted for these differences disappear, it does appear that weighting can correct for these biases. As stated earlier, when weighted for race, sex, and education, within these categories, the age distributions of the LSAF and CPS are similar. What cannot be adjusted is the fact that nonrespondents are likely more shy than respondents. Yet this difference did not lead to any differences between initial respondents and refusal conversion respondents. The apparent impact of this difference on the representativeness of these results is statistically zero.

Because a listed sample of Asian surnames was used for more than half of the Asian American respondents, it is important to ensure the representativeness of that portion of the sample. The random group of Asian Americans was compared with the listed sample after both samples were weighted by the CPS data. This comparison was made by age, education, sex, ethnicity, and a variety of attitudinal variables. There are no significant differences between these two groups on any of these measures, and these groups are statistically the same after the proper weights are applied.

Several questions depended upon the racial identity of the respondent. However, there were two situations anticipated that might prove to make assessing the racial identity of the respondent more difficult. First is the situation of those who identified themselves as being of mixed race, and second is the situation of those who refused to give their race or gave their race as "other." In both cases these individuals were dropped from the analysis presented in this book.

Variables

Obviously there are demographic and social differences between the racial groups that may help to explain some of the results found in the preceding chapters. In the following models, several independent variables are calculated to control for possible effects.

First, several demographic variables were calculated for the models. In addition to "age," "income,"[20] and "male," a dummy variable, these variables included the following: "education," which was determined by the number of years of schooling the respondent had completed; "political view," which measured political orientation on a seven-point scale ranging from "very liberal" to "very conservative"; "attendance," which indicated the respondent's frequency of church attendance; "conservative protestant," which was a dummy variable indicating whether the respondent was a fundamentalist or an evangelical Protestant; and "south," "west," and "northeast," which denoted the region of the country the respondent lived in[21] (in Table A.3, "north central" was used instead of "west"); "immigrant," which was used to designate whether the respondent was born in the United States; "own house," which measured whether the respondent owned his or her own home; "suburb" and "central city," which measured whether the respondent lived in the suburbs or in the central city; and "married," which measured whether the respondent was currently married.

The model in Table A.3 required certain specialized variables. Regarding "racial composition of friends," the respondents could answer that all, most, half, few, or none of their circle of friends were members of their own race. The "age" variable was specialized in this model through multiplication by a factor of 10. Four proxy variables were also included—"educational quality," "crime level," "housing values increasing," and "housing value relative to others in neighborhood—which are obtained by the random switching of values in Question 92 on the survey and allow for control of the proxy variables that can explain demand for housing. Finally, because people with children may have different values concerning their housing choices than other individuals, the dummy variable "children under 18" was added to measure whether the respondents had children of such age living with them. Theoretically, such individuals should be even less likely to exhibit a willingness to move into a residential area with high crime or low educational quality.

Several racial variables were also constructed to allow an analysis of the effects of race within the models. "White," "black," "Hispanic," and "Asian" are dummy variables respectively used to indicate whether the respondent is European American, African American, Hispanic American, or Asian American. Only these four racial groups are included in the models in Tables A.2, A.4, and A.5.

Since it has been argued that weighted data create larger standard errors than unweighted data,[22] resulting in regression models with a larger number of false negatives, all models were constructed using unweighted data. In the tables, the dependent variables are located at the tops of columns. The independent variables are located along the leftmost column. Unstandardized betas appear as main entries, with standard errors in parentheses.

Regression Analysis of
Bivariant Comparisons Found in the LSAF

In this section I will discuss the regression tables I applied to support the assertions in this book. Tables A.2 and A.3 support the analysis in Chapter 3; Tables A.4 and A.5 buttress the work in Chapter 4. While there are interesting nonracial effects to be found in some of these models, I will ignore results that do not have direct bearing on the racial differences discussed in the earlier chapters.

In Table A.2 the results of a regression analysis on the tendency of certain racial groups to support the exogamy of their children can be observed. The four models in this table consist respectively of European American respondents, African American respondents, Hispanic American respondents, and Asian American respondents. I constructed dummy variables to indicate which race the respondent was questioned about. Those who were asked about African Americans as potential in-laws are represented by the "black in-laws" variable. Respectively, "Hispanic in-laws" and "Asian in-laws" represent those who were asked about Hispanic Americans and Asian Americans. Theoretically there is also a "white in-laws" variable, which represents those asked about European Americans. However, this group is the reference group in the second, third, and fourth models. "Asian in-laws" are the reference group in the first model.[23]

Even after the application of social and demographic controls, European Americans who were asked about having African American in-laws are significantly more likely to reject racial exogamy than those asked about other racial groups. Other regression models with "Hispanic in-laws" as the reference group (not shown here but available from the author upon request) indicate that there is no significant preference of European Americans for either Hispanic Americans or Asian Americans. The only significant racial effect of this examination of European Americans is their rejection of

Table A.2   Unstandardized Betas and Standard Errors Predicting Acceptance of Racial Exogamy

	European Americans	African Americans	Hispanic Americans	Asian Americans
Black in-laws	-0.881[c]		-0.718[b]	-0.819[a]
	(0.126)		(0.270)	(0.409)
Hispanic in-laws	-0.077	0.028		-0.249
	(0.128)	(0.226)		(0.397)
Asian in-laws		0.268	0.334	
		(0.223)	(0.271)	
Age	-0.025[c]	-0.012	-0.011	-0.029[a]
	(0.003)	(0.006)	(0.009)	(0.013)
Income	-0.008	-0.067	0.032	-0.009
	(0.020)	(0.039)	(0.051)	(0.058)
Male	-0.117	-0.068	-0.584[a]	-1.198[c]
	(0.106)	(0.196)	(0.229)	(0.331)
Education	0.061[b]	0.109[b]	0.072[a]	0.058
	(0.021)	(0.036)	(0.032)	(0.082)
Political view	-0.123[c]	-0.054	-0.100	-0.165
	(0.036)	(0.997)	(0.068)	(0.123)
Attendance	-0.004	0.050	0.043	-0.032
	(0.032)	(0.064)	(0.070)	(0.103)
Conservative				
Protestants	-0.484[b]	0.286	0.155	-0.167
	(0.162)	(0.556)	(0.666)	(0.574)
South	-0.575[c]	-0.499[a]	-0.835[a]	-0.544
	(0.130)	(0.238)	(0.380)	(0.619)
West	0.244	0.059	-0.435	-0.679
	(0.151)	(0.379)	(0.365)	(0.564)
Northeast	0.016	-0.880[b]	-0.148	-0.263
	(0.163)	(0.309)	(0.423)	(0.601)
Immigrant	0.325	1.112[a]	-0.013	-0.930[a]
	(0.328)	(0.461)	(0.256)	(0.367)
R^2	0.144	0.118	0.137	0.209
N	1,427	248	270	158

Source: LSAF.
Notes: Unstandardized betas are main entries. Standard errors are in parentheses.
a. $p < 0.05$.
b. $p < 0.01$.
c. $p < 0.001$.

African Americans. For African American respondents, the race of the potential in-law is not significant. My inability to find strongly predictive variables for African Americans is likely related to the high overall level of support, and thus lack of variation, among

African Americans for interracial marriage. For Hispanic Americans, potentially having a European American or Asian American in-law is significantly positive when compared to the possibility of having an African American in-law. A model (not shown here) that used "black in-laws" as the reference group showed no evidence that Hispanic Americans preferred European Americans to Asian Americans. Rejection of African Americans was the main racial effect. Asian Americans are also significantly more likely to favor European American in-laws relative to the possibility of having African American in-laws. A model (not shown here) that used "black in-laws" as the reference group showed no evidence that Asian Americans significantly preferred European Americans to Hispanic Americans, and the preference of Asian Americans for Hispanic American in-laws over African American in-laws is significant at the 0.1 level. These findings reinforce the basic argument of the first portion of Chapter 3—that the rejection of African Americans drives attitudes about American racial exogamy.

Table A.3 reports the OLS (ordinary least squares) regression on the LSAF data concerning the likelihood of white respondents buying a home.[24] Each model consists of European Americans who were asked about a given racial group, and the dependent variable is the likelihood of whites to purchase a home in the given neighborhood. The first model consists only of whites asked about having Asian Americans in their neighborhood, the second model consists only of whites asked about having Hispanic Americans in their neighborhood, and the third model consists only of whites asked about having African Americans in their neighborhood. The most important observation to note is that only in the third model does racial composition matter as to whether whites will move into a neighborhood. In neither the first nor second models is racial composition significant in predicting the response of European Americans toward moving into a new neighborhood, suggesting that having Hispanic or Asian neighbors does not discourage whites from buying a house. Only black neighbors deter whites from locating into a neighborhood once all race proxy factors are controlled.

The strength of the finding is seen in the t-scores ($t = -7.0$) in the third model, indicating that having black neighbors is the third most important factor for these white respondents. Only crime level and educational quality are more important to these respondents than the black racial composition of a neighborhood. The proper way to interpret these results is that a higher number of blacks has a similar,

Table A.3 OLS Regression of the Likelihood of Buying a House on Racial Composition, Variables for Which Race Serves as a Proxy, and Selected Variables: White Americans, 1999–2000

	Asians		Hispanics		Blacks	
Racial Composition	-0.01	-0.03	0.02	0.04	-0.07[b]	-0.20
	(0.01)		(0.02)		(0.01)	
Proxy Variables						
Educational quality	0.70[b]	0.28	0.74[b]	0.30	0.80[b]	0.33
	(0.10)		(0.10)		(0.09)	
Crime level	-0.71[b]	-0.28	-0.86[b]	-0.34	-0.93[b]	-0.38
	(0.10)		(0.10)		(0.09)	
Housing values increasing	0.28[b]	0.11	0.29[b]	0.12	0.32[b]	0.13
	(0.10)		(0.10)		(0.09)	
House value relative to others in neighborhood	0.29[b]	0.12	-0.09	-0.03	0.24[b]	0.10
	(0.10)		(0.10)		(0.09)	
Control Variables						
Male	-0.08	-0.02	0.23	0.05	0.10	0.03
	(0.16)		(0.17)		(0.15)	
Education	-0.03	-0.03	-0.01	-0.01	-0.03	-0.05
.	(0.03)		(0.03)		(0.03)	
Own house	0.34	0.07	-0.53[a]	-0.12	-0.20	-0.04
	(0.22)		(0.21)		(0.19)	
Age x 10	-0.09	-0.08	0.06	0.05	-0.13[a]	-0.11
	(0.06)		(0.06)		(0.05)	
South	-0.08	-0.02	0.03	0.01	-0.25	-0.06
	(0.22)		(0.24)		(0.22)	
North central	0.60[b]	0.13	-0.04	-0.01	0.09	0.02
	(0.23)		(0.24)		(0.23)	
Northeast	0.28	0.05	0.22	0.04	-0.06	-0.01
	(0.26)		(0.27)		(0.23)	
Central city	0.18	0.04	-0.42[a]	-0.10	-0.11	-0.03
	(0.20)		(0.19)		(0.18)	
Suburb	0.33	0.07	-0.33	-0.07	-0.09	-0.02
	(0.20)		(0.22)		(0.20)	
Immigrant	0.27	0.02	0.42	0.04	-0.02	-0.00
	(0.48)		(0.45)		(0.48)	
Married	-0.31	-0.07	-0.22	-0.05	0.19	0.05
	(0.19)		(0.19)		(0.17)	
Children under 18	-0.18	-0.04	0.14	0.03	-0.27	-0.06
	(0.19)		(0.19)		(0.18)	
Racial composition of friends[c]	0.20[a]	0.08	0.12	0.05	0.29[b]	0.12
	(0.10)		(0.10)		(0.09)	
Intercept	2.47[b]	(0.74)	3.09[b]	(0.75)	3.65[b]	(0.70)
Sample size	548		518		531	
R[2]		0.240		0.242		0.348

Source: LSAF.

Notes: Unstandardized betas are main entries. Standardized betas are second entries. Standard errors are in parentheses.

a. p < 0.05 (two-tailed test).

b. p < 0.01 (two-tailed test).

c. Racial composition of friends is measured on a 5-point scale, from 1 = all friends are white to 5 = no friends are white.

although weaker, effect upon whites as a higher level of crime and lower quality of education. Just as a high crime rate and a low quality of schools are seen as social dysfunctions that discourage whites from moving into a neighborhood, so too can a higher percentage of blacks in a neighborhood be seen as a social dysfunction for European Americans.

It is possible that the effects found in Table A.3 are due to the fact that whites with children under eighteen are less likely to purchase a home when the percentage of blacks in a neighborhood rises. This possibility was tested by creating two separate models, one with whites having children under eighteen, the other with whites not having children under eighteen. The results of these models can be found in an article I coauthored on this topic.[25] There was a larger effect on whites who had children, but whites without children were still negatively influenced by black neighborhood composition. This result is particularly chilling, since if having children makes whites especially likely to avoid blacks, then it will be very difficult to create racial understanding through interracial contact with the younger generation.

Table A.4 explores the predictions of the social attitudes that were discussed in Chapter 4. In the models in this table, African Americans are the reference group, with "white," "Hispanic," and "Asian" dummy variables used to represent the other racial groups. "Male," "age," "education," "income," "political view," "south," "west," "northeast," and "immigrant" are controlled in these models. The racialized variables discussed in Chapter 4 are used as dependent variables. In six of the seven models, after the appropriate demographic/social controls are applied, European Americans are still significantly different from African Americans—the exception being attitudes toward welfare. This is not surprising, since one of the criteria by which I picked the racialized variables was whether whites significantly differed from blacks in a bivariant comparison. The more interesting findings are to be discovered by comparing African Americans to Hispanic and Asian Americans.

Latino Americans are significantly less likely to support integrated churches, less likely to want to talk about race, more likely to want to spend money on prisons, and less supportive of school vouchers than are African Americans. In regression analysis not shown here (available from the author upon request), I used European Americans as a reference group. This analysis indicated that Latino Americans are significantly more likely to support affirmative action and welfare than are European Americans—but they did not significantly differ from whites on any of the other racial measures. Asian Americans are significantly less likely to want to talk about race, less likely to support affirmative action, and more likely to spend money on prisons than are African Americans. In a regression analysis (not shown here) where European Americans are the reference group, Asian Americans are significantly less likely to talk about race and to support affirmative action than are European Americans—but they did not significantly differ from whites on any of the other racial measures.

A final way to test for differences between multiple groups among several variables is through the use of a technique called discriminate analysis, which is basically the reverse of multivariate analysis of covariance. In multivariate analysis of covariance, a researcher uses the group to which a respondent belongs to predict the dependent variables linked to that respondent. For example, I can use the fact that a respondent is white to predict that he or she does not support affirmative action. Of course, such a prediction is imperfect, but generally research indicates that whites are less supportive of affirmative action than are minority racial groups. In discriminate analysis the dependent variables are used to help predict the group a respondent belongs to. So the main question is how well the set of racialized variables that I found in the LSAF can be used to predict racial identity. I will use discriminate analysis to assess whether a black/nonblack dichotomy better predicts the racialized attitudes of Americans than a white/nonwhite structure.

Of course, divisions between these racial groups are not clearcut. As I have stated in this book, some of the racialized variables (e.g., the able-bodied receiving welfare) do not indicate the black/nonblack divide cleanly. Theoretically I assert that this indicates that the assimilation of nonblack minorities is not yet complete. But despite anomalies, if the black/nonblack divide is a better predictor, there should be more evidence showing that nonblack minorities tend to have racialized attitudes closer to those of European Americans than to those of African Americans. This would indicate that the pressure toward assimilation is more powerful than minority group alienation in predicting the racialized attitudes of Latino and Asian Americans. The standardized canonical discriminate function coefficients, eigenvalues, and canonical correlations of the discriminate analysis can be seen in Table A.5.

Table A.4 Unstandardized Betas and Standard Errors Predicting Selected Social Attitude Variables

	Should Integrate Churches	Should Talk About Race	Support Affirmative Action	Spend Money on Prisons	Cut Income Tax	Able-Bodied Should Not Receive Welfare	School Choice
Male	0.458[b] (0.100)	-0.199[a] (0.096)	0.432[c] (0.094)	0.193 (0.106)	-0.182[a] (0.090)	0.021 (0.086)	0.093 (0.082)
Age	0.001 (0.003)	-0.001 (0.003)	-0.001 (0.003)	0.001 (0.003)	-0.003 (0.003)	-0.013[c] (0.003)	0.005 (0.003)
Education	-0.042[a] (0.019)	.0159[c] (0.018)	0.018 (0.018)	0.093[c] (0.020)	0.048[b] (0.017)	0.046[b] (0.016)	0.056[c] (0.015)
Income	0.021 (0.019)	0.065[c] (0.018)	0.032 (0.017)	0.001 (0.020)	-0.050[b] (0.017)	-0.048[b] (0.016)	0.026 (0.015)
Political view	0.035 (0.032)	-0.179[c] (0.030)	0.180[c] (0.030)	-0.102[a] (0.033)	-0.106[c] (0.028)	-0.108[c] (0.027)	-0.103[c] (0.026)
South	0.183 (0.129)	-0.593[c] (0.123)	0.231 (0.120)	-0.374[a] (0.135)	-0.012 (0.115)	0.112 (0.110)	-0.023 (0.104)
West	0.034 (0.145)	-0.068 (0.140)	0.334[a] (0.136)	-0.017 (0.152)	-0.248 (0.129)	0.294[a] (0.124)	-0.019 (0.118)
Northeast	-0.076 (0.156)	-0.011 (0.150)	0.083 (0.146)	-0.010 (0.165)	-0.209 (0.141)	0.147 (0.133)	-0.015 (0.128)
White	0.367[a] (0.156)	-0.926[c] (0.151)	0.950[c] (0.144)	-0.772[c] (0.166)	-0.381[b] (0.141)	-0.003 (0.134)	0.304[a] (0.128)
Hispanic	0.439[a] (0.221)	-1.026[c] (0.213)	0.335 (0.206)	-0.813[c] (0.234)	-0.104 (0.200)	0.223 (0.191)	0.407[a] (0.181)
Asian	0.376 (0.259)	-1.532[c] (0.248)	0.667[b] (0.239)	-0.825[a] (0.271)	-0.430 (0.231)	0.001 (0.220)	0.373 (0.210)
Immigrant	0.431[a] (0.181)	0.024 (0.174)	-0.131 (0.170)	0.161 (0.190)	-0.219 (0.163)	0.231 (0.156)	-0.324[a] (0.148)
R^2	0.025	0.110	0.071	0.036	0.027	0.042	0.029
N	2,090	2,136	1,987	2,134	2,129	2,152	2,066

continues

Source: LSAF.
Notes: Unstandardized betas are main entries. Standard errors are in parentheses.
a. p < 0.05.
b. p < 0.01.
c. p < 0.001.

Table A.5 Discriminant Analysis Results for Whites, Blacks, Hispanics, and Asians

	Whites v. Hispanics	Whites v. Asians	Blacks v. Hispanics	Blacks v. Asians	Whites v. Hispanics and Asians	Blacks v. Hispanics and Asians
Support affirmative action	0.466	-0.137	0.841	0.487	0.219	0.749
Cut income tax	-0.006	-0.027	-0.103	-0.092	-0.009	-0.094
Should talk about race	-0.492	0.091	-0.249	-0.019	-0.249	-0.176
Should integrate churches	0.099	0.968	0.392	0.797	0.697	0.587
Spend money on prisons	-0.311	-0.307	-0.147	-0.113	-0.396	-0.149
Able-bodied should not receive welfare	0.754	0.107	0.219	-0.018	0.520	0.099
School choice	-0.241	-0.292	-0.057	-0.031	-0.348	-0.059
Eigenvalue	0.006	0.010	0.042	0.048	0.007	0.033
Canonical correlation	0.077	0.101	0.201	0.213	0.084	0.179

Source: LSAF.
Note: Standardized canonical discriminate function coefficients reported.

The first four models in Table A.5 compare whites and blacks respectively to Hispanics and Asians. I did not compare whites to blacks because the definition by which I choose the racialized variables predicates that whites and blacks will significantly differ from each other on these variables. What is important is whether whites or blacks have attitudes that are similar to the nonblack minority groups. To answer this question, either the eigenvalue or canonical correlation of each equation can be used; the choice does not matter, since the eigenvalue is equal to the squared canonical correlation. Larger canonical correlations indicate a greater difference between the groups (identical groups have a correlation of zero). Respectively, the eigenvalues of whites compared to Hispanics and Asians are 0.006 and 0.010, while the eigenvalues of blacks compared to those groups are 0.042 and 0.048. Respectively, this translates into canonical correlation scores for whites compared to Hispanics and Asians of 0.077 and 0.101, and for blacks compared to Hispanics and Asians of 0.201 and 0.213. The scores indicate that these racialized variables are better able to discriminate between blacks and Latinos/Asians than between whites and Latinos/Asians. Thus there is a greater difference in the scores between African Americans and nonblack minorities than between European Americans and nonblack minorities. This greater difference makes it easier for a researcher to predict the racialized attitudes from group membership in the pairing involving African Americans.

Given the strength of the first four models, I predict that comparisons of blacks to both Hispanics and Asians in a single group will reveal more distinctions than comparisons of whites to both Hispanics and Asians. This is indeed the case. In the last two models, I compared European Americans and African Americans to both Hispanics and Asians grouped together. This is a truer test of whether a white/nonwhite or a black/nonblack dichotomy better explains the racialized attitudes of both Hispanics and Asians. Once again the eigenvalue and canonical correlation scores of whites compared to Hispanics and Asians are lower, 0.007 and 0.084 respectively, than the scores of blacks compared to those two groups, 0.033 and 0.179 respectively. Whites are not as far from the attitudes of nonblack minorities as are blacks. Therefore the racialized attitudes of blacks are relatively more distinct than the racialized attitudes of whites from the perspectives of Hispanics and Asians.

African Americans have more distinctive racial attitudes than the other three racial groups. But this finding is only applicable as it pertains to the seven measures of racial attitudes under discussion. I have already acknowledged that this research is limited by the relatively low number of racial measures that are utilized in the Lilly research. An important extension to this work should be a discriminate analysis that incorporates more racial variables than the seven captured in this research. Such future research would either give the alienation thesis more support or serve to refute some of the assertions I have made in this book.

To summarize, the results of Table A.2 and A.3 indicate that African Americans suffer from social rejection that is qualitatively different from that suffered by other racial minorities, and this rejection comes from both nonblack racial minorities and majority group members. Table A.4 suggests that while the racial attitudes of nonblack minorities still differ from those of majority group members, their racial attitudes are more distinct from African Americans than from European Americans—confirming the basic conclusions of Chapter 4. With the exceptions of measures toward affirmative action and welfare, for which the attitudes of Hispanic Americans are at least as indicative of an alienated status as those of African Americans, all of the models in Table A.4 indicate powerful evidence of an alienated social reality for African Americans. In five of the seven models there is moderate to strong evidence that nonblack minorities possess racial attitudes that are more akin to dominant group attitudes than to African Americans' racial concerns. While these models do not consistently support the alienation thesis, they do warrant the use of discriminate analysis to perceive whether a black/nonblack framework is a better fit for racialized attitudes than a white/nonwhite structure. Discriminate analysis in Table A.5 supports the ability of a black/nonblack framework to better explain racialized attitudes—upholding the predictions of the alienation thesis. While it is clear that Hispanic and Asian Americans have not completely accepted the perspectives of European Americans, there is evidence in the LSAF that at least some of their attitudes on racialized issues are influenced by a desire to maintain the racial status quo.

Selected Questions from the
Lilly Survey of Social Attitudes and Relationships

Could we speak with the person who is over 18 and will have the next birthday in your family? (If no, may we interview you?)

First we'd like to ask a few questions to make sure we are talking to a wide range of Americans.

Screen: How long have you lived at your current residence? [If less than 3 months: "Thank you for your time." Otherwise, proceed with the interview.]

Q1. Are you currently married, or are you living with someone in a marriage-like relationship, widowed, divorced, separated, or have you never been married? [If say divorced and separated, code as divorced. If say marriage-like relationship and divorced/separated/ widowed, code as marriage-like.]
　　1) Married [go to Q2]
　　2) Living with someone [go to Q2]
　　3) Widowed [go to Q2]
　　4) Divorced
　　5) Separated [go to Q2]
　　6) Never married
　　7) Don't know [go to Q2]
　　8) Refused

Q2. [If Q1 = 1–3, or 5 or 7] Have you ever been divorced?
　　1) Yes
　　2) No
　　3) Don't know
　　4) Refused

Q3. What race or ethnic group do you consider yourself? [If necessary] That is, are you white, black American, Hispanic, Asian American, Pacific Islander, American Indian, or of mixed race? [If say "human," ask: "Would you mind telling us your ethnicity?"]
　　1) White/Caucasian/Anglo
　　2) Black/African American
　　3) Hispanic/Latino/a
　　4) Asian/Asian American
　　5) Pacific Islander
　　6) American Indian/Native American
　　7) Mixed
　　8) Gave ethnicity [coded in Q4]

9) Other (only if volunteered and cannot be placed in categories 1–7)

10) Don't know

11) Refused

Q4. [Interviewer: If Q3 = 1–5, or 7, read categories under appropriate racial group.]

[If say Asian]
Are you:
  Chinese
  Filipino
  Japanese
  Asian Indian
  Korean
  Vietnamese

Or something else? Other:
Mixed (if volunteered)

[If say Hispanic]
Are you:
  Mexican
  Cuban
  Puerto Rican
  Other Caribbean

Or something else? Other:
Mixed (if volunteered)

[If say Mixed]
What ethnic/racial groups are part of your heritage?

Q5. Do you identify with one of these more than the others?

Q6. [If Q1 = 1–2] What race or ethnicity is your [spouse/partner]?

1) White (includes European, Middle Eastern)

2) Black (includes African American, African, Dominican, other black)

3) Hispanic (includes Mexican, Cuban, Puerto Rican, other Latin American)

4) Asian (includes Asian and Pacific Islander ethnicities)

5) American Indian (includes Native American and tribes)

Now I would like to ask you a few more background questions.

Q12. Do you consider yourself to be Protestant, Catholic, Jewish, Muslim, nothing in particular, or something else?

1) Protestant (includes Baptists, Methodists, Presbyterians, Mormons, Reformed)

2) Catholic

3) Jewish
4) Eastern Orthodox Christian
5) Muslim
6) Buddhist
7) Nothing in particular/Not religious
8) "Just a Christian" [go to Q15]
9) Other: [go to Q16]
10) Refused [go to Q17]
11) Don't know [go to Q19]

Q13. How often have you been attending [church/synagogue/mosque/temple] services in the last year?
1) Never
2) Less than once a month
3) Once a month
4) 2–3 times a month
5) Once a week
6) More than once a week
7) Don't know
8) Refused

Now think of your circle of friends, people that you like to do things with and have conversations with. They may be people you see often, or because they may live far away, they may be people you primarily keep in contact with by calling or writing.

Q33. For your circle of friends, how many [their race] are among these people:
1) All
2) Most
3) About half
4) Few
5) None
6) Don't know

I am going to read you a list of statements. For each, please tell me whether you agree or disagree, and if you do so strongly, moderately, or slightly.

Q48. I support affirmative action policies.

Q53. The federal income tax should be cut.

Q55. Able-bodied people should not receive welfare.

Q56. The number of immigrants who can legally enter the United States should be reduced.

Q57. There is too much talk today in the United States about racial issues.

Q58. We need a program of parental school choice.

Q59. Religious congregations should actively seek to become racially integrated.

Q61. We should spend more money on prisons so that we can put criminals away for a long time.

Q63. We should give businesses special tax breaks for locating in largely [rotate racial group] areas.

Q64. Compared to other racial groups, [rotate racial group] on average tend to prefer to live on welfare.

Q65. Compared to other racial groups, [rotate racial group] on average tend to be patriotic to the United States.

Q66. Compared to other racial groups, [rotate racial group] on average tend to be arrogant.

Q67. I would be upset if I had a child who wanted to marry [a/an] [rotate racial group, other than respondent's own racial group].

I would like to get your thoughts on a few other questions.

Q92. Imagine that you are looking for a new house and that you have two school-aged children. You find a house that you like much better than any other house—it has everything that you'd been looking for, it is close to work, and it is within your price range. Checking on the neighborhood, you find that

a. the public schools are of [low, medium, high] quality,

b. the neighborhood is [5–100%, randomly chosen (if 0%, then say 100% of respondent's race) [Black, Hispanic, Asian, White] (do not ask respondent's own race)],

c. the other homes in the neighborhood are of [lower, equal, higher] value than the home you are considering,

d. property values are [declining, stable, increasing],

e. and the crime rate is [low, average, high]. [rotate order that present variables]

How likely or unlikely do you think it is that you would buy this home?

> Very unlikely
> Moderately unlikely
> Slightly unlikely
> Slightly likely
> Moderately likely
> Very likely

Q94. In the United States, we generally refer to 5 racial groups: Whites, Blacks, Hispanics, Asians, and American Indians. Do you personally think that any one of these groups experiences more discrimination than the other groups? YES NO

> If yes, which group?

Q105. On a political scale of 1 to 7—with 1 being extremely liberal, 4 being middle of the road, and 7 being extremely conservative—how would you describe yourself politically?

> 1) Extremely liberal
> 2) Liberal
> 3) Slightly liberal
> 4) Moderate, middle of the road
> 5) Slightly conservative
> 6) Conservative
> 7) Extremely conservative
> 8) Don't know
> 9) Refused

[For Christians only—Protestant or Catholic, if Q12 = 1–2, 8.]

These next few questions are questions we are asking of the Christians we are interviewing.

Q121. [If Q12 = 1 or 3, or Q16 = 1–9, 11–13, 15–30] When it comes to your religious identity, would you say you are a fundamentalist, evangelical, mainline, or theologically liberal Christian, or do none of these describe you?
1. Fundamentalist
2. Evangelical
3. Mainline
4. Theologically liberal
5. None of these
6. Other (must volunteer)
7. Don't know
8. Refused

You are being very helpful. We are almost done. Just a couple of final background questions, and that will be it.

Q129. [If not sure about respondent's sex] Are you male or female?

Q130. How many children do you currently live with and raise? [includes stepchildren]
1) 0
2) 1
3) 2
4) 3
5) 4
6) 5
7) 6
8) 7
9) 8
10) 9 or more
11) Don't know
12) Refused

Q131. [If Q130 = 2] How old is your child?

Q132. [If Q130 = 3–10] How old is your oldest child?

Q133. [If Q130 = 3–10] How old is your youngest child?

Q134. What year were you born?

Q135. In what state or country were you born? Code state or country of birth (If say, "U.S.": Ask, "And what state?").

Q136. From age 8–18, in what state or country did you live the longest? Code state or country of birth.

Q137. [If Q135 and Q136 = country other than United States] Since you moved to the United States, in which state did you live the longest?

Q138. In what state or country was your father born?

Q139. And in what state or country was your mother born?

Q140. [If owner] Could you tell me what the present value of your home is—I mean about what would it bring if you sold it today? [If not sure, "Could you just give me a rough estimate?"]
    [If renter] About how much rent do you pay a month?

Q141. How many rooms do you have (for your family), not counting bathrooms?

Q142. What is the highest grade of school, year in college, or graduate degree you have completed?

Q145. Do you live in a city, a suburb, a small town, or in the country?

Q147. Now here is the last question. I am going to read you a list of income categories. Please tell me to stop when a category I read best describes your total household income before taxes.
    1) Less than 10,000
    2) Between 10,000 and 20,000
    3) Between 20,000 and 30,000
    4) Between 30,000 and 40,000
    5) Between 40,000 and 50,000

6) Between 50,000 and 60,000
7) Between 60,000 and 70,000
8) Between 70,000 and 80,000
9) Between 80,000 and 90,000
10) Between 90,000 and 100,000
11) More than 100,000
12) Don't know
13) Refused (Prompt if necessary: "Remember, your answers are totally anonymous, and we don't need to know your exact income, just an income bracket within ten thousand dollars. It would really help us out." [Wait for YES or NO before reading answer categories.])

Notes

1. See, for example, Bobo and Klugel 1997; Sniderman and Piazza 1993; Firebaugh and Davis 1988; Weitz 1992; and Kuklinski and Cobb 1997.
2. Tuch, Sigelman, and Martin 1997; Bunzel 1991; Tripp 1992.
3. As noted in Cox and Nkomo 1990.
4. Obviously, any racial breakdown will have a category of "other," since inevitably there will be people who do not easily fall into racial categories. Nevertheless, it is important to minimize the number of people in that category so that racial identity questions will have more explanatory power.
5. Gallup Organization 1997.
6. Because nonblack minorities were not classified, it is impossible to conduct the types of sophisticated analysis necessary to sufficiently assess the attitudes of those minority groups. For example, the 1998 GSS data generated 2,832 subjects. Given that African Americans compose about 13 percent of the U.S. population, Hispanic Americans about 13 percent, Asian Americans about 3 percent, and Native Americans about 1 percent, the 1998 GSS should obtain about 368 African Americans, 368 Hispanics, 84 Asian Americans, and 28 Native Americans. With such numbers, a comparison of African Americans and Hispanic Americans to majority group members is possible, since there would be more than 200 of both African Americans and Hispanic Americans, enough to create meaningful comparisons. In reality the 1998 GSS survey obtained 400 African Americans and 191 individuals classified as "others." Since "others" likely include Hispanic Americans, Asian Americans, Native Americans, multiracial individuals, and anyone else whose racial identity is not easily classified, this number indicates an underrepresentation of nonblack minorities. Even if nonblack minorities were properly classified, the small numbers in these groups prohibit valid comparison between nonblack racial groups and whites or blacks.

7. There are surveys sponsored by the Inter-University Consortium for Political and Social Research (ICPSR) that also examine social attitudes. These surveys tend to be funded by news organizations such as ABC/Washington Post and CBS/New York Times and come with their own biases. Like the other three minor polls, these surveys have asked race questions beyond the "white/black/other" categories used in the GSS and Gallup polls. However, these surveys also share the same shortcomings of those minor polls in that they do not include sufficient numbers of nonblack racial minority respondents.

8. For example, in the 1998 GSS there were several questions assessing racial attitudes asked about African Americans and European Americans. However, there were no questions asked about Hispanic or Asian Americans.

9. Jaret 1995: 177.

10. The exception was in the fall 1997 Southern Focus Poll, which asked: "On a scale of 0 to 100, how would you rate Hispanic Americans?" However, this question was only posed to the 400 national respondents in that particular survey—not to all respondents in the different surveys sponsored by the Southern Focus Poll.

11. Commonly this is done though geographically targeted interviews. Nevertheless, the problem with this method is that minorities who live in areas where there are high numbers of their own race might have different social attitudes than minorities who live in majority white areas.

12. Because of the low absolute number of Native Americans who dwell in the United States, cost considerations prohibited an attempt to oversample that group.

13. The respondents were also asked to assess their ethnic groups. The groups used as ethnic categories can be seen in the questionnaire in this appendix. While such ethnic groupings are useful for other types of analysis, this book will focus upon differences between racial groups, rather than ethnic differences within racial groups.

14. One of the difficulties of capturing attitudes toward so many groups is the creation of a high number of questions. This is especially problematic when utilizing a phone survey, which limits the number of questions that can be asked. To compensate for this possibility, on certain questions the racial groups asked about were randomly alternated. The number of respondents interviewed allows for intragroup comparisons about whether the attitudes of individuals in a certain group toward a given situation are correlated to which group they are asked about. For example, in respondents' assessment of racial exogamy, this technique allows me to investigate whether it matters to European Americans if their child marries a black or a Hispanic.

15. Salvatore and Lareau 1999.

16. Eduardo Bonilla-Silva (2001) provides this type of rich analysis with his assessment of the color-blind storylines that European Americans tend to use to justify their support for the status quo. But while Bonilla-Silva also examines some of the attitudes of African Americans, he, like the vast majority of researchers who investigate racial attitudes, fails to incorporate any examination of nonblack racial minorities. Thus his work does not allow

for an examination of whether Hispanic and Asian Americans are more likely to accept a Eurocentric or an Afrocentric perspective on racial issues.

17. This lumping together of different Asian groups can be seen in the
tragic case of Vincent Chin—a Chinese American who was killed in 1982
because he was believed to be a Japanese American.

18. Actually, nearly 2,700 subjects were called for this part of the project, with 200 European Americans given a shortened survey due to a com-
puter error. As far as the research of this book is concerned, these individuals were only included in the Lilly question, discussed in Chapter 3, that
dealt with the attitudes of whites toward residential segregation when different minority groups were rotated as potential neighbors.

19. Mangione 1995: 61.

20. Respondents were given eleven categories, in increments of
$10,000, to classify their income.

21. Regional designations were determined by GSS categories.

22. Winship and Radbill 1994.

23. Each model was tested for possible interactive effects of "white in-
laws," "Hispanic in-laws," and "Asian in-laws." Any interactive effects that
exist are minor and did not alter the main findings of this study.

24. While I am a coauthor of the article that came from this analysis
(Emerson, Yancey, and Chai 2001), primary credit is owed to Michael
Emerson, who was the lead author of that paper and who by far did the
lion's share of the work.

25. Emerson, Yancey, and Chai 2001.

References

ABC/Washington Post Poll (1989).

Alba, Richard D. (1995). "Assimilation's Quiet Tide." *The Public Interest* no. 119 (spring): 3–18.

——— (1990). *Ethnic Identity: The Transformation of White America.* New Haven, Conn.: Yale University Press.

Alba, Richard D., and John R. Logan (1991). "Variations of Two Themes: Racial and Ethnic Patterns in the Attainment of Suburban Residence." *Demography* 28:431–453.

Aldridge, Delores P. (1978). "Interracial Marriage: Empirical and Theoretical Considerations." *Journal of Black Studies* 8:355–368.

Allport, Gordon (1958). *The Nature of Prejudice.* Garden City, N.Y.: Doubleday.

Alvarez, Lizette (1997). "Doubts Rising on Election in California, Gingrich Says." *New York Times,* September 26, p. A23.

Alvirez, David, and Frank D. Bean (1976). "The Mexican American Family." In C. H. Mindel and R. W. Habenstein, eds., *Ethnic Families in America: Patterns and Variations.* New York: Elsevier North-Holland, pp. 271–292.

Andersen, Margaret L., and Patricia Hill Collins (1998). *Race, Class, and Gender: An Anthology.* Belmont, Calif.: Wadsworth.

Anderson, Talmadge (1992). "Comparative Experience Factors Among Black, Asian, and Hispanic Americans." *Journal of Black Studies* 23 (1): 27–38.

Ansell, Amy Elizabeth (1997). *New Right, New Racism: Race and Reaction in the United States and Britain.* Washington Square, N.Y.: New York University Press.

Anti-Defamation League (1993). *Highlights from an Anti-Defamation*

League Survey on Racial Attitudes in America. New York: Anti-Defamation League.

Arnesen, Eric (2001). "Whiteness and the Historians' Imagination." *International Labor and Working-Class History* 60:3–32.

Artze, Isis (2000). "To Be and Not to Be—The Question Is: Can Latinos Simultaneously Integrate into America and Preserve Their Identity?" *Hispanic* 13, no. 10 (October): 32.

Arvizu, John, and Chris Garcia (1996). "Latino Voting Participation: Explaining and Differentiating Latino Voting Turnout." *Hispanic Journal of Behavioral Sciences* 18 (2): 104–128.

Asante, Molefi Kete (1991–1992). "Afrocentric Curriculum." *Educational Leadership* 49:28–31.

Bai, Matt, and Michael Isikoff (2000). "Clouds over the Sunshine State." *Newsweek,* November 20, pp. 16–25.

Bailey, Beth L. (1988). *From Porch to Back Seat: Courtship in Twentieth-Century America.* Baltimore: Johns Hopkins University Press.

Barrera, Mario (1988). *Beyond Aztlan: Ethnic Autonomy in Comparative Perspective.* South Bend, Ind.: University of Notre Dame Press.

Barringer, Herbert R., Robert W. Gardener, and Michael J. Levin (1993). *Asians and Pacific Islanders in the United States.* New York: Russell Sage Foundation.

Barthes, Roland (1976). *Mythologies.* Trans. Annette Lavers. New York: Hill and Wang.

Bash, Harry (1979). *Sociology, Race, and Ethnicity.* New York: Gordon and Brench.

Bell, Derrick (1992). *Faces at the Bottom of the Well.* New York: Basic Books.

Bell, Myrtle P., David A. Harrison, and Mary E. McLaughlin (1997). "Asian American Attitudes Toward Affirmative Action in Employment: Implications of the Model Minority Myth." *Journal of Applied Behavioral Science* 33 (3): 356–377.

Bellah, Robert N., Richard Madsen, William M. Sullivan, Ann Swindler, and Steven M. Tipton (1985). *Habits of the Heart: Individualism and Commitment in American Life.* Berkeley: University of California Press.

Berthoff, Rowland (1953). *British Immigrants in Industrial America, 1790–1950.* Cambridge: Harvard University Press.

Blauner, Robert (1989). *Black Lives, White Lives.* Berkeley: University of California Press.

——— (1972). *Racial Oppression in America.* New York: Harper and Row.

Blinder, Norman E., and J. L. Polinard (1997). "Mexican American and Anglo Attitudes Towards Immigration Reform: A View from the Border." *Social Science Quarterly* 78 (2): 324–337.

Bloom, Allen (1987). *The Closing of the American Mind: How Higher Education Has Failed Democracy and Impoverished the Souls of Today's Students*. New York: Simon and Schuster.

Bobo, Lawrence (2000). "Race and Beliefs About Affirmative Action: Assessing the Effects of Interests, Group Threat, Ideology, and Racism." In David O. Sears, Jim Sidanius, and Lawrence Bobo, eds., *Racialized Politics: The Debate About Racism in America*. Chicago: University of Chicago Press, pp. 137–164.

——— (1983). "White Opposition to Busing: Symbolic Racism or Realistic Group Conflict?" *Journal of Personality and Social Psychology* 45:1196–1210.

Bobo, Lawrence, and Franklin D. Gilliam Jr. (1990). "Race, Sociopolitical Participation, and Black Empowerment." *American Political Science Review* 84 (2): 377–393.

Bobo, Lawrence D., and Vincent L. Hutchings (1996). "Perceptions of Racial Group Competition: Extending Blumer's Theory of Group Position to a Multiracial Social Context." *American Sociological Review* 61:951–972.

Bobo, Lawrence D., and James R. Kluegel (1997). "Status, Ideology, and Dimensions of Whites' Racial Beliefs and Attitudes: Progress and Stagnation." In Steven A. Tuch and Jack K. Martin, eds., *Racial Attitudes in the 1990s: Continuity and Change*. Westport, Conn.: Praeger, pp. 93–120.

Bobo, Lawrence D., James R. Kluegel, and Ryan A. Smith (1997). "Laissez-Faire Racism: The Crystallization of a Kinder, Gentler, Antiblack Ideology." In S. A. Tuch and J. K. Martin, eds., *Racial Attitudes in the 1990s*. Westport, Conn.: Praeger, pp. 15–42.

Bobo, Lawrence D., and Camille L. Zubrinsky (1996). "Attitudes on Residential Integration: Perceived Status Differences, Mere In-Group Preference, or Racial Prejudice?" *Social Forces* 74:883–909.

Bogardus, Emory (1968). "Comparing Racial Distance in Ethiopia, South Africa, and the United States." *Sociology and Social Research* 52:149–156.

Bonilla-Silva, Eduardo (2001). *White Supremacy and Racism in the Post–Civil Rights Era*. Boulder: Lynne Rienner.

——— (1997). "Rethinking Racism: Towards a Structural Interpretation." *American Sociological Review* 62:465–480.

Bonilla-Silva, Eduardo, and Amanda Lewis (1997). "The 'New Racism':

Toward an Analysis of the U.S. Racial Structure, 1960s–1990s." Unpublished manuscript.

Bradshaw, Benjamin S., and Frank D. Bean (1970). "Intermarriage Between Persons of Spanish and Non-Spanish Surnames: Changes from the Mid-Nineteenth to the Mid-Twentieth Century." *Social Science Quarterly* 51:389–395.

Brown, Dee (1970). *Bury My Heart at Wounded Knee: An Indian History of the American West.* New York: Bantam Books.

Brown, Nancy G., and Ramona E. Douglass (2003). "Evolution of Multiracial Organizations: Where We Have Been and Where We Are Going." In Loretta I. Winters and Herman L. Debose, eds., *New Faces in a Changing America: Multiracial Identity in the Twenty-first Century.* Thousand Oaks, Calif.: Sage, pp. 111–124.

Browning, Rufus P., Dale R. Marshall, and David Tabb (1990). "Has Political Incorporation Been Achieved? Is It Enough?" In Rufus P. Browning, Dale R. Marshall, and David H. Tabb, eds., *Racial Policy in American Cities.* New York: Longman, pp. 212–230.

——— (1984). *Protest Is Not Enough: The Struggle of Blacks and Hispanics for Equality in Urban Politics.* Berkeley: University of California Press.

Bunzel, John H. (1991). "Black and White at Stanford." *Public Interest* 105:61–77.

Busto, Rudy V. (1999). "The Gospel According to the Model Minority? Hazarding an Interpretation of Asian American Evangelical College Students." In David K. Yoo, ed., *New Spiritual Homes: Religion and Asian Americans.* Honolulu: University of Hawaii Press, pp. 169–187.

Buttny, Richard (1999). "Discursive Constructions of Racial Boundaries and Self-Segregation on Campus." *Journal of Language and Social Psychology* 18 (3): 247–268.

Buzbee, Sally S. (1995). "NEA Fears Support for Schools May Fade." *Chattanooga News,* July 4, p. A7.

Campbell, Donald T. (1965). "Ethnocentric and Other Altruistic Motives." In Robert Levine, ed., *Nebraska Symposium on Motivation.* Lincoln: University of Nebraska Press.

Carr, Leslie G. (1997). *"Color-Blind" Racism.* Thousand Oaks, Calif.: Sage.

Chavez, L. (1990). "Rainbow Collision." *New Republic* 203 (21): 14–16.

Cherlin, Andrew J. (1996). *Public and Private Families: An Introduction.* Albany: State University of New York Press.

Choi, J. M., K. A. Callaghan, and J. W. Murphy (1995). *The Politics of Culture: Race, Violence, and Democracy.* Westport, Conn.: Praeger.

Clark, William A. V. (1991). "Residential Segregation and Neighborhood Racial Segregation: A Test of the Schelling Segregation Model." *Demography* 28:1–19.

———— (1989). "Residential Segregation in American Cities: Common Ground and Differences in Interpretation." *Population Research and Policy Review* 8:193–197.

———— (1986). *Residential Segregation in American Cities.* Albany: State University of New York Press.

Cobb, Kim (2001). "High Court to Hear School Voucher Case: People on Both Sides Eager for Ruling." *Houston Chronicle,* September 26, p. A12.

Cohn, D'Vera (2000). "Biracial Parents Defy Check Boxes: Couples Say They Don't Want Their Kids Defined by Color." *Washington Post,* July 17, p. B01.

Cornell, Stephen, and Douglass Hartmann (1998). *Ethnicity and Race: Making Identities in a Changing World.* Thousand Oaks, Calif.: Pine Forge Press.

Cose, Ellis (1997). *Color-Blind: Seeing Beyond Race in a Race-Obsessed World.* New York: HarperCollins.

Cox, T., and S. Nkomo (1990). "Invisible Men and Women: A Status Report on Race as a Variable in Organization Behavior Research." *Journal of Organizational Behavior* 11:419–431.

Dalmage, Heather M. (2000). *Tripping on the Color Line: Black-White Multiracial Families in a Racially Divided World.* New Brunswick, N.J.: Rutgers University Press.

Dalton, Harlon L. (2002). "Failing to See." In Paula S. Rothenberg, ed., *White Privilege: Essential Readings on the Other Side of Racism.* New York: Worth, pp. 15–18.

———— (1996). *Racial Healing: Confronting the Fear Between Blacks and Whites.* New York: Anchor Books.

Daniel, G. Reginald (1996). "Black and White Identity in the New Millennium." In Maria P. P. Root, ed., *The Multiracial Experience: Racial Borders as the New Frontier.* Thousand Oaks, Calif.: Sage, pp. 121–139.

Daniels, Rogers (1969). *The Politics of Prejudice.* New York: Atheneum.

Danigelis, Nicholas (1977). "A Theory of Black Political Participation in the United States." *Social Forces* 56:31–47.

Davis, Darren W., and Christian Davenport (1997). "The Political and

Social Relevancy of Malcolm X: The Stability of African-American Political Attitudes." *Journal of Politics* 57 (2): 550–565.

Davis, F. James (1991). *Who Is Black? One Nation's Definition.* University Park: Pennsylvania State University Press.

Dawson, Michael C. (2000). "Slowly Coming to Grips with the Effects of the American Racial Order on American Policy Preferences." In David Sears, Jim Sidanius, and Lawrence Bobo, eds., *Racialized Politics: The Debate About Racism in America.* Chicago: University of Chicago Press, pp. 344–357.

Day, Jennifer C. (1996). "Population Projections of the United States by Age, Sex, Race, and Hispanic Origin: 1995 to 2050." *Current Population Reports* ser. P-25, no. 1130. Washington, D.C.: U.S. Government Printing Office.

de la Garza, Rodolfo (1992). *Latino Voices: Mexican, Puerto Rican, and Cuban Perspectives on American Politics.* Boulder: Westview Press.

de la Garza, Rodolfo, O. Louis DeSipio, F. Chris Garcia, John Garcia, and Angelo Falcon, eds. (1992). *Latino Voices: Mexican, Puerto Rican, and Cuban Perspectives.* Boulder: Westview Press.

Delgado, Richard, and Jean Stefancic (2000). "Latino/a Critical Legal Studies: Review Essay." *Aztlan* 25 (2): 161–189.

Dinnerstein, Leonard, and David M. Reimers (1982). *Ethnic Americans: A History of Immigration and Assimilation.* New York: Harper and Row.

Doane, Ashley W., Jr. (1997). "Dominant Group Ethnic Identity in the United States: The Role of 'Hidden' Ethnicity in Intergroup Relations." *Sociological Quarterly* 38 (3): 375–397.

Downey, Dennis J. (1999). " From Americanization to Multiculturalism: Political Symbols and Struggles for Cultural Diversity in Twentieth-Century American Race Relations." *Sociological Perspectives* 42 (2): 249–278.

Doyle, Ruth T., and Olga Scarpetta (1982). *Hispanics in New York: Religious, Cultural, and Social Experiences.* 2nd ed. New York: Office of Pastoral Research and Planning.

D'Souza, Dinesh (1995). *The End of Racism.* New York: Free Press.

Dyer, Richard (1997). *White.* New York: Routledge.

Edsall, Tom, and Mary D. Edsall (1991). *Chain Reaction: The Impact of Race, Rights, and Taxes on American Politics.* New York: Norton.

Emerson, Michael O., Rachel T. Kimbro, and George Yancey (2002). "Contact Theory Extended: The Effects of Prior Racial Contact on Current Social Ties." *Social Science Quarterly.* Forthcoming.

Emerson, Michael O., and David Sikkink (1997). "White Attitudes,

White Actions: Education and the Reproduction of a Racialized Society." Paper presented at the annual meeting of the American Sociological Association, Toronto.

Emerson, Michael O., and Christian Smith (2000). *Divided by Faith: Evangelical Religion and the Problem of Race in America*. Oxford: Oxford University Press.

Emerson, Michael O., Christian Smith, and David Sikkink (1999). "Equal in Christ, but Not in the World: White Conservative Protestants and Explanations of Black-White Inequality." *Social Problems* 46 (3): 398–417.

Emerson, Michael O., George Yancey, and Karen Chai (2001). "Does Race Matter in Residential Segregation: Exploring the Preferences of White Americans." *American Sociological Review* 66:922–935.

Eschbach, Karl (1995). "The Enduring and Vanishing American Indian: American Indian Population Growth and Intermarriage in 1990." *Ethnic and Racial Studies* 18, no. 1 (January): 89–107.

Espiritu, Yee Le (1996). *Asian American Women and Men: Labor, Laws, and Love*. Thousand Oaks, Calif.: Sage.

Esterchild, Elizabeth M., and Rodney A. McDanel (1998). "Race, Gender, and Income." *Race, Gender, and Income* 5 (2): 124–138.

Fairchild, Henry Pratt (1925). *Immigration*. New York: Macmillan.

Fang, Carolyn Y., Jim Sidanius, and Felicia Pratto (1998). "Romance Across the Social Status Continuum." *Journal of Cross-Cultural Psychology* 29 (2): 290–305.

Farley, John E. (1983). "Metropolitan Housing Segregation in 1980: The St. Louis Case." *Urban Affairs Quarterly* 18:347–359.

Farley, Reynolds, Suzanne Bianchi, and Diane Colasanto (1979). "Barriers to the Racial Integration of Neighborhoods: The Detroit Case." *Annual of the American Academy of Political and Social Science* 441 (January): 97–113.

Farley, Reynolds, Maria Krysan, Tara Jackson, Charlotte Steeh, and Keith Reeves (1993). "Causes of Continued Racial Residential Segregation in Detroit: 'Chocolate City, Vanilla Suburbs' Revisited." *Journal of Housing Research* 4 (1): 1–38.

Farley, Reynolds, Howard Schuman, Suzanne Bianchi, Diane Colasanto, and Shirley Hatchett (1978). "Chocolate City, Vanilla Suburbs: Will the Trend Toward Racially Separate Communities Continue?" *Social Science Research* 7:319–344.

Feagin, Joe R. (2000). *Racist America: Roots, Current Realities, and Future Reparations*. New York: Routledge.

Feagin, Joe R., and Clairece B. Feagin (1996). *Racial and Ethnic Relations*. 5th ed. Upper Saddle River, N.J.: Prentice-Hall.

Feagin, Joe R., and Melvin P. Sikes (1994). *Living with Racism: The Black Middle-Class Experience*. Boston: Beacon Press.

Feder, Don (1996). "The 104th Congress: Verdict Pending." *American Enterprise* 7 (January–February): 40–42.

Ferber, Abby L. (1998). *White Man Falling: Race, Gender, and White Supremacy*. Lanham, Md.: Rowman and Littlefield.

Field, Suzanne (1997). "What's Wrong with Assimilation?" *Plain Dealer*, March 21, p. 11B.

Fields, Barbara (2001). "Whiteness, Racism, and Identity." *International Labor and Working-Class History* 60:48–56.

Fineman, Howard (1995). "Race and Rage." *Newsweek*, April 2, p. 25.

Firebaugh, Glenn, and K. E. Davis (1988). "Trends in Antiblack Prejudice, 1972–1984: Region and Cohort Effects." *American Journal of Sociology* 94 (2): 251–272.

Flanigan, William H., and Nancy H. Zingale (1998). *Political Behavior of the American Electorate*. Washington, D.C.: Congressional Quarterly Press.

Ford, W. S. (1986). "Favorable Intergroup Contact May Not Reduce Prejudice: Inconclusive Journal Evidence, 1960–1984." *Sociology and Social Research* 70:256–258.

Frady, M. (1996). *Jesse: The Life and Pilgrimage of Jesse Jackson*. New York: Random House.

Francis, Emerich K. (1976). *Interethnic Relations: An Essay in Sociological Theory*. New York: Elsevier.

Franklin, Clyde W., and Walter Pillow (1994). "The Black Male's Acceptance of the Prince Charming Ideal." In Robert Staples, ed., *The Black Family: Essays and Studies*. Belmont, Calif.: Wadsworth, pp. 97–103.

Free, Marvin D., Jr. (1997). "The Impact of Sentencing Reforms on African Americans." *Journal of Black Studies* 28:268–286.

Frey, William H. (1979). "Central City White Flight: Racial and Nonracial Causes." *American Sociological Review* 44:425–448.

Fugita, Stephen S., and David J. O'Brien (1991). *Japanese American Ethnicity: The Persistence of Community*. Seattle: University of Washington Press.

Gallagher, Charles A. (2002a). "Playing the White Ethnic Card: Using Ethnic Identity to Deny Contemporary Racism." Forthcoming in Ashley Doane and Eduardo Bonilla-Silva, eds., *Deconstructing Whiteness, Deconstructing White Supremacy*. New York: Routledge.

———— (2002b). "Racial Redistricting: Expanding the Boundaries of Whiteness." Paper presented at the annual meeting of the American Sociological Association, Chicago.

Gallup, George, Jr., and D. Michael Lindsay (2000). *Surveying the Religious Landscape: Trends in U.S. Beliefs.* Harrisburg, Pa.: Morehouse.

Gallup Organization (1997). *Black/White Relations in the U.S.* Princeton: Gallup Organization.

Gans, Herbert J. (1992). "Second Generation Decline: Scenarios for the Economic and Ethnic Futures of the Post-1965 American Immigrants." *Ethnic and Racial Studies* 15 (April): 173–192.

———— (1979). "Symbolic Ethnicity." *Ethnic and Racial Studies* 2 (1): 1–20.

Garcia, Ignacio M. (1996). "Backwards from Aztlan: Politics in the Age of Hispanics." In Roberto M. DeAnda, ed., *Chicanas and Chicanos in Contemporary Society.* Boston: Allyn and Bacon, pp. 191–204.

Geertz, Clifford (1963). "The Integrative Revolution: Primordial Sentiments and Civil Politics in the United States." In Clifford Geertz, ed., *Old Societies and New States: The Quest for Modernity in Asia and Africa.* New York: Free Press, pp. 105–157.

George, Douglas (2001). "Social Attitudes on Assimilation and Pluralism in the United States." Paper presented at the annual meeting of the Southwestern Social Science Association, Fort Worth, Tex.

Geschwender, James A. (1978). *Racial Stratification in America.* Dubuque, Ia.: William C. Brown.

Gibson, Margaret (1989). *Accommodation Without Assimilation: Sikh Immigrants in an American High School.* Ithaca, N.Y.: Cornell University Press.

Gilens, Martin (1998). "Racial Attitudes and Race-Neutral Social Policies: White Opposition to Welfare and the Politics of Racial Inequality." In Jon Hurwitz and Mark Peffley, eds., *Perception and Prejudice: Race and Politics in the United States.* New Haven, Conn.: Yale University Press.

———— (1996). "'Race Coding' and White Opposition to Welfare." *American Political Science Review* 90:563–604.

Giles, Michael, and Kaenan Hertz (1994). "Racial Threat and Partisan Identification." *American Political Science Review* 88:317–326.

Giroux, Henry A. (1997). *Channel Surfing: Race Talk and the Destruction of Today's Youth.* New York: St. Martin's Press.

Gitlin, T. (1995). *The Twilight of Common Dreams: Why America Is Wracked by Culture Wars*. New York: Henry Holt.

Glazer, Nathan G. (1993). "Is Assimilation Dead?" *Annals of the American Academy* 530:122–136.

——— (1967). *Affirmative Discrimination*. Cambridge: Harvard University Press.

Glazer, Nathan G., and Patrick Moynihan (1963). *Beyond the Melting Pot*. Cambridge: MIT Press.

Glenn, Norval, and David Weiner (1979). "Some Trends in the Social Origins of American Sociologists." *American Sociologist* 10:291–302.

Gonzales, Roberto O., and Michael La Velle (1985). *The Hispanic Catholic in the United States*. New York: Northeast Catholic Pastoral Center for Hispanics.

Gordon, Milton M. (1964). *Assimilation in American Life*. New York: Oxford University Press.

Grebler, Leo, Joan W. Moore, and Ralph C. Guzman (1970). *The Mexican-American People*. New York: Free Press.

Grieco, Elizabeth M., and Rachel C. Cassidy (2001). "Overview of Race and Hispanic Origin." *Census 2000 Brief*. Washington, D.C.: U.S. Department of Commerce, U.S. Census Bureau.

Gutierrez, David G. (1995). *Walls and Mirrors: Mexican Americans, Mexican Immigrants, and the Politics of Ethnicity*. Berkeley: University of California Press.

Gutierrez, Ramon A. (1995). "Ethnic Studies: Its Evolution in American Colleges and Universities." In David Theo Goldberg, ed., *Multiculturalism: A Critical Reader*. Cambridge, Mass.: Blackwell, pp. 114–139.

Gutmann, A., ed. (1994). *Multiculturalism: Examining the Politics of Recognition*. Princeton: Princeton University Press.

Hacker, Andrew (1992). *Two Nations: Black and White, Separate, Hostile, Unequal*. New York: Ballantine Books.

Harris, David R. (1999). "'Property Values Drop When Blacks Move In, Because': Racial and Socioeconomic Determinants of Neighborhood Desirability." *American Sociological Review* 64 (3): 461–479.

Harris, Ernest (1996). "Blacks and Hispanics Clash Politically in Cities." *Headway* 8 (3): 22.

Harris, Shanette M. (1994). "Black Male Masculinity and Same Sex Friendships." In Robert Staples, ed., *The Black Family: Essays and Studies*. Belmont, Calif.: Wadsworth, pp. 82–90.

Hartigen, John (1999). *Racial Situations: Class Predicaments of Whiteness in Detroit.* Princeton: Princeton University Press.

Heaton, Tim B., and Cardell K. Jacobson (2000). "Intergroup Marriage: An Examination of Opportunity Structures." *Sociological Inquiry* 70 (1): 30–41.

Herberg, Will (1955). *Protestant-Catholic-Jew.* Garden City, N.Y.: Doubleday.

Herring, Cedric, and Charles Amissah (1997). "Advance and Retreat: Racially Based Attitudes and Public Policy." In Steven A. Tuch and Jack K. Martin, eds., *Racial Attitudes in the 1990s: Continuity and Change.* Westport, Conn.: Praeger, pp. 121–143.

Hilliard, A. G. (1988). "Conceptual Confusion and the Persistence of Group Oppression Through Education." *Equality and Excellence* 1:36–43.

Hirschman, Charles (1983). "America's Melting Pot Reconsidered." In R. H. Turner, ed., *Annual Review of Sociology.* Palo Alto, Calif.: Annual Review, pp. 397–423.

Hoffman, John P., and Alan S. Miller (1997). "Social and Political Attitudes Among Religious Groups: Convergence and Divergence over Time." *Journal for the Scientific Study of Religion* 36:52–70.

Hoskins, L. (1968). *I Have a Dream: The Quotations of Martin Luther King Jr.* New York: Grosset and Dunlap.

Hughes, Michael G., and Bradley R. Hertel (1990). "The Significance of Color Remains: A Study of Life Chances, Mate Selection, and Ethnic Consciousness Among Black Americans." *Social Forces* 68 (4): 1–16.

Hughes, Michael, and Steven A. Tuch (2000). "How Beliefs About Poverty Influence Racial Policy Attitudes." In David O. Sears, Jim Sidanius, and Lawrence Bobo, eds., *Racialized Politics: The Debate About Racism in America.* Chicago: University of Chicago Press, pp. 165–190.

Hughes, R. (1993). *The Culture of Complaint: The Fraying of America.* New York: Oxford University Press.

Hunt, Larry L., and Matthew O. Hunt (1999). "Regional Patterns of African American Church Attendance: Revisiting the Semi-Involuntary Thesis." *Social Forces* 78 (2): 779–791.

Hurh, Won Moo (1994). "Majority Americans' Perception of Koreans in the United States: Implications of Ethnic Images and Stereotypes." In H. Kwon, ed., *Korean Americans: Conflict and Harmony.* Chicago: Center for Korean Studies, pp. 3–21.

Hurh, Won Moo, and Kwang Chung Kim (1989). "The 'Success' Image of Asian Americans: Its Validity and Its Practical and Theoretical Implications." *Ethnic and Racial Studies* 12 (October): 512–536.

Ignacio, Lemuel F. (1976). *Asian Americans and Pacific Islanders.* San Jose, Calif.: Filipino Development Association.

Ignatiev, Noel (1995). *How the Irish Became White.* New York: Routledge.

Isaacs, Harold R. (1975). *Idols of the Tribe: Group Identity and Political Change.* Cambridge: Harvard University Press.

Jackman, Mary R., and Marie Crane (1986). "'Some of My Best Friends Are Black . . .': Interracial Friendship and Whites' Racial Attitudes." *Public Opinion Quarterly* 50:459–486.

Jackson, Sandra, and Jose Solis (1995). *Beyond Comfort Zones in Multiculturalism: Confronting the Politics of Privilege.* Westport, Conn.: Bergin and Garvey.

Jacobson, Cardell K., Tim B. Heaton, and Rutledge M. Dennis (1990). "Black-White Differences in Religiosity: Item Analysis and a Formal Structural Test." *Sociological Analysis* 51:257–270.

Jacobson, Matthew F. (1998). *Whiteness of a Different Color: European Immigrants and the Alchemy of Race.* Cambridge: Harvard University Press.

Jakubs, John. F. (1986). "Recent Racial Segregation in U.S. SMSAs." *Urban Geography* 7:146–163.

James, David R. (1994). "The Racial Ghetto as a Race-Making Situation: The Effects of Residential Segregation on Racial Inequalities and Racial Identity." *Law and Social Inquiry* 19 (2): 407–432.

Jaret, Charles (1995). *Contemporary Racial and Ethnic Relations.* New York: HarperCollins.

Jenkins, Richard (1996). *Social Identity.* New York: Routledge.

Jones, James M. (1981). "The Concept of Racism and Its Changing Reality." In B. P. Bowser and R. G. Hunt, eds., *Impacts of Racism on White Americans.* Beverly Hills, Calif.: Sage, pp. 27–49.

Kain, John F. (1986). "The Influence of Race and Income on Racial Segregation and Housing Policy." In John M. Goering, ed., *Housing Desegregation and Federal Policy.* Chapel Hill: University of North Carolina Press, pp. 99–118.

Kang, Connie K. (1995). "Building Bridges to Equality." *Los Angeles Times,* January 7, p. A1.

Kasarda, John D. (1992). "Why Asians Can Prosper Where Blacks Fail." *Wall Street Journal,* May 28, p. A18.

Keith, Vera M., and Cedric Herring (1991). "Skin Tone and Stratification in the Black Community." *American Journal of Sociology* 97 (3): 760–778.

Kennedy, Ruby Jo Reeves (1944). "Single or Triple Melting Pot? Intermarriage Trends in New Haven, 1870–1940." *American Journal of Sociology* 49:331–339.

Kilson, Martin (1995). "Affirmative Action." *Dissent* 42 (fall): 469–470.

Kim, Claire J. (2000–2001). "Playing the Racial Trump Card: Asian Americans in Contemporary Politics." *Amerasia Journal* 26 (3): 35–65.

Kinder, Donald R., and Lynn M. Sanders (1996). *Divided by Color: Racial Politics and Democratic Ideals*. Chicago: University of Chicago Press.

Kirschenman, Joleen, and Kathryn M. Neckerman (1991). "'We'd Love to Hire Them, But . . .': The Meaning of Race for Employers." In Christopher Jencks and Paul Peterson, eds., *The Urban Underclass*. Washington, D.C.: Brookings Institution, pp. 203–234.

Kitano, Harry H. L., and Roger Daniels (1988). *Asian Americans: Emerging Minorities*. Englewood Cliffs, N.J.: Prentice-Hall.

Kluegel, James R. (1990). "Trends in Whites' Explanation of the Black-White Gap in Socioeconomic Status, 1977–1989." *American Sociological Review* 55:512–525.

Korgen, Kathleen O. (1998). *From Black to Biracial: Transforming Racial Identity Among Americans*. Westport, Conn.: Praeger.

Kornblum, William (2000). *Sociology in a Changing World*. 5th ed. Fort Worth, Tex.: Harcourt.

Kovel, Joel (1984). *White Racism: A Psychohistory*. New York: Columbia University Press.

Kozol, Jonathan (1992). *Savage Inequalities: Children in America's Schools*. New York: Harper Perennial.

Kuklinski, James H., and Michael D. Cobb (1997). "Racial Attitudes and the 'New South.'" *Journal of Politics* 59 (2): 323–349.

Kuklinski, James H., Paul M. Sniderman, Kathleen Knight, Thomas Piazza, Philip E. Tetlock, Gordon R. Lawrence, and Barbara Mellers (1997). "Racial Prejudice and Attitudes Toward Affirmative Action." *American Journal of Political Science* 41 (2): 402–419.

Kymlicka, Will (1996). *Multicultural Citizenship*. Oxford: Clarendon Press.

Ladd, Seymour, and Martin Lipset (1975). *The Divided Academy: Professors and Politics*. New York: McGraw-Hill.

Lake, Robert (1981). *The New Suburbanites: Race and Housing in the Suburbs*. New Brunswick, N.J.: Rutgers University, Center for Urban Policy Research.

Lee, Elisa (1993). "Silcon Valley Study Finds Asian Americans Hitting the Glass Ceiling." *AsianWeek,* October 8, p. 21.

Lee, Kenneth (1996). "Separate and Unequal." *American Enterprise* 7:63–64.

Levine, L. W. (1996). *The Opening of the American Mind.* Boston: Beacon Press.

Lewis, Curtis P., Jr. (1971). *Apes and Angels: The Irish in Victorian Caricature.* Washington, D.C.: Smithsonian Institution Press.

Lewis, Richard (1994). "Racial Discrimination Encountered by Individuals Who Are Interracially Married." *Diversity: A Journal of Multicultural Issues* 2:49–63.

Lewis, Richard, and George Yancey (1995). "Biracial Marriage in the United States: An Analysis of Variation in Family Member Support." *Sociological Spectrum* 15:443–462.

Lie, John (1995). "From International Migration to Transnational Diaspora." *Contemporary Sociology* 24 (4): 303–306.

Lieberson, Stanley (1980). *A Piece of the Pie: Black and White Immigrants Since 1880.* Berkeley: University of California Press.

Lincoln, C. Eric, and Lawrence H. Mamiya (1990). *The Black Church in the African American Experience.* Durham, N.C.: Duke University Press.

Lindsey, Daryl (2000). "The Stakes Are a Bit Higher for Us." http://salon.com/news/feature/2000/02/16/naacp.

Lipsitz, George (1998). *The Possessive Investment in Whiteness: How White People Profit from Identity Politics.* Philadelphia: Temple University Press.

Loewen, James W. (1988). *The Mississippi Chinese: Between Black and White.* Prospect Heights, Ill.: Waveland Press.

Logan, John R., Richard D. Alba, and Thomas L. McNulty (1994). "Ethnic Economies in Metropolitan Regions: Miami and Beyond." *Social Forces* 72 (March): 691–724.

Loury, Glenn C. (1998). "Color-Blinded." *New Republic* 219:12.

Lusane, Clarence (1999). "Assessing the Disconnect Between Black and White Television Audiences." *Journal of Popular Film & Television* 27 (1): 12–20.

Lyman, Stanford M. (1992). "The Assimilation-Pluralism Debate: Toward a Postmodern Resolution of the American Ethnoracial Dilemma." *International Journal of Politics, Culture, and Society* 6 (2): 181–210.

Lynxwiler, John (1999). "The Impact of Religiosity of Race Variations in Abortion Attitudes." *Sociological Spectrum* 19 (3): 359–377.

Mack, Raymond W. (1996). "Whose Affirmative Action?" *Society* 33 (March–April): 41–43.

Maki, Mitchell T., Harry H. L. Kitano, S. Megan Berthold, and Roger Daniels (1999). *Achieving the Impossible Dream: How Japanese Americans Obtained Redress (The Asian American Experience).* Urbana: University of Illinois Press.

Mangione, Thomas W. (1995). *Mail Surveys: Improving the Quality.* Thousand Oaks, Calif.: Sage.

Manning, Marble (2000). *How Capitalism Underdeveloped Black America: Problems in Race, Political Economy, and Society.* Boston: South End Press.

Marsh, David (1995). "Cops 'n' Gangstas." *The Nation* 260 (25): 408–409.

Martinez, Elizabeth (1994). "Seeing More Than Black and White: Latinos, Racism, and the Cultural Divides." *Z Magazine* 7 (May): 56–60.

Mason, Philip (1970). *Patterns of Dominance.* New York: Oxford University Press.

Massey, Douglas S., and Nancy Denton (1996). *American Apartheid: Segregation and the Making of the Underclass.* Cambridge: Harvard University Press.

——— (1988). "Residential Segregation of Blacks, Hispanics, and Asians by Socioeconomic Status and Generation." *Social Science Quarterly* 69:797–817.

——— (1987). "Trends in the Residential Segregation of Blacks, Hispanics, and Asians: 1970–1980." *American Sociological Review* 52:802–825.

Massey, Douglas S., and Eric Fong (1990). "Segregation and Neighborhood Quality: Blacks, Hispanics, and Asians in the San Francisco Area." *Social Forces* 69:15–32.

Massey, Douglas S., and Brendan P. Mullan (1984). "Processes of Hispanic and Black Spatial Assimilation." *American Journal of Sociology* 89:836–874.

Matute-Bianchi, Maria Eugenia (1991). "Situational Ethnicity and Patterns of School Performance Among Immigrant and Nonimmigrant Mexican-Descent Students." In Margaret Gibson and John U. Ogbu, eds., *Minority Status and Schooling: A Comparative Study of Immigrant and Involuntary Minorities.* New York: Garland, pp. 205–247.

McAdam, D. (1982). *Political Process and the Development of Black Insurgency, 1930–1970.* Chicago: University of Chicago Press.

McConahay, J. B. (1986). "Modern Racism, Ambivalence, and the Modern Racism Scale." In John F. Dovidio and Samuel L. Gaertner, eds., *Prejudice, Discrimination, and Racism.* Orlando, Fla.: Academic Press, pp. 91–125.

McDaniel, Antonio (1996). "The Dynamic Racial Composition of the United States." In Obie Clayton Jr., ed., *An American Dilemma Revisited: Race Relations in a Changing World.* New York: Harper & Row, pp. 269–287.

McIntosh, Peggy (2002). "White Privilege: Unpacking the Invisible Knapsack." In Paula S. Rothenberg, ed., *White Privilege: Essential Readings on the Other Side of Racism.* New York: Worth, pp. 97–102.

McKeever, Matthew, and Stephen L. Klineberg (1999). "Generational Differences in Attitudes and Socioeconomic Status Among Hispanics in Houston." *Sociological Inquiry* 69 (1): 33–50.

McLemore, Dale S., and Harriett D. Romo (1998). *Race and Ethnic Relations in America.* 5th ed. Boston: Allyn and Bacon.

——— (1949). "Discrimination and the American Creed." In R. M. MacIver, ed., *Discrimination and the National Welfare.* New York: Institute for Religious and Social Studies, pp. 99–126.

McWilliams, Carey (1968). *North from Mexico: The Spanish-Speaking People of the United States.* New York: Greenwood.

Merton, Robert K. (1941). "Intermarriage and Social Structure." *Psychiatry* 4:361–374.

Metzger, L. Paul (1971). "American Sociology and Black Assimilation: Conflicting Perspectives." *American Journal of Sociology* 76 (4): 627–647.

Miller, John J. (1995). "Asian Americans Head for Politics: What Horse Will They Ride?" *American Enterprise* 6 (2): 56–58.

Moore, Joan W., and Harry Pachon (1985). *Hispanics in the United States.* Englewood Cliffs, N.J.: Prentice-Hall.

——— (1975). *Mexican Americans.* 2nd ed. Englewood Cliffs, N.J.: Prentice-Hall.

Moore, Solomon, and Robin Fields (2002). "The Great 'White' Influx." *Los Angeles Times,* July 21, p. A1.

Moskos, Charles C., and John S. Butler (1996). *All That We Can Be.* New York: Basic Books.

Mueller, Carol M. (1988). "The Empowerment of Women Polling and the Women's Voting Bloc." In Carol M. Mueller, ed., *The Politics of the Gender Gap: The Social Construction of Political Influence.* Newbury Park, Calif.: Sage, pp. 16–36.

Munford, Clarence J. (1996). *Race and Reparations: A Black Perspective for the Twenty-first Century.* Trenton, N.J.: African World Press.

Murguia, Edward (1982). *Chicano Intermarriage.* San Antonio, Tex.: Trinity University Press.

Myrdal, Gunnar (1944). *An American Dilemma.* New York: Harper and Brothers.

Nadeau, Richard, Richard G. Niemi, and Jeffrey Levine (1993). "Innumeracy About Minority Populations." *Public Opinion Quarterly* 57 (3): 332–347.

Nash, Phil T., and Frank Wu (1997). "Asian Americans Under Glass: Where the Furor over the President's Fundraising Has Gone Awry— and Racist." *The Nation* 264 (12): 15–16.

National Roster of Black Elected Officials (1997).

National Roster of Hispanic Elected Officials (1994).

Newman, Williams M. (1973). *American Pluralism.* New York: Harper and Row.

Noble, Kenneth B. (1995). "Attacks Against Asian-Americans Are Rising." *New York Times,* December 13, p. A14.

Norrander, Barbara (1999). "The Evolution of the Gender Gap." *Public Opinion Quarterly* 63 (4): 566–576.

Ogbu, John (1978). *Minority Education and Caste: The American System in Cross Cultural Perspective.* New York: Academic Press.

Ohnuma, Keiko (1991). "Study Finds Asians Unhappy at CSU." *AsianWeek,* August 8, p. 5.

Oliver, Melvin L., and Thomas Shapiro (1995). *Black Wealth/White Wealth: A New Perspective on Racial Inequality.* New York: Routledge.

Olzak, Susan, Suzanne Shanahan, and Elizabeth West (1994). "School Desegregation, Interracial Exposure, and Antibusing Activity in Contemporary Urban America." *American Journal of Sociology* 100:196–241.

Omi, Michael, and Howard Winant (1994). *Racial Formation in the United States.* 2nd ed. New York: Routledge.

Orfield, Gary, Susan Eaton, and the Harvard Project on School Desegregation (1996). *Dismantling Desegregation: The Quiet Reversal of Brown v. Board of Education.* New York: New Press.

O'Sullivan, John (2000). "Preferences for (Almost) All." *National Review* 52 (7): 22–24.

Owen, Carolyn A., Howard C. Eisner, and Thomas R. McFaul (1981). "A Half-Century of Social Distance Research: National Replication of the Borgardus Studies." *Sociology and Social Research* 66:80–98.

Pagnini, Deanna L., and S. Philip Morgan (1990). "Intermarriage and Social Distance Among U.S. Immigrants at the Turn of the Century." *American Journal of Sociology* 96:405–432.

Parrillo, Vincent N. (1997). *Stranger to These Shores.* 5th ed. Boston: Allyn and Bacon.

Parsons, Talcott (1965–1966). "Full Citizenship for the Negro American? A Sociological Problem." In Talcott Parsons and Kenneth B. Clark, eds., *The Negro American.* Boston: Houghton Mifflin, pp. 709–754.

Patchen, Martin (1999). *Diversity and Unity: Relations Between Racial Ethnic Groups.* Chicago: Nelson-Hall.

Patterson, Orlando (1977). *Ethnic Chauvinism: The Reactionary Impulse.* New York: Stein and Day.

Pavalko, Ronald (1981). "Racism and the New Immigration: Towards a Reinterpretation of the Experiences of White Ethnics in American Society." *Sociology and Social Research* 65:56–77.

Penalosa, Fernando (1970). "The Changing Mexican-American in Southern California." In John H. Burma, ed., *Mexican Americans in the United States.* Cambridge, Mass.: Schenkman, pp. 41–51.

Perry, H. L. (1995). "A Theoretical Analysis of National Black Politics in the United States." In Huey L. Perry and Wayne Parent, eds., *Blacks and the American Political System.* Gainesville: University Press of Florida, pp. 41–50.

Petersen, William (1971). *Japanese Americans.* New York: Random House.

Pettigrew, Thomas F. (2000). "Systematizing the Predictors of Prejudice." In David O. Sears, Jim Sidanius, and Lawrence Bobo, eds., *Racialized Politics: The Debate About Racism in America.* Chicago: University of Chicago Press, pp. 280–301.

———— (1985). "New Black-White Patterns: How Best to Conceptualize Them." In Ralph H. Turner and James F. Short, eds., *Annual Review of Sociology.* Palo Alto, Calif.: Annual Review.

Pierce, Paulette (1988). "The Roots of the Rainbow Coalition." *Black Scholar* 19 (2): 12–16.

Pomper, Gerald M. (1997). "The Presidential Election." In Gerald M. Pomper, ed., *The Election of 1996.* Chatham, N.J.: Chatham House, pp. 173–204.

Population Projections Program (2000). Washington, D.C.: U.S. Census Bureau, Population Division.

Porterfield, Ernest (1978). *Black and White Mixed Marriages.* Chicago: Nelson.

Portes, Alejandro, and Robert L. Bach. 1985. *Latin Journey.* Berkeley: University of California Press.

Portes, Alejandro, and Min Zhou (1993). "The New Second Generation: Segmented Assimilation and Its Variants." *Annals of the American Academy of Political and Social Science* 530 (November): 74–97.

Pratto, Felicia, Jim Sidanius, L. M. Stallworth, and B. F. Malle (1994). "Social Dominance Orientation: A Personality Variable Predicting Social and Political Attitudes." *Journal of Personality and Social Psychology* no. 67: 741–763.

Quirk, Paul J. (1989). "The Election." In Michael Nelson, ed., *The Elections of 1988.* Washington, D.C.: Congressional Quarterly Press, pp. 63–92.

Reed, Adolph, Jr. (2001). "Response to Eric Arnesen." *International Labor and Working-Class History* 60:69–80.

Roberts, Steven V. (1995). "Affirmative Action on the Edge." *U.S. News and World Report,* February 13, p. 32.

Robinson, Randell N. (2001). *The Debt: What America Owes to Blacks.* New York: E. P. Dutton.

Rockquemore, Kerry Ann, and David L. Brunsma (2002). *Beyond Black: Biracial Identity in America.* Thousand Oaks, Calif.: Sage.

Rodriguez, Clara (2000). *Changing Race: Latinos, the Census, and the History of Ethnicity in the United States.* New York: New York University Press.

Roediger, David R. (1991). *The Wages of Whiteness: Race and the Making of the American Working Class.* New York: Verso.

Root, Maria P. P. (2001). *Love's Revolution: Interracial Marriage.* Philadelphia: Temple University Press.

——— (1996). "A Bill of Rights for Racially Mixed People." In Maria P. P. Root, ed., *The Multiracial Experience: Racial Borders as the New Frontier.* Thousand Oaks, Calif.: Sage, pp. 3–14.

Rose, Tricia (1994). "Rap Music and the Demonization of Young Black Males." In Thelma Golden, ed., *Black Male: Representations of Masculinity in Contemporary American Art.* New York: Whitney Museum of American Art, pp. 149–157.

Ross, Andrew (1994). "The Gangsta and the Diva." In Thelma Golden, ed., *Black Male: Representations of Masculinity in Contemporary American Art.* New York: Whitney Museum of American Art, pp. 159–166.

Rossi, Peter H., and S. L. Nock (1982). *Measuring Social Judgements: The Factorial Survey Approach.* Beverly Hills, Calif.: Sage.

Rothenberg, Paula (1998). *Race, Class, and Gender in the United States: An Integrated Study.* New York: St. Martin's Press.

Russell, Kathy, Midge Wilson, and Ronald Hall (1992). *The Color Complex: The Politics of Skin Color Among African Americans.* New York: Harcourt Brace Jovanovich.

Salvatore, Saporito, and Annette Lareau (1999). "School Selection as a Process: The Multiple Dimensions of Race in Framing Educational Choice." *Social Problems* 46 (3): 418–439.

Samuelson, William, and Richard Zeckhauser (1988). "Status Quo Bias in Decision Making." *Journal of Risk and Uncertainty* 1:7–59.

San Francisco Chronicle (1997). Editorial: "Multiracial Checkoff Is a Vote for Accuracy." June 8, p. 10.

San Juan, E., Jr. (1998). *From Exile to Diaspora: Versions of the Filipino Experience in the United States.* Boulder: Westview Press.

Schaefer, Richard T. (1998). *Racial and Ethnic Groups.* 7th ed. New York: Longman.

Schiraldi, Vincent (1995). "Blacks Are Target of 57 Percent of 'Three Strikes' Prosecutions in Los Angeles." *Overcrowded Times* 6 (2): 7.

Schlesinger, A. M. (1992). *The Disuniting of America.* New York: W. W. Norton.

Schneider, Michael (1997). "Black Viewers Turn Away from Big 4 to UPN, Says Study." *Electronic Media* 16 (8): 1–2.

Schneider, William (1996). "Is It a Time for Mending or Ending?" *National Journal* 28 (30): 1982.

Schuman, Howard (1996). "Attitudes vs. Actions Versus Attitudes vs. Attitudes." *Public Opinion Quarterly* 36:347–354.

Schuman, Howard, Suzanne Bianchi, Diane Colasanto, and Shirley Hatchett (1978). "'Chocolate City, Vanilla Suburbs': Will the Trend Towards Racially Separate Communities Continue?" *Social Science Research* 7:319–344.

Schuman, Howard, and Lawrence Bobo (1988). "Survey-Based Experiments on White Racial Attitudes Toward Residential Integration." *American Journal of Sociology* 94:273–299.

Schuman, Howard, and Stanley Presser (1996). *Questions and Answers in Attitude Surveys: Experiments on Question Form, Wording, and Context.* Thousand Oaks, Calif.: Sage.

Schuman, Howard, and Charlotte Steeh (1996). "The Complexity of Racial Attitudes in America." In Silvia Pedraza and Ruben G. Rumbaut, eds., *Origins and Destinies: Immigration, Race, and*

Ethnicity in America. Belmont, Calif.: Wadsworth, pp. 455–469.

Schuman, Howard, Charlotte Steeh, Lawrence Bobo, and Maria Krysan (1997). *Racial Attitudes in America: Trends and Interpretations*. Rev. ed. Cambridge: Harvard University Press.

Scott, Jacqueline, and Howard Schuman (1988). "Attitude Strength and Social Action in the Abortion Dispute." *American Sociological Review* 53:785–793.

Scott, Marvin B., and Stanford M. Lyman (1968). "Accounts." *American Sociological Review* 33:40–62.

Sears, David O., P. J. Henry, and Rick Kosterman (2000). "Egalitarian Values and Contemporary Racial Policy." In David O. Sears, Jim Sidanius, and Lawrence Bobo, eds., *Racialized Politics: The Debate About Racism in America*. Chicago: University of Chicago Press, pp. 75–117.

Sears, David O., John J. Hetts, Jim Sidanius, and Lawrence Bobo (2000). "Race in American Politics." In David O. Sears, Jim Sidanius, and Lawrence Bobo, eds., *Racialized Politics: The Debate About Racism in America*. Chicago: University of Chicago Press, pp. 1–43.

Shils, Edward (1957). "Primordial, Personal, Sacred, and Civil Ties: Some Particular Observations on the Relationships of Sociological Research and Theory." *British Journal of Sociology* 8:130–145.

Sigelman, Lee, and Susan Welch (1993). "The Contact Hypothesis Revisited: Black-White Interaction and Positive Racial Attitudes." *Social Forces* 71 (3): 781–795.

Skogan, Wesley G. (1995). "Crime and the Racial Fears of White Americans." *Annals of the American Academy of Political and Social Science* 539 (May): 59–71.

Sleeter, C., and C. Grant (1988). *Making Choices for Multicultural Education*. New York: Merrill.

Sleeter, Christine E., and Peter L. McLaren (1995). *Multicultural Education, Critical Pedagogy, and the Politics of Difference*. Albany: State University of New York Press.

Smith, Christopher B. (1994). "Back and to the Future: The Intergroup Contact Hypothesis Revisited." *Sociological Inquiry* 64 (4): 438–455.

Smith, Tom W. (1998). "Public Opinion on Abortion." National Opinion Research Center, www.norc.uchicago.edu/library/abortion.htm.

Sniderman, Paul M., and Thomas Piazza (1993). *The Scar of Race*. Cambridge: Harvard University Press.

Song, Tae-Hyon (1991). "Social Contact and Ethnic Distance Between Koreans and the U.S. Whites in the United States." Paper, Western Illinois University.

Southwest Voter Registration Project (1984). *The Hispanic Electorates.* San Antonio, Tex.: Hispanic Policy Development Project.

Sowell, Thomas (1984). *Civil Rights: Rhetoric or Reality?* New York: Quill.

Spencer, Martin E. (1994). "Multiculturalism, Political Correctness, and the Politics of Identity." *Sociological Forum* 9 (December): 547–567.

Spickard, Paul R. (1992). "The Illogic of American Racial Categories." In Maria P. P. Root, ed., *Racially Mixed People in America.* Thousand Oaks, Calif.: Sage, pp. 12–23.

——— (1989). *Mixed Blood: Intermarriage and Ethnic Identity in Twentieth-century America.* Madison: University of Wisconsin Press.

Spigner, Clarence (1990). "Black/White Interracial Marriages: A Brief Overview of U.S. Census Data, 1980–1987." *Western Journal of Black Studies* 14 (4): 214–216.

St. John, Craig, and Nancy A. Bates (1990). "Racial Composition and Neighborhood Evaluation." *Social Science Research* 1:47–61.

St. John, Nancy H. (1975). *School Desegregation Outcomes for Children.* New York: Wiley.

Statistical Abstract of the United States (1998). Washington, D.C.: U.S. Government Printing Office.

Steeh, Charlotte, and Maria Krysan (1996). "Affirmative Action and the Public, 1970–1995." *Public Opinion Quarterly* 60 (1): 128–159.

Steeh, Charlotte, and Howard Schuman (1992). "Young White Adults: Did Racial Attitudes Change in the 1980s?" *American Journal of Sociology* 98:340–367.

Steele, C. Hoy (1985). "The Acculturation/Assimilation Model in Urban Indian Studies: A Critique." In Norman R. Yetman, ed., *Majority and Minority: The Dynamics of Race and Ethnicity in America.* 4th ed. Boston: Allyn and Bacon, pp. 332–339.

Steele, Shelby (1996). "Self-Segregation Should Be Condemned." In P. A. Winters, ed., *Race Relations: Opposing Viewpoints.* San Diego, Calif.: Greenhaven Press, pp. 209–215.

Suarez-Orozco, Marcelo M. (1987). "Becoming Somebody: Central American Immigrants in U.S. Inner-City Schools." *Anthropology and Education Quarterly* 18 (4): 287–299.

Szymanski, Albert (1983). *Class Structure: A Critical Perspective.* New York: Praeger.

Tachiki, Amy (1971). Introduction to Amy Tachiki, Eddie Wong, Franklin Odo, and Buck Wong, eds., *Roots: An Asian American Reader*. Los Angeles: Regents of the University of California, pp. 1–5.

Takagi, Dana Y. (1992). *The Retreat from Race: Asian-American Admissions and Racial Politics*. New Brunswick, N.J.: Rutgers University Press.

Takaki, Ronald (1989). *Strangers from a Different Shore: A History of Asian Americans*. Boston: Little, Brown.

Tatum, Beverly D. (1999). *Why Are All the Black Kids Sitting Together in the Cafeteria? And Other Conversations About Race*. New York: Basic Books.

Taub, Richard P., Garth D. Taylor, and Jan D. Dunham (1984). *Paths of Neighborhood Change*. Chicago: Aldine.

Taylor, Marlee C. (1998). "How White Attitudes Vary with the Racial Composition of Local Population: Numbers Count." *American Sociological Review* 63:512–535.

Taylor, Robert Joseph, Linda M. Chatters, Rukmalie Jayakody, and Jeffrey S. Levin (1996). "Black and White Differences in Religious Participation: A Multi-Sample Comparison." *Journal for the Scientific Study of Religion* 35:403–410.

Thompson, Becky W. (2001). *A Promise and a Way of Life: White Antiracist Activism*. Minneapolis: University of Minnesota Press.

Tonry, Michael (1996). *Malign Neglect: Race, Crime, and Punishment in America*. Oxford: Oxford University Press.

Torrecilha, Ramon S., Lionel Cantu, and Quan Nguyen (1999). "Puerto Ricans in the United States." In Anthony Gary Dworkin and Rosalina J. Dworkin, eds., *The Minority Report: An Introduction to Racial, Ethnic, and Gender Relations*. 3rd ed. Fort Worth, Tex.: Harcourt Brace.

Tripp, Luke (1992). "The Political Views of Black Students During the Reagan Era." *Black Scholar* 22 (3): 45–52.

Tuch, Steven A. (1988). "Race Differences in the Antecedents of Social Distance Attitudes." *Sociology and Social Research* 72:181–184.

Tuch, Steven A., Lee Sigelman, and Jack K. Martin (1997). "Fifty Years After Myrdal: Blacks' Racial Policy Attitudes in the 1990s." In Steven A. Tuch and Jack K. Martin, eds., *Racial Attitudes in the 1990s: Continuity and Change*. Westport, Conn.: Praeger, pp. 226–238.

Tucker, Belinda M., and C. Mitchell-Kernan (1990). "New Trends in Black American Interracial Marriage: The Social Structural Context." *Journal of Marriage and the Family* 52:209–218.

Tversky, Amos, and Daniel Kahneman (1990). "Rational Choice and the Framing of Decisions." In Karen Cook and Margaret Levi, eds., *The Limits of Rationality*. Chicago: University of Chicago Press, pp. 60–89.

Twine, France Winddance (1997). "Brown-Skinned White Girls: Class, Culture, and the Construction of White Identity in Suburban Communities." In Ruth Frankenberg, ed., *Displacing Whiteness: Essays in Social and Cultural Criticism*. Durham, N.C.: Duke University Press.

Ulmer, Jeffrey T., and John H. Kramer (1996). "Court Communities Under Sentencing Guidelines: Dilemmas of Formal Rationality and Sentencing Disparity." *Criminology* 34:383–407.

U.S. Bureau of the Census (1993). "Hispanic Origin by Race" [CD-ROM]. *1990 Census of Population and Housing Summary*. Tape file 3c, 010 United States.

——— (1992). *The Hispanic Population of the United States: March 1992 (Current Population Reports*, tab. P20-459). Washington, D.C.: U.S. Government Printing Office.

U.S. Commission on Civil Rights (1992). *Civil Rights Issues Facing Asian Americans in the 1990s*. Washington, D.C.: U.S. Government Printing Office.

U.S. Department of Commerce (1997). *Bureau of the Census*.

Valenzuela, Angela, and Sanford M. Dornbusch (1996). "Familism and Assimilation Among Mexican-Origin and Anglo High School Adolescents." In Roberto M. DeAnda, ed., *Chicanas and Chicanos in Contemporary Society*. Boston: Allyn and Bacon, pp. 53–62.

Virtanen, Simo V., and Leonie Huddy (1998). "Old-Fashion Racism and New Forms of Racial Prejudice." *Journal of Politics* 60 (2): 311–332.

Walker, Samuel, Cassia Spohn, and Miriam DeLonc (1996). *The Color of Justice: Race, Ethnicity, and Crime in America*. Belmont, Calif.: Wadsworth.

Warren, Jonathan W., and France Winddance Twine (1997). "White Americans: The New Minority? Non-Blacks and the Ever-Expanding Boundaries of Whiteness." *Journal of Black Studies* 28 (2): 200–218.

Waters, Mary (2000). "Multiple Ethnicities and Identity in the United States." In Paul Spickard and W. Jeffrey Burroughs, eds., *We Are a People: Narrative and Multiplicity in Constructing Ethnic Identity*. Philadelphia: Temple University Press, pp. 23–40.

——— (1999). *Black Identities: West Indian Immigrant Dreams and American Realities*. Cambridge: Harvard University Press.

———— (1998). "Multiple Ethnic Identity Choices." In Wendy F. Katlin, Ned Landsman, and Andrea Tyree, eds., *Beyond Pluralism: The Conception of Groups and Group Identities in America.* Urbana: University of Illinois Press, pp. 28–46.

———— (1990). *Ethnic Options: Choosing Identities in America.* Berkeley: University of California Press.

Weakliem, David L. (1997). "Race Versus Class? Racial Composition and Class Voting, 1936–1992." *Social Forces* 75 (3): 939–956.

Weglyn, Michi (1976). *Years of Infamy: The Untold Story of America's Concentration Camps.* New York: Morrow.

Wei, William (1993). *The Asian American Movement.* Philadelphia: Temple University Press.

Weis, Lois (1988). *Class, Race, and Gender in American Education.* Albany: State University of New York Press.

Weitz, Rose (1992). "College Students' Images of African American, Mexican American, and Jewish American Women." Paper presented at the annual meeting of the American Sociological Association, Pittsburgh.

Welch, Susan, and Lee Sigelman (2000). "Getting to Know You? Latino-Anglo Social Contact." *Social Science Quarterly* 81 (1): 67–83.

———— (1993). "The Politics of Hispanic Americans: Insights from National Surveys, 1980–1988." *Social Science Quarterly* 74 (1): 76–94.

———— (1992). "A Gender Gap Among Hispanics: A Comparison with Blacks and Anglos." *Western Political Quarterly* 45 (1): 181–200.

———— (1989). "A Black Gender Gap." *Social Science Quarterly* 70:120–133.

West, Cornell (1994). *Race Matters.* New York: Vintage Books.

Wildman, Stephanie M., with Adrienne D. Davis (2002). "Making Systems of Privilege Visible." In Paula S. Rothenberg, ed., *White Privilege: Essential Readings on the Other Side of Racism.* New York: Worth, pp. 89–95.

Williams, Kim M. (2003). "From Civil Rights to the Multiracial Movement." In Loretta I. Winters and Herman L. Debose, eds., *New Faces in a Changing America: Multiracial Identity in the Twenty-first Century.* Thousand Oaks, Calif.: Sage, pp. 85–98.

Wilson, William J. (1980). *The Declining Significance of Race.* 2nd ed. Chicago: University of Chicago Press.

Winant, Howard (1994). *Racial Conditions: Politics, Theory, Comparisons.* Minneapolis: University of Minnesota Press.

Winnick, Louis (1990). "America's Model Minority." *Commentary* 90:23.

Winship, Christopher, and Larry Radbill (1994). *Sociological Methods and Research* 23 (2): 230–257.

Yancey, George (2002). "Who Interracially Dates? Examinations of the Characteristics of Those Who Have Interracially Dated." *Journal of Comparative Family Studies* 33 (2): 179–190.

——— (2001). "Racial Attitudes: Differences in Racial Attitudes of People Attending Multiracial and Uniracial Congregations." *Research in the Social Scientific Study of Religion* 12:185–206.

——— (1999). "An Examination of Effects of Residential and Church Integration upon Racial Attitudes of Whites." *Sociological Perspectives* 42 (2): 279–304.

——— (1994). "The Utilization of Weber's Elective Affinity to Reconcile the Macro and Micro Schools Within Sociology of Science." Ph.D. diss., University of Texas at Austin.

Yancey, George, and Michael O. Emerson (n.d.). "Integrated Sundays: An Exploratory Study into the Formation of Multiracial Churches." Unpublished paper.

Yetman, Norman R. (1999). *Majority and Minority: The Dynamics of Race and Ethnicity in American Life.* 6th ed. Boston: Allyn and Bacon.

Yinger, John (1995). *Closed Doors, Opportunities Lost: The Continuing Costs of Housing Discrimination.* New York: Russell Sage Foundation.

Yip, Alethea (1997). "Jump in Violence Against APAS." *AsianWeek,* September 19, pp. 13–15.

Zack, Naomi (2001). "American Mixed Race: The U.S. 2000 Census and Related Issues." *Harvard Black Letter Law Journal* 17. Forthcoming.

Zilber, Jeremy, and David Niven (1995). "'Black' Versus 'African American': Are Whites' Political Attitudes Influenced by the Choice of Racial Labels?" *Social Science Quarterly* 76 (3): 655–665.

Zinsmeister, Karl (1987). "Asians: Prejudice from Top and Bottom." *Public Opinion* 10:8–10, 59.

Zubrinsky-Charles, Camille (2000). "Neighborhood Racial-Composition Preferences: Evidence from a Multiethnic Metropolis." *Social Problems* 47 (3): 379–407.

Index

African Americans, 21, 115–117, 125, 159–160, 162–163; alienation of, 4, 13–15, 44, 116, 139, 159; alienation of, compared to that of Native Americans, 46–47, 51–52; culture, 158; deserve special research attention, 18, 153–154; discrimination faced by, 51–53, 56–57; experiences distinct from Hispanic and Asian Americans, 126, 143; inability to assimilate, 12–15, 57–58, 80, 83, 125, 141–142, 153; inability to find powerful allies, 132, 141, 155–157; one-drop rule, 48–50, 142; racial identity, 12, 97; rejection of, 45–46, 64, 70, 81–83, 151–152; and segmented assimilation, 7, 135–136; segregation of, 19, 45, 63–64, 72–73, 115; social attitudes of, 11, 89–90, 96; social position of, 9, 67, 90, 118, 143, 150; socioeconomic status of, 56
Afro-Anglo culture, 13, 82
Alienation thesis, 13, 67, 104, 139, 149, 154–159; assumptions of, 132–133; explains maintenance of status quo, 17
Allport, Gordon, 93
Amissah, Charles, 67–69
Anglo-conformity, 29, 67, 138
Arnesen, Eric, 35
Asian Americans, 91, 143, 155–157; ability to assimilate, 7, 38, 43–44, 114, 130–132, 141; acceptance by majority group, 81, 139–140, 142, 151; adopt racial identity of majority group, 111, 115, 131, 138, 155, 157; believe blacks face more discrimination, 54–55; developing thinner racial identity, 9–10, 37–38, 83, 92, 132, 137; facing alienation, 13–15; facing prejudice and/or discrimination, 15, 42–43, 52, 104, 126, 154; immigration of, 41–42, 130, 134; model minority, 56; phenotypically different from European Americans, 42, 127, 130–131; and racialized attitudes, 93–94, 100, 107–111,

225

About the Book

George Yancey marshals compelling evidence to show that the definition of who is "white" is changing rapidly, with nonblack minorities accepting the perspectives of the current white majority group
and, in turn, being increasingly assimilated. In contrast, African
Americans continue to experience high levels of alienation. To
understand the racial reality in the United States, Yancey demonstrates that it is essential to discard the traditional white/nonwhite
dichotomy and to explore the implications of the changing color of
whiteness.

George Yancey is assistant professor of sociology at the University
of North Texas.